THE UNION OF MOLDAVIA
AND WALLACHIA, 1859

T0364291

THE UNION OF MOLDAVIA AND WALLACHIA, 1859

An Episode in Diplomatic History

BY

W. G. EAST, M.A.

Assistant in Historical Geography
London School of Economics
formerly Scholar of
Peterhouse

THIRLWALL
PRIZE ESSAY
FOR 1927

CAMBRIDGE
AT THE UNIVERSITY PRESS
1929

CAMBRIDGE UNIVERSITY PRESS
Cambridge, New York, Melbourne, Madrid, Cape Town,
Singapore, São Paulo, Delhi, Tokyo, Mexico City

Cambridge University Press
The Edinburgh Building, Cambridge CB2 8RU, UK

Published in the United States of America by
Cambridge University Press, New York

www.cambridge.org
Information on this title: www.cambridge.org/9781107601314

First published 1929
First paperback edition 2011

A catalogue record for this publication is available from the British Library

ISBN 978-1-107-60131-4 Paperback

In Memoriam

PREFACE

THIS essay is an attempt to investigate, from the standpoint of diplomatic and international history, a question which confronted and divided the Great Powers of Europe during the years 1855–59, namely, whether or not the Principalities of Moldavia and Wallachia should be politically united under either a foreign or native prince. I have not been specially concerned with this question as one of domestic or national history. Reference has been made to the efforts and aspirations of Rumanians themselves, but attention has been centred on the conflicting policies of the Powers whose co-operation or failure to co-operate determined, for the time being, the destinies of the nascent Rumanian state. Accordingly, I have endeavoured in Chapter I to present only a summary of the history of Moldavia and Wallachia such as makes intelligible the diplomatic events which followed the Crimean War. I have tried to examine and to describe the way in which the question of uniting the Principalities reacted on the interrelations of the Powers, in particular, how it served not only to facilitate a Franco-Russian understanding but also to embitter Franco-Austrian relations and to jeopardise the Anglo-French alliance. Further, an attempt has been made to account for Napoleon III's zealously pro-unionist policy, and to unravel the tangle of circumstances which led to the diplomatic rupture at Constantinople and to the healing compromise at Osborne in August, 1857.

It is thirty-one years since Louis Thouvenel in his *Trois années de la question d'Orient 1856–1859* called attention to the importance of the union of Moldavia and Wallachia as an international issue bequeathed by the Crimean War. His book, vivid and stimulating though it is, merely comprises a selection from the papers of his father, who was French Ambassador at the Porte, and cannot be regarded as either a complete or an impartial study of the union of the Principalities. Dr Lane-Poole in his *Life of Lord Stratford de Redcliffe*, who was Thouvenel's colleague and opponent at Constantinople, scarcely alludes in his last chapters to the vigorous efforts by which Lord Stratford opposed the union of the Principalities during the last two years of his long "Eastern drama." Professor T. W. Riker's recent article in *The English Historical Review*[1], which appeared after this essay was written, helps to elucidate one portion only of this problem.

The present essay is based primarily on the collections of Foreign Office MSS., diplomatic and consular, in the Public Record Office at London and the Cambridge Gaol. Of these, the official correspondence between the Constantinople Embassy and the Foreign Office (F.O. 195 and F.O. 78) is the most valuable, and has been used in conjunction with the French despatches published in Thouvenel's *Trois années* and, more particularly, in Sturdza's *Actes et documents relatifs à l'histoire de la régénération de la Roumanie*. Thanks to a grant from the Worts Fund at Cambridge, I was enabled to make some use of Foreign Office correspondence at the Vienna State Archives (for which I have used the abbreviation V.S.A. in the footnotes). The *Stratford Canning Papers* at the Public Record Office provide a rich source for the years 1856–57. They contain a number of private letters expressing Stratford's views on the Principalities and on the diplomatic situation generally, written to Lords Clarendon, Cowley and Lyons, and to Alison, Gardner and others. In addition there are

[1] xlii. pp. 227–244. *The Concert of Europe and Moldavia in* 1857.

private letters from Clarendon, Sir Henry Bulwer, and from Baron Prokesch-Osten, the Austrian Internuncio at Constantinople. Two minor unpublished sources are *The Bloomfield Papers*, which throw light on Prussian policy, at the Public Record Office, and *The Layard Papers* at the British Museum which include a few relevant letters from Sir Austen Layard and from Alison who was Secretary to the Embassy at Constantinople. The published authorities used—State Papers, collections of treaties, authorities on Rumanian history, and various diplomatic studies—are given at the end of this book.

I am much indebted to Dr H. W. V. Temperley, F.B.A., of Peterhouse, for invaluable advice and encouragement. I am grateful to Miss Malcolm-Smith, M.A., Ph.D., of Newnham College, who kindly gave me copies of certain documents. Dr L. Grosz, of the Vienna Archives, and Frl. Dr A. Kaldegg, of the University of Vienna, courteously assisted me. I am also indebted to Mr Wright for his help at the Cambridge Gaol, and to my friends Mr J. A. Fordham, I.C.S., of Downing College, and Dr H. Lauterpacht, of the London School of Economics, who very kindly and very critically read my proofs. To Miss W. Hunt, B.Sc., my colleague in the Geography Department at the London School of Economics, I am grateful for both the suggestion and the execution of the map.

W. G. E.

January 1929

CONTENTS

CHAPTER ONE

MOLDAVIA AND WALLACHIA BEFORE THE CRIMEAN WAR

"The Muscovites have gone into Moldavia. Who the Devil could prevent them?...Here is one infernal affair to begin with."

ALISON to LAYARD, July 17, 1848.[1]

[1] *The Layard Papers*, Add. MS. 38,978.

MOLDAVIA AND WALLACHIA BEFORE
THE CRIMEAN WAR

THE Principalities of Moldavia and Wallachia, out of whose union in the nineteenth century arose the independent state of Rumania, appear as distinct political units in the fourteenth century under the rule of lords who successfully threw off their feudal allegiance to the neighbouring Magyar kingdom. The fourteenth and fifteenth centuries witnessed a succession of civil and foreign wars during which the princes of Moldavia and Wallachia acknowledged the suzerainty of one or other of the great Powers surrounding them—Hungary, or Poland or Turkey. With the rise of the latter Power to predominance in the Balkans began a long and important phase in Rumanian history which ended only in 1878 when the Sultan abandoned his rights of suzerainty. Struggle as he could, Mircea the Great of Wallachia was unable to prevent the expansion of the Turks beyond the Danube: victorious at Kossovo in 1389 and at Nicopolis in 1396, they forced him on two occasions to accept their suzerainty. Separated from Wallachia by the River Milcov and the Lower Sereth, Moldavia, which stretched from Bukovina in the north to the Dniester in the east and to the Danube mouth in the south, was compelled to suffer a similar fate. Her excellent geographical position commanded the Danube route westwards, the Pruth and Sereth routes northwards into Hungary, Russia and Poland, and the natural avenue southwards into the Balkans afforded by the Dobruja. Already in the thirteenth century, under the favouring influences of Tatar rule, she showed promise of commercial development and prosperity. Later under her great ruler Stephen III, who did homage to the King of Poland in 1462, an unequal struggle was waged with the Turks. Stephen indirectly aided the Turkish cause by attacking the prince of Wallachia, the terrible Vlad "The Impaler", whose hatred of the Turks might have served their common end. Despite Stephen's victory at Racova in 1475, the Turks won a great battle near Neamtu in the heart of Moldavia in 1476, and at length, eight years later, captured Kilia and Cetatea-Alba. The inevitable result of these successes was the submission of Bogdan, Stephen's son, in 1511.

The engagements by which the princes of Moldavia and Wallachia acknowledged the Sultan's suzerainty—usually described as treaties or capitulations—formed the legal basis of the claim of those countries to political independence. Copies of these documents[1] are described as *tractatuli*: in form, that of 1391, which inscribed Wallachia on the Porte's list of countries subject to its protection, approximates rather to a capitulation than to a treaty, since it purports to be a concession made out of the *grande clémence* of the Sultan. Other *tractatuli*, one relating to Wallachia in 1460 and two made with Moldavia in 1511 and 1634, are in form rather more like treaties. The capitulation of 1391 left the Wallachian prince free to exercise full powers of internal and external sovereignty; Christian princes were to be elected by the boyars and the Metropolitan, who was in Wallachia head of the Orthodox Church; and a yearly fixed tribute was to be paid to the Porte. The treaty of 1460 reiterated these clauses and added certain others: the Porte was not to interfere in the affairs of the Principality, nor were Turks either to own

---

[1] Sturdza, *Actes et documents relatifs à l'histoire de la régénération de la Roumanie*, I, 1–8. The capitulation of 1391 is often dated 1393. Sir Henry Bulwer, British Commissioner to the Principalities during 1856–58, wrote, after due enquiry, that the treaties so frequently referred to by the local divans did not exist in either Principality in the original and were not known to exist anywhere else. Sturdza gives the sources for his copies, *op. cit.* p. 8.

land or dwell there; the tribute, newly fixed, was to be collected by a Turkish envoy; finally, no Wallachian subject was to be summoned by the Porte before any court "in the Ottoman possessions". The treaties with Moldavia, though similar in content, are more detailed in form. In that of 1511, the Porte recognised Moldavia as a free and unconquered country subject to its own prince and laws: princes were to be elected for life by the Moldavian nation and confirmed by the Porte; the prince was to maintain an armed troop; the Christian religion was to be free; no Turk was to hold land or build mosques; the prince might have a house and church for an agent at Constantinople; the Sultan was to receive *as a present* 4000 ducats yearly; finally, the Sultan undertook to defend Moldavia from invasion, whilst the prince agreed to support the Sultan with his troop in time of war. The treaty of 1634 confirmed all these articles. In addition it increased the Sultan's yearly tribute and secured for him a preference in purchasing supplies at the ports of Galatz, Ismail and Kilia.

During the sixteenth, seventeenth and eighteenth centuries the Porte sought to transform its legal suzerainty into what became in practice something akin to full sovereignty. It is true that in 1599 Michael the Brave, hospodar of Wallachia, extended his rule over Moldavia and Transylvania and created an independent principality. His principality, comparable in geographical form with the Greater Rumania of to-day, represented the outcome of personal ambition rather than a premature attempt to realise Rumanian national aspirations, and fell to pieces at his death in 1601. More and more the office of hospodar was filled by means of bribery at Constantinople. In the eighteenth century Phanariot rule was instituted, first in Moldavia and then in Wallachia. The Phanariot princes were Greeks from the Phanar quarter of Constantinople who were directly appointed by the Porte. And since the latter regarded these appointments as a source of income, the unfortunate hospodars ruled for short periods[1] and were not infrequently assassinated or interchanged between the two Principalities, which thus suffered constantly the evils of maladministration.

The rise of Russia in the eighteenth century to the rank of a great military power and the series of Russo-Turkish wars which ensued from the time of Peter the Great onwards, mark a new period during which Turkish influence in the Principalities was consistently diminished, to the advantage of Russia. The treaties and conventions which regulated Russo-Turkish relations from 1774 until 1849 embody specific engagements on the part of the Porte towards the Principalities. Russia's interest in these countries was primarily strategical; nor did she fail to assert as a principle of policy support of her Orthodox co-religionists on the Danube. Broadly, these treaties show that although Russia was intent on acquiring for herself privileges and sometimes territory in the Principalities, nevertheless she aimed consistently and successfully at recovering for them, subject to her own protection, that internal independence of the Porte to which they had some theoretical claim.

By the Treaty of Kutchuk-Kainardji[2] in 1774 the Sultan

---

[1] Using as a basis Prof. Iorga's Chronological Table of Ruling Princes in his *History of Roumania*, pp. 266–273, it can be shown that (i) in Wallachia from 1394 until 1822 (when the Porte appointed native princes) 105 princes ruled during a period, allowing for interregna, of 417 years, and (ii) in Moldavia from 1517 until 1822, 107 princes ruled during a period of 294 years. That is, from the time each Principality fell under Turkish influence until 1822, the average reign for a ruler was in Wallachia 4·0 years and in Moldavia 2·7 years.

[2] Hertslet, *Treaties, etc., between Turkey and Foreign Powers* 1535–1855, pp. 463–475.

agreed not only that Russia should reappoint a Minister at the Porte, but also that she should appoint consuls and vice-consuls wherever she wished, with the ostensible purpose of encouraging trade; he agreed, too, to Russia's claim to protect the Christian religion and its churches in Turkey. Russia returned Moldavia and Wallachia to Turkey on certain conditions: they were to receive a complete amnesty, freedom of worship, and freedom from taxation for two years; the tribute was to be fixed at a moderate sum; the "sovereigns" of the Principalities were to be represented at the Porte by *chargés d'affaires* of the Greek Orthodox religion whom the Porte agreed to recognise as diplomatic persons. The Russian Minister at the Porte was to be allowed to intercede on behalf of the Principalities. In accordance with this treaty and not without considerable objection on the part of the Porte, a Russian consul, a Greek, was appointed at Bukarest in 1781;[1] Austria, the Empire, Prussia and France similarly sent representatives, whilst in 1803 British interests were confided to Francis Summerers, a Greek, who acted as consul-general, although his appointment was never confirmed by the Foreign Office.[2] The Convention of Ainali-Kavac of 1779 was explanatory of the previous treaty, the terms of which it reiterated; it specified further that the tribute should be brought to the Porte every two years by native agents, and it limited the Russian Minister's right of intercession to the specific provisions of the convention. In 1792 at Jassy Russia again restored Bessarabia and Moldavia, which she had overrun—this despite the partitioning zeal which she had recently shown in Poland; the Treaty of Jassy confirmed the earlier engagements and added some provisions of a purely temporary nature. As a result of Russian intervention, the Porte issued two hatti-sheriffs in 1784 and 1802. The first[3]

---

[1] Xénopol, *Histoire des Roumains de la Dacie Trajane*, II, 240–241.
[2] See Appendix I.   [3] Xénopol, *op. cit.* II, 244.

stipulated that the hospodars should be dismissed only for insubordination, that Turks were not to own land in the Principalities, and that the tribute, definitely fixed, should be brought to the Porte by agents of the hospodars. The hatti-sheriff of 1802,[1] the result of an agreement with Russia, declared that hospodars would be appointed for seven years, during which time they would be irremovable except in the case of misconduct proved *after a Russo-Turkish enquiry*; that the hospodars should, subject to the views of the Russian Minister, assess taxes; that the Porte should pay the current prices for supplies of grain, sheep, wool, *etc.*; that offices should be bestowed on natives and Greeks of good character; and lastly, that the hospodars should re-establish the national guard. It is indicative of Russia's growing power in the Principalities that she secured her own nominees as hospodars in 1802.[2]

During the years 1806 to 1808 the Principalities figured prominently in international politics. At Constantinople General Sebastiani, the French Ambassador, succeeded in inducing the Porte, which was then strongly pro-French and anti-Russian, to recall the hospodars of Moldavia and Wallachia (August 24, 1806).[3] Russia, with full British concurrence, violently protested against this breach by the Porte of the agreement of 1802. Sebastiani sought further to obtain the closure of the Bosphorus to Russian warships. The British Ambassador, Arbuthnot, was instructed peremptorily to demand the reinstatement of the hospodars and the right for Russian warships to pass the Straits; in the event of non-compliance with these demands he was to end his mission.[4] The news of Napoleon's victory at

---

[1] Hertslet, *op. cit.* p. 762.
[2] Xénopol, *op. cit.* II, 261.
[3] F.O. 78. 51, Arbuthnot to C. J. Fox, Aug. 25/06.
[4] F.O. 78. 52, Instructions from Lord Howick, Nov. 20/06.

Jena encouraged the Turks in their pro-French attitude, although the presence of a British squadron off the Dardanelles exercised a restraining influence. Napoleon sent an agent to the Porte in December, 1806, who stated that the Emperor would not make peace with Prussia until he had humbled Russia and freed the Principalities from dependence on that Power.[1] A Russian army crossed the Dniester and occupied the Principalities; the Turks declared war on Russia; Arbuthnot broke off relations with the Porte by quitting his post secretly, under the cover of night; and finally Great Britain joined in the war. The Franco-Russian alliance at Tilsit suddenly re-orientated French policy in Turkey. At Erfurt in 1808 Napoleon, involved in the Spanish war and distrustful of Austrian policy, desired to renew his alliance with the Czar, and in the secret convention which they signed Alexander I was able to exact the right to acquire the Principalities (which he still occupied) as a *quid pro quo* for his military support of Napoleon in the event of Austria declaring war on France. In 1812, however, by the Treaty of Bukarest, Russia secured only Bessarabia: the Pruth valley, which provides an easy path to the Russian invader, and the Danube from the confluence of the Pruth *via* Kilia to the sea, thus formed the north-eastern boundary between Russia and Turkey.

The outbreak of the Greek rebellion in Moldavia under Demetrius Ypsilanti in 1821 indirectly benefited the Principalities. Seeing that the Czar, true to his Holy Alliance principle of resistance to revolution, was discountenancing the revolt, and acutely mindful of the oppression of their Greek hospodars, the Moldavian boyars offered no support, but shrewdly used the favourable moment to demand of the Porte (among other things) the appointment of native princes. In Wallachia at the same time

---

[1] F.O. 78. 52, Arbuthnot to Howick, Dec. 1/06.

Tudor Vladimirescu raised among the peasants (he was himself the son of a peasant) a social rebellion against the oppression of the nobility, but when Ypsilanti entered Wallachia the revolt assumed an anti-Greek tone. The Czar advised the Wallachian Divan through his consul at Bukarest to demand help from the Porte against the Greeks. The hospodars, who as Greeks favoured their national movement, sought safety in flight; the Porte appointed Greek kaïmakams or temporary governors and sent troops which defeated the Greek rebels. The boyars of each Principality again sent delegations to the Porte, and the latter, free from Russian tutelage since the Czar had just broken off diplomatic relations, wisely appointed native hospodars in 1822. The Czar strongly objected to the retention of Turkish troops in the Principalities and to the increase of Turkish power there; he protested further that the Porte was converting the local corps of Mussulman police, the *beschlis*, into Ottoman troops. Separating his differences with the Porte in respect of the Principalities from those arising out of the Greek rebellion, the new Czar Nicholas I addressed an ultimatum to the Porte in 1826, one demand of which was that the *status quo* of 1821 should be restored in the Principalities; the immediate result was the Convention of Ackerman[1]—"explanatory" of the Treaty of Bukarest—which aimed in its own words "à remettre en vigueur tous les privilèges dont la Moldavie, la Valachie et la Servie doivent jouir sous l'influence tutélaire du Cabinet de Pétersbourg".

By this convention the Porte agreed to respect all the privileges which by treaties or hatti-sheriffs had been

---

[1] Hertslet, *op. cit.* pp. 530–538. Copies of treaties and conventions relating to the Principalities between 1774 and 1849 are conveniently collected in G. Bibesco, *Règne de Bibesco*, vol. 1, but they contain small verbal differences from those in Martens' collections and in Hertslet *supra.*

bestowed upon the Principalities. In a "separate act" forming part of the convention the affairs of the Principalities were specifically dealt with. The boyar assemblies were to elect native princes who, if satisfactory to the Porte, would be nominated and invested by the Sultan for a period of seven years; only if the Porte's objection to an elected candidate was equally shared by Russia, would another election be demanded; moreover a hospodar was to be dismissed only for a serious *délit* which after due enquiry had been proved by the two Courts. Hospodars were to pay attention to the representations of the Russian Minister and consuls. In the case of the dismissal, abdication or death of a reigning prince, the administration was to be temporarily entrusted to kaïmakams chosen by the assemblies. Further, the *beschlis* were to remain, as hitherto, under the control of the hospodars and in numerical strength as before the year 1821. The provisions of the hatti-sheriff of 1802 relating to tribute and the payment for supplies were expressly reaffirmed. Finally, in view of the need for reorganisation after the disturbances of 1821, the hospodars were to draw up in co-operation with their assemblies a *règlement* or body of organic law.

Despite the cession to Austria of the Banat in 1718 and Bukovina in 1775 and that of Bessarabia to Russia in 1812, the Principalities escaped the wholesale partition which the decadence of Turkey and the military strength of Austria and Russia rendered a likely contingency. The Czar's dramatic intervention in the Napoleonic conflict after 1812, an important factor in the overthrow of Napoleon, was important also in saving the Principalities from the political extinction threatened by the Convention of Erfurt. Certainly after 1812 Russian policy towards Turkey, either out of inclination or of necessity, took the form of acquiring, not territory, but treaty rights to interfere in the affairs of the Ottoman Empire. At the Congress of Vienna of 1814–15 the Near Eastern Question was ignored; the Turkish Empire still remained outside the Concert of Europe; the Holy Alliance, as the alliance of Christian monarchs, significantly perhaps, excluded the Sultan; and it seemed that Russia was tacitly enunciating a Monroe doctrine with regard to Turkey:

No Convention of Guarantee [so ran Russia's declaration of war on Turkey in 1828], no political combination, connected the fate of the Ottoman Empire with the healing Acts of 1814 and 1815, under the protection of which civilised and Christian Europe reposed.[1]

From 1828 until 1834 Russia occupied the Principalities, and it seemed again, especially in view of Polignac's scheme[2] in 1829 for recasting the map of Europe to the benefit of France and Russia, that annexation might ensue. According to Lord Augustus Loftus,[3] Sultan Mahmud offered in 1829 to cede Moldavia and Wallachia to Russia in lieu of a war indemnity, but the offer was rejected by Count Orloff, the Russian plenipotentiary, on the ground that Russia had no desire to annex provinces whose "liberal and democratic tendencies" would be dangerous to the Russian state. Indeed, Russia repudiated annexation as both unnecessary and unwise: Count Kisseleff, who governed the Principalities during the Russian occupation, wrote to Count Nesselrode,[4] September 3, 1831:

---

[1] Hertslet, *The Map of Europe by Treaty*, II, 777.
[2] The scheme was a territorial rearrangement of the map of Europe which was to be proposed to Russia and Prussia, had the Ottoman Empire succumbed to Russian arms in 1829. A copy of the project, which is believed to be unpublished, may be found enclosed in a despatch from Cowley to Clarendon, no. 1619, Dec. 28/56, and marked "most confidential" (F.O. 27. 1140).
[3] *Diplomatic Reminiscences* (First Series), I, 343.
[4] G. Bibesco, *op. cit.* I, 24–25.

qu'il ne considérait pas comme utile la réunion des Principautés à l'Empire de Russie, si jamais la Porte venait à re-
noncer à leur suzeraineté,...surtout si la Russie est décidée à
ne pas voir d'un œil indifférent les empiètements qu'ils (les
Turcs) ne manqueront pas de faire sur les privilèges garantis
aux Principautés;

and the Russian Chancellor himself agreed that conquest
was superfluous since Russia was already master of the
Principalities.[1]

The Russo-Turkish war of 1828 brought the Russians
to Adrianople where peace was signed in 1829. The Treaty
of Adrianople stipulated that the Principalities should be
held by Russia until the last payments of the indemnity
of one and a half million Dutch ducats had been paid by
the Porte. The treaty stated clearly the nature of the re-
lationships which connected Turkey and Russia to the
Principalities: the latter, it declared, had been placed by
a capitulation under the suzerainty of the Sultan; Russia
occupied the position of guarantor, having guaranteed
their privileges by her treaties with the Porte. The Treaty
of Adrianople contained a "separate act" relating to the
Principalities which modified or extended the provisions
contained in the Convention of Ackerman: native princes
were to be elected for life; the Principalities were
to enjoy a national and independent administration together with freedom of worship and commerce; the Porte
engaged not to maintain any fortified place on the left
bank of the Danube, or any Mussulman settlement; further,
only those Mussulman merchants who were furnished
with firmans should trade there. The hospodars were

---

[1] W. Miller, *The Balkans* (3rd ed.), p. 92. In 1834 Nesselrode's
instructions to Prince Lieven, Ambassador at London, avowed
Russia's desire "at heart" to respect the independence and integrity
of Turkey and to strengthen the authority of the Sultan (F.O. 65. 212;
Palmerston to Bligh, Feb. 28/34).

empowered in co-operation with their assemblies to raise a militia, with a view particularly to establishing a sanitary cordon at the frontiers. The Porte agreed to cease commandeering supplies of labour and foodstuffs in return for a yearly payment additional to the tribute as fixed in the year 1802; it was to receive also at every appointment of a hospodar a sum equal to the usual annual tribute. Finally, the Porte promised to accept the new constitution which, adumbrated in the Ackerman convention, was already being elaborated, whilst the Russian consuls in the Principalities were specifically authorised to watch over its working. Henceforth, the suzerainty of the Sultan was reduced to slender proportions: he could invest native princes elected for life, but could not reject or dismiss them without Russia's concurrence; he could bestow honours and exact a limited tribute; and he could direct foreign policy,[1] so long as in so doing he did not infringe the privileges guaranteed to the Principalities.

The Russian proclamation in 1828 that they entered the Principalities "as brothers" did not square with their tyrannical conduct, which aroused resentment among both the boyars and the peasants.[2] The Czar's appointment of General Kisseleff, an able and conciliatory administrator, as Commander-in-Chief and "President Plenipotentiary of the Divans of Moldavia and Wallachia",[3] in November,

---

[1] The Treaty of Adrianople made no allusion to any powers of external sovereignty possessed by the Principalities. Actually, Wallachia was represented at Vienna by a *chargé d'affaires*, M. Philippsborn, in 1844; see *Règne de Bibesco*, I, 224. Moldavia made a convention with Austria in 1837 "for the extradition of vagabonds and deserters", the text of which is given in A. A. C. Sturdza, *Règne de Michel Sturdza*, annex IV, pp. 276-282. The hospodars were, further, represented at the Porte by *chargés d'affaires*. Consuls in the Principalities were accredited by the Sultan. Only the shadow of external sovereignty was left to the Principalities.

[2] F.O. 97. 402, despatches from Blutte during 1828-29.

[3] G. Bibesco, *op. cit.* I, 10 and Iorga, *op. cit.* p. 219.

1829, was successful in winning the confidence of the Moldo-Wallachians. Under his guidance the new constitution, the *Règlement Organique*, was completed. This was the work of a committee composed of two members selected by the assembly and two by Kisseleff from each Principality; it worked in two sections, one for Moldavia, and the other for Wallachia, and was presided over by Minciaky, the Russian consul. The Wallachian boyars addressed a petition to Kisseleff demanding that the *Règlement* should be submitted to their assembly for discussion and modification, and alluding to a member of the committee who had been dismissed, ostensibly on account of illness but more probably, as the British consul explained, on account of "indocility".[1] Actually, the *Règlement* was sent to St Petersburg for "correction", then submitted to the assemblies of each Principality, under Kisseleff's presidency, where it was approved with slight amendment, and lastly communicated to the Porte.[1] Many of the boyars, who formed the only political class, were won over to the Russian cause by a generous bestowal of Orders, uniforms, and jewelled snuff-boxes,[2] and by the protection of their privileges in the new constitution. Even so, opposition amounting to rebellion arose in Moldavia, where proximity to Russia, the memory of the annexation of Bessarabia, and the initial success of the Poles in their revolt against the Czar in 1830–31, served to increase the indignation of the boyars against the Russians. The boyars claimed that the right to reform their constitution resided in them alone,[3] and papers were found in the streets of Jassy bearing the exhortation,

---

[1] F.O. 97. 402, Blutte to Cowley, Feb. 22/30. A copy of the *Règlement* of Moldavia is published in Hertslet, *British and Foreign State Papers*, XXXII, 586.
[2] F.O. 78. 238, Blutte to Ponsonby, Aug. 29/34.
[3] F.O. 97. 403, Blutte to Cowley, May 16/31.

"À bas le règlement, citoyens, plutôt la mort".[1] Another protest took the form of a memorial,[2] drawn up by Michael Sturdza and other boyars, which was addressed to the Czar and advocated the union of Moldavia and Wallachia under a foreign prince after the example of Greece; Blutte, British consul at Bukarest, actually forwarded the memorial to Lord Heytesbury, Ambassador at St Petersburg, who protested against this "extraordinary correspondence" sent at the request of Sturdza, whom he styled "their (the boyars') clever man".[3] Had Russia been seriously embarrassed by the Polish rising, something might have resulted from Moldavian opposition. Russia's success over the Polish rebels showed the futility of resistance: "The fall of Warsaw", wrote Blutte on October 3, 1831, "has served to put an end to the hopes founded by the inhabitants of these Provinces...of being possibly delivered from the exclusive protection of Russia".[4] The boyars could do nothing therefore but, at the command of their masters, accept the *Règlement*, adopt European costumes, and shave off their beards.[4]

The Russians signed the Treaty of St Petersburg with the Porte in January, 1834, and evacuated the Principalities, although they continued to hold for a time a number of military roads which would facilitate their intervention, and retained troops at Silistria until 1836.[5] In accordance with the treaty the Sultan issued the *Règlement* in the form of a hatti-sheriff; he was to fix the number of troops which should form native militias in the Principalities, and to receive an increased tribute assessed at three million Turkish

[1] F.O. 97. 403, Blutte to Cowley, Jan. 28/31.
[2] F.O. 97. 402, Blutte to Heytesbury, Jan. 29/30.
[3] F.O. 97. 402, Heytesbury to Aberdeen, May 1/30.
[4] F.O. 97. 403, Blutte to Forbes.
[5] F.O. 97. 404, Blutte to Lamb, Apr. 11/34 and Colquhoun to Palmerston, Sept. 11/36.

piastres a year.[1] The period of the Russian occupation had
been one of abject misery to the inhabitants of the Principalities who had suffered from plague and cholera, from
famine in 1828, from extortion, and even, in 1829, from
an earthquake. In the alleviation of the famine by bringing
supplies from Russia and establishing granaries, Kisseleff
did efficient work; no less did he successfully combat
disease by instituting sanitary cordons and other means.
The constitution with which Russia endowed the Principalities has been criticised as a reactionary code and as the
instrument of Russian domination.[2] The first criticism is,
in the main, reasonable; it should be noted, however, that
it was against his own wishes and in deference to boyar
feelings[3] that Kisseleff confirmed the boyar privileges of
immunity from taxation and sole participation in national
office, and left the peasants in a condition of subjection
even worse than hitherto.[4] In other respects, the *Règlement* was a boon to backward countries which had long
suffered from chronic maladministration: among other
important reforms the judicial system was reorganised,
militia and police systems were established, elective assemblies replaced the pre-existing nominated divans, and
a scheme of public education was prescribed. Further,
although (as will be seen) the *Règlement* strengthened

[1] Moldavia's share of the tribute after 1834 was 700,000 piastres,
i.e. nearly one quarter of the whole; her approximate annual revenue,
as estimated in the *Règlement*, was 6,652,575 piastres; her tribute
amounted therefore to 10 per cent. of her annual revenue. Moldavian
tribute was increased to 1,500,000 piastres by the Convention of Paris,
1858.

[2] Cp. Xénopol, *op. cit.* II, 419.

[3] See the views of Kisseleff stated in Damé, *Histoire de la Roumanie
Contemporaine*, pp. 10, 18 and 26 n. 1. Prof. Iorga, *op. cit.* p. 219,
describes Kisseleff as "the egalitarian, Voltairean, and passionate
lover of liberty". Cp. Xénopol, *op. cit.* II, 408: "esprit large et libéral,
caractère droit, ferme, doué d'une activité et d'une force de travail
véritablement hors ligne".

[4] Cp. Ifor L. Evans, *The Agrarian Revolution in Roumania*, pp. 29–34.

Russia's position with regard to the Principalities, it must be recognised that Russian domination was in many ways beneficial to the Principalities. William Wilkinson, who was consul of the Levant Company at Bukarest, referring to the period before 1820, wrote that the intervention of the Russian consuls often saved the Moldo-Wallachians from the extortion and oppression of their rulers;[1] whilst M. Bois-le-Comte, who was carrying out "a sort of semi-official investigation of the political and moral state of the Principalities" in 1834, contended (erroneously, according to the anti-Russian British consul, Blutte) that the inhabitants should be grateful to the Russians to whom they owed all their civilisation.[2]

With the withdrawal of the Russians Moldavia and Wallachia entered upon a period of nominal self-government, under what has often been inaccurately described as a Russian "protectorate". Certainly Russia retained an effective control over Moldo-Wallachian politics. One article of the *Règlement* ran thus:

Aucune des dispositions de la Constitution ne pourra être abolie ou changée sans le consentement de la Cour Protectrice;[3]

another enabled the hospodar, in cases of deadlock, to complain to the "suzerain" and "protecting" Courts against his assembly—a right which the assembly equally possessed against the hospodar. The Treaty of St Petersburg ignored, as an exceptional case, the right of the Principalities to elect their own princes. Before her withdrawal Russia secured her own candidates as hospodars—

[1] Cited by G. Bengesco, *op. cit.* p. xiv.
[2] F.O. 97. 404, quoted in Blutte to Ponsonby, May 9/34.
[3] F.O. 97. 404, Colquhoun to Palmerston, Dec. 4/36 "separate". Kisseleff printed one hundred copies of the *Règlement* in the Wallachian tongue, for which he was officially reproved. These copies did not contain the article quoted above.

Alexander Ghika and Michael Sturdza—who were invested by the Sultan and swore an oath of allegiance to Kisseleff on behalf of the Czar.[1] The power of the Russian consuls was considerable: the Porte ordered the hospodars to comply with their wishes as much as possible,[2] and Nesselrode made it clear to the hospodars that dismissal would be the result of their disobedience.[3] Indeed, the hospodar of Wallachia was removed in 1842 in favour of Prince Bibesco, and in 1847, at the instance of Russia, Church property in Wallachia was secularised.[4] As the predominant partner in the dualism by which the Principalities were governed, Russia could interfere continually and effectively at Bukarest and Jassy. Nevertheless her control, as defined by the Treaty of Adrianople, was not that of a "protectorate" but that of an exclusive "guarantee" of the privileges granted by the Sultan to the Principalities. In 1848 the Porte affirmed that Russia was only the guarantor and not the protector of the Principalities,[5] although in 1855 at the Conference of Vienna it joined with Great Britain, France and Austria in asserting that Russia had exercised the powers of a protectorate, which Russia herself denied.[6] Sir Stratford Canning agreed that "guarantor" described Russia's relationship.[7] Count Walewski, the French Foreign Minister, considered the question one of mere words.[8] At Vienna in 1855 the less precise term "protection" was adopted, but finally at the

[1] F.O. 97. 404, Blutte to Ponsonby, May 9/34.
[2] F.O. 97. 404, Colquhoun to Palmerston, Aug. 11/36, private.
[3] F.O. 97. 404, letter from Nesselrode to Boutenieff, June 21/36, enclosed in Colquhoun to Palmerston, Oct. 10/36, separate.
[4] F.O. 195. 281, Colquhoun to Palmerston, Mar. 25/47, enclosed in Colquhoun to Wellesley, Mar. 31/47.
[5] F.O. 196. 29, Stratford to Palmerston, Oct. 2/48.
[6] Hertslet, *British and Foreign State Papers*, XLV, protocol 1.
[7] F.O. 196. 29, to Palmerston, Jan. 18/49, no. 11.
[8] Sturdza, *Actes et documents, etc.*, II, 772, circular from Walewski, May 23/55.

Congress of Paris in 1856 the term "protectorate" was
retained.

The Paris revolution of February, 1848 had its counter-
part in the Principalities, particularly in Wallachia. The
practice had grown up among the boyars of sending their
sons to Paris for their education, and M. Lamartine, who
became Foreign Minister in the republican government
which succeeded on the fall of Louis Philippe,

had some connexion with Moldo-Wallachian students in
Paris, having promised a lively interest in the affairs of the
Principalities, and having accepted the office of Patron of a
Moldo-Wallachian Society established at Paris, hence there
exists a certain degree of excitement among the young men,
and a very considerable portion of sympathy with the proceedings in France.[1]

The disturbances in Wallachia marked a definite reaction
against the Russian ascendency. By 1848, as Palmerston
noted,[2] feeling in the Principalities had undergone a
striking change: whereas in 1828 Russia appeared as the
deliverer from the misrule of the Turks, in 1848 Turkey
was regarded as the protector against the severity of
Russia. To the latter Power Moldavia and Wallachia owed
their deliverance from Phanariot hospodars and the establishment of an ordered and nominally autonomous rule.
To young Wallachian leaders who had learnt the catch-
words of Western liberalism, the Czar was too reactionary,
too powerful and too meddlesome a master. Constantine
Rosetti, in common with other leaders, advocated[3] liberty
of the Press, responsibility of ministers, and the equitable
distribution of the burden of taxation among all classes
of society. John Ghika aspired to the purchase of complete independence of the Porte, and believed that the

[1] F.O. 195. 281, Colquhoun to Cowley, Mar. 24/48.
[2] F.O. 195. 316, to Normanby, Oct. 24/48.
[3] F.O. 195. 281, Colquhoun to Stratford, Apr. 6/48, confidential.

geographical position of Wallachia as a frontier province of Turkey was such that the Great Powers might be prevailed upon to fix on the form of government to be established and guarantee her independence.[1] Generally, however, the revolutionary leaders in Wallachia desired to abolish the Russian protection; they did not advocate the abolition of Turkish suzerainty, and in the main, like Tell and Eliad—members of the Provisional Government whom Palmerston thought "well informed and very intelligent"[2] —they approved the Turkish connexion.

The reform movement at Jassy, although essentially moderate in its aims, led, as the Russian consul had predicted, to armed intervention, when General Duhamel, acting entirely without instructions and anticipating an order not to intervene,[3] entered Moldavia with some 4000 troops in July, 1848—drawn there by a bribe of 6000 ducats from the Russophile hospodar, Sturdza.[4] Meanwhile at Bukarest Prince Bibesco abdicated, a Provisional Government was set up, and the original copy of the *Règlement Organique* was burnt during a popular demonstration.[5] Letters were sent from the Provisional Government to Great Britain, France and Austria, requesting their "interest and mediation in the work of regeneration";[6] Palmerston, in reply, professed "sincere interest in their welfare", but declined mediation unsolicited by the Porte.[7] Russian troops entered Bukarest. Nesselrode avowed that Russia's aim was not aggressive but that, in accordance with treaty stipulations, she had

[1] Note 3, p. 19.
[2] F.O. 195. 322, to Stratford, Apr. 7/49.
[3] *Lettres et Papiers du Chancelier Comte de Nesselrode*, IX, 130–131: letter from Nesselrode to Baron Meyendorff.
[4] F.O. 196. 29, Stratford to Palmerston, July 15 and 19/48.
[5] F.O. 195. 281, Colquhoun to Palmerston, Sept. 22/48, private.
[6] F.O. 195. 281, Colquhoun to Stratford, June 26/48.
[7] F.O. 195. 314, to Voynesco, July 17/48.

intervened to restore order.[1] Indeed he maintained that
Wallachia should not be regarded as a civilised European
country, and that a good public servant was scarcely to
be found there.[2] At Constantinople, the attitude of Ali
Pasha, the Foreign Minister, betrayed a struggle between
"a sense of dignity and a fear of consequences",[3] but the
Porte refused to admit Russia's claim to treaty rights of
intervention.[4] Sulieman Pasha was sent to Bukarest, as
Commissioner, to effect necessary reforms, but his recall
was demanded and obtained by Russia, who intended to
deal sternly with the authors of government "à la française".
Sir Stratford Canning, the British Ambassador, advised
the Porte in June, 1848, merely "to wait and watch";
later he urged it firmly to resist the efforts of Russia to
substitute "the rights of protection for the obligations of
a guarantee".[3] He wrote in July, 1848, that "circumstances are ripe for some restoration of Turkish influence",[5] and fearing that Russia held aggressive designs
against Turkey, enquired on November 20 of Sir William
Parker, Vice-Admiral in charge of the Mediterranean fleet,
how much help he could offer, if called upon, either alone or
in concert with the French fleet.[6] Colquhoun, the British
consul at Bukarest, wrote (November 24): "I think it
more than likely that some collision (between the Russian
and Turkish troops) must take place".[7] None, however,
of importance occurred and although the Ottoman Council
"faced the possible contingency of war",[8] pacific counsels
prevailed. Indeed, Russian attention was focussed on

[1] F.O. 195. 314, Brunnow to Palmerston, July 17/48, *particulière*.
[2] F.O. 195. 314, Bloomfield to Palmerston, Aug. 1/48.
[3] F.O. 196. 29, Stratford to Palmerston, Dec. 4/48.
[4] F.O. 196. 29, Stratford to Palmerston, Oct. 2/48.
[5] F.O. 196. 29, Stratford to Palmerston, July 15/48.
[6] F.O. 196. 29.
[7] F.O. 195. 321, to Stratford, confidential.
[8] F.O. 196. 29, Stratford to Palmerston, Feb. 16/49.

Hungary, not on Turkey,[1] and General Grabbe was sent by the Czar in April, 1849 to conclude a peaceful settlement with the Porte.[2] The result of this mission was the *Acte* of Balta-Liman:[3] joint military occupation was continued and the *Règlement* confirmed, the assemblies were abolished and replaced by more narrowly oligarchic divans, whilst new hospodars were appointed for a term of seven years, by the two Courts acting together, at the end of which time the future of the Principalities was to be reconsidered. None of the desired reforms, such as freedom of the Press or equality of taxation, was effected, and reaction triumphed in the Principalities.

The project of a political fusion of Moldavia and Wallachia was not, by the year 1849, envisaged as practical policy: in the social and economic conditions of those countries, fundamental reforms were seriously needed, whilst, politically, freedom from Russian tutelage was more immediately desired. Even so, signs were not lacking at this time which foreshadowed dimly the eventual creation of a Rumanian state. The Phanariot régime, by frequently interchanging hospodars between the two Principalities, and inflicting common suffering at the hands of the Turks, had served to emphasise the common interests of two countries which were geographically and linguistically united. The idea of union had occurred to the Russians during their occupation of 1828 to 1834: Kisseleff in a new commission from the Czar in 1833 had been styled Governor-General of the "United Principalities";[4] the *Règlement* was the work of a single committee, although it worked in two sections, and contained (article ccccxxv) the significant statement:

[1] F.O. 196. 29, Stratford to Palmerston, Feb. 3/49, confidential. See C. Sproxton, *Palmerston and the Hungarian Revolution*, pp. 81–82.
[2] *Ibid.* pp. 86–87.
[3] Hertslet, *The Map of Europe, etc.* 11, 1090. Balta-Liman and Ainali-Kavac are both districts of Constantinople.
[4] F.O. 97. 404, Blutte to Lamb, Feb. 8/33.

Les avantages et les conséquences salutaires résultant de la réunion de ces deux peuples ne sauraient être révoqués en doute. Les éléments de la fusion du peuple Moldo-Valaque sont déjà posés dans ce règlement par l'uniformité des bases administratives des deux pays;[1]

whilst it stipulated further that a mixed commission nominated by the two hospodars should draw up a common code of Moldo-Wallachian law. A great advance was made towards union when, in 1847, by a convention between the two countries custom duties were abolished; article 8 of this convention referred to the "United Principalities", and thenceforth the two peoples became accustomed to the idea of a common frontier.[2] No less important than these positive measures was the growth of national literature and feeling, especially after 1830. In this cultural movement the Rumanians of Transylvania,[3] long subject to Austro-Magyar rule, took the lead, their teachers, both clerical and secular, being fully conscious of the linguistic and racial affinities which connected them with the Moldo-Wallachians. In this intercourse geographical factors assisted, for the Carpathians, together with Transylvania which they encircle and defend, appear to have formed historically the centre of refuge and diffusion of the Rumanian peoples, preserving them from effacement at the hands of invaders,[4] and fostering inter-

[1] Note 1, p. 14.   [2] See Damé, op. cit. p. 47.

[3] There are of course no reliable figures as to the Rumanian-speaking population in Hungary at this time, but the figures given in *A Handbook of Roumania* (published 1920) show that in pre-war Hungary as a whole there were 2,900,000 Rumanians, whilst in Transylvania alone the Rumanian element formed 55 per cent. of the total population. With the exception of the Kutso Vlachs of Macedonia, the Rumanian peoples were geographically enclosed between the Danube, the Theiss and the Dniester: see pp. 85–86, *op cit. supra.*

[4] On the migrations and settlements in Dacia in pre-historic and historical times, and the creation of Rumanian nationality, see V. Pârvan, *Dacia*, J. B. Bury, *The Invasion of Europe by the Barbarians*, and Prof. R. W. Seton-Watson, "Roumanian Origins," in *History*, vol. VII, no. 28.

relations, by means of their passes and summer pasturage, between the peoples on their opposing slopes.[1] The defeat of the Hungarians in 1849, although by Russian arms, was greeted on both sides of the Carpathians as a Rumanian victory over the common enemy. Wallachian liberals, exiled from 1848 until 1857 as the result of Russian intervention in the Principalities, spread abroad, especially in France and England, some knowledge of Rumanian affairs and ambitions;[2] whilst in the Principalities themselves the nationalist teaching of men like George Lazar, John Eliad, Bolintineanu, and Alexandrescu had awakened the sentiment of national pride and aspiration. Without the active interest and assistance of the Great Powers, however, small chance existed of transforming into reality the vague dreams of national regeneration which were shaping in a few minds. That interest and assistance were nearer at hand in 1849 than contemporary statesmen might have guessed, for the Crimean War broke out in 1854, perhaps unnecessarily, and left in its train, quite unintentionally, a number of questions to tax the ingenuity of European statesmanship. One of these questions was the future of Moldavia and Wallachia.

[1] Cp. *A Handbook of Roumania*, chs. I and IV. Permanent occupation of the Carpathians stops at the 2500 ft. contour line, but there are "large areas of comparatively level pasture land at high elevations". The Rumanians are essentially a mountain people, and until recently population was denser in the hill regions than in the plains. The Carpathian boundary of the Principalities was almost entirely a watershed; the rivers Jiu and Olt, however, rise on its northern flank and cut deep passes through the mountain wall, thus affording natural avenues of communication. See map *infra*.

[2] Much of the writings of Rumanian exiles is published in Sturdza, *op. cit.* vols. II–IV: for a full bibliography of this propagandist literature see G. Bengesco, *op. cit.* See also N. Iorga, *Histoire des relations entre la France et les Roumains*, and Xénopol, *op. cit.* vol. II.

CHAPTER TWO

THE PRINCIPALITIES AND THE GREAT POWERS, 1855–56

"Those poor devils of old Romans have always the piper to pay."

ALISON to LAYARD, June 10, 1853.[1]

[1] *The Layard Papers*, Add. MS. 38,981.

CHAPTER TWO

THE PRINCIPALITIES AND THE GREAT
POWERS, 1855-56

THE Crimean War made the question of the Principalities one of European importance. The first phase of the war took place in the Principalities: a Russian army crossed the Pruth in July, 1853, only three years after the termination of the previous occupation; the Porte declared war and successfully defeated the Russians in their attempts to secure Vidin and Silistria, strategical points on the right bank of the Danube. The intervention of France and Great Britain transferred the theatre of war to the Crimea, whilst, in accordance with an Austro-Turkish convention[1] of June 14, 1854, Austria occupied the Principalities, which Russia evacuated. Great Britain and France declared, in the Convention of London[2] of April 10 to which Austria and later Sardinia acceded, that the integrity of the Ottoman Empire, violated by Russia's occupation of the Principalities, was an object of the war. An equally important aim of the Allies was the abolition of the "protectorate" which Russia had exercised over the Principalities. Consequently Article I in the Memorandum[3] presented to Russia in December, 1854, by Great Britain, France and Austria, stipulated as a condition of peace that Russia's exclusive "protectorate" should be abolished, and that the privileges granted to Moldavia and Wallachia by Turkey should be placed under the Collective Guarantee of the Five Powers—Great Britain, France, Austria, Turkey and Russia. The Five Powers sent plenipotentiaries to Vienna in March, 1855, ostensibly to make peace, although in reality the secret aim of both parties to the war was to win the active co-

---

[1] Hertslet, *The Map of Europe, etc.* II, 1213.
[2] *Ibid.* II, 1193.
[3] *Ibid.* II, 1225.

operation of Austria.[1] Prussia, who was not a member of the Alliance and occupied the position of armed neutrality, refused[2] to send a representative to the Conference. Negotiations failed to produce peace, as Lord John Russell, the British plenipotentiary, had anticipated,[3] but the question of Moldavia and Wallachia was discussed and the conflicting interests and policies of the Powers were revealed.

Great Britain had little knowledge of the Principalities and only a moderate interest in their affairs. There are, it is true, traces of early commercial intercourse between the two countries: English manufactured goods entered the Principalities by way of the Dantzig fairs as early as the mid-fifteenth century, whilst in the sixteenth century Moldavian oxen reached England by way of the Baltic.[4] A commercial treaty, which was signed between Queen Elizabeth and Peter the Lame of Moldavia in 1588, permitted English merchants to reside in Moldavia for purposes of trade and fixed the customs duty at 3 per cent.[5] With the beginning of the nineteenth century, when consular relations began, the East India and Levant Companies had established business connexions in the Principalities. William Wilkinson who succeeded Summerers as "acting" British consul-general at Bukarest in 1813 was actually consul in the employment of the Levant Company.[6] Wilkinson, in a letter to Castlereagh in 1814, gives a glimpse of the extent of British commercial

[1] F. Charles-Roux's *Alexandre, Gortchakoff et Napoléon III*, contains a good account of the Conference. See also *The Later Correspondence of Lord John Russell*, edited by Dr G. P. Gooch.

[2] L. Thouvenel, *Pages de l'histoire du Second Empire*, p. 34.

[3] *The Later Correspondence of Lord John Russell*, II, 190, letter to Sir G. Grey, Feb. 13/55.

[4] N. Iorga, *Les premières relations entre l'Angleterre et les pays Roumains du Danube* (1427 à 1611), printed in C. Bémont, *Mélanges d'Histoire*, p. 565.

[5] Note 4 above, and *A Handbook of Roumania*, p. 117.

[6] See Appendix I.

activity in the Principalities: there were one hundred merchants enjoying British protection dwelling at Bukarest, Jassy and Galatz; often more than ten English vessels reached Galatz in a season; whilst he estimated the consumption of British products in the Principalities at £40,000 a year.[1] In 1849 Lord Dudley Stuart raised the question in the House of Commons: "What are Moldavia and Wallachia and what has been their political condition?", to which Palmerston replied.[2] Austen Layard, who had acquired some knowledge of Near Eastern affairs as an attaché under Sir Stratford Canning at Constantinople, won the gratitude of Rumanian leaders in 1855 by his supposed advocacy in Parliament of the cession of Bessarabia to Moldavia and the creation of a Rumanian state on the Lower Danube[3]: gratitude in this instance was, it seems, anticipatory, for in none of his Parliamentary speeches did Layard propose such an innovation.[4] In Gladstone the Moldo-Wallachians possessed a staunch Parliamentary supporter. A public meeting at Brighton in favour of the union of the Principalities was noted with stern disapproval by the Turkish Ambassador.[5] It was held on October 6, 1856 at the Town Hall, under the chairmanship of the Mayor; D. Bratianu, a former member of the Wallachian government and a keen advocate abroad of Moldo-Wallachian unity, was present, whilst certain parliamentarians, including Lord Brougham, Gladstone, Roebuck, and Otway, sent letters stating their full

[1] F.O. 78. 82, Oct. 1/14.
[2] Hansard, *Parliamentary Debates* (3rd Series), vol. CIII, Mar. 22/49.
[3] *The Layard Papers*, Add. MS. 39,065, letter to Layard from Rumanian leaders in Paris, May 17/55. For the facts of Layard's career see *Catalogue of Additional Manuscripts* at the British Museum. This corrects statements in the *Dictionary of National Biography*.
[4] In his Parliamentary speeches Layard indicated only his sympathy for the Moldo-Wallachians, his condemnation of the Russian "protectorate", and his objection to the Austrian occupation.
[5] *The Layard Papers*, Add. MS. 38,985, Musurus to Layard, Oct. 8/56.

sympathy with the objects of the meeting and their regret at inability to attend. The motion which was passed unanimously read thus:

That this meeting is in favour of the union of Moldavia and Wallachia, in order to make a free and powerful nation of the Roumans, as the best barrier against Austria and Russia; and that the meeting expresses its earnest hopes that the Government of England will, in conjunction with France, insist on the fulfilment of the resolutions of the Paris Conference, in adopting the views and satisfying the just expectations, of the Rouman people as to their internal government;[1]

whilst a petition in these terms to the Queen was approved, although (to quote the *Brighton Gazette*):[2]

Mr Mathews, a mechanic, and a chartist said..."as to a petition to the British Government, it was worth about as much as the snap of a finger. But since they had allowed us to petition perhaps we might as well do it." (A laugh.)

The Brighton meeting, however, was probably an isolated event, and *The Brighton Guardian* reported significantly that "the meeting was but thinly attended".[3] *The Quarterly Review* was justified in commenting in April, 1858, on the "gross and Egyptian darkness of understanding" which prevailed in England on the question of the Principalities.[4]

The fate of those countries in 1855 touched only lightly British policy in the Near East, which had the double aim of crippling Russian power and of preserving Ottoman integrity. The latter aim was justified, not only on political but also on commercial grounds, since, as Palmerston informed

---

[1] *The Brighton Examiner*, Oct. 7/56.
[2] Oct. 9/56; the *Brighton Gazette* published a small leader on the Principalities. Rather undecided in tone, it stressed the practical difficulties in the way of union, *e.g.* would the Principalities, if united, be strong enough to act as a barrier to Austria and Russia?
[3] Oct. 8/56.   [4] Article viii.

the Commons, "there was no foreign country with which we carried on intercourse in which the tariff was so low and so liberal as that of Turkey".[1] British views on the future of the Principalities in 1855 are summed up in the instructions[2] given to Lord John Russell for his guidance at Vienna. The first aim was to abolish Russia's "exclusive protectorate", which (the instruction declared) had already lapsed, since Russo-Turkish treaties had been abrogated by the war:

> Russia shall no longer have to plead special Treaty engagements with herself (*sc.* the Porte) as justifying her single interference with the Sovereign Power, in regard to the relations between that Power and the established authorities in the Provinces.

On the termination of Russia's influence Moldavia and Wallachia would not revert to the "immediate subjection of the Porte". The Sultan would resume his suzerainty and the Principalities would no longer

> look to Russia as the arbitress of their destinies, and pay that court and deference to her which should be reserved for the Sultan alone.

Great Britain did not consider that internal changes should be made in the Principalities, and suggested the return to the *status quo ante bellum*:

> There would be no occasion to interfere, at least in principle, with the system of local self-government established in those Provinces, or to place the rulers of the Provinces in more direct dependence on the Sovereign Power than they now are.

There were several matters, however, which Lord John Russell was authorised to discuss: the Sultan's tribute might be increased, and the Sultan might be allowed to have garrisons in Moldavia and Wallachia as in Serbia.

---

[1] Note 2, p. 28.
[2] *Parliamentary Papers* (1854–55), LV, 265–270, dated Feb. 22/55.

The right of investing hospodars, treaty-making power, and the recognition of consular agents would remain vested in the Porte. Beyond these points Lord John Russell's instructions did not go: although desirous of improvements in the Principalities, Great Britain was not prepared to discuss further questions, such as political union, national representation, and hereditary hospodars, until the Porte had stated its views. It is significant, too, that no mention was made in the instructions of the idea of a Collective Guarantee, although that idea formed part of Article I of the December Memorandum.

To Austria the future of the Principalities was a matter of much greater concern. Her troops under General Coronini occupied the Principalities in 1854, and except for a garrison at Bukarest the Turks withdrew. The ruling hospodars were left in office, Gregory A. Ghika in Moldavia, and Barbu Stirbey, Austria's faithful adherent, in Wallachia. Question was raised in the House of Commons in May, 1855, about an alleged proclamation of martial law by the Austrian general, but Palmerston explained that the law in question related only to the desertion of Austrian troops and to persons inciting them to desertion.[1] Gladstone characterised the Austrian occupation as "a still heavier infliction"[2] than that of Russia which preceded it. Lord Stratford described public opinion in the Principalities as decidedly averse from Austria, whose control was identified "with the domineering pretensions of Russia unsoftened by historical traditions or by religious sympathies".[3] In the material sphere the Austrians showed

[1] Hansard, *op. cit.* cxxxviii, Mar. 24/55.
[2] *Ibid.* cl, 43, May 4/58.
[3] *Memorandum printed for use of Foreign Office, Dec.* 22/55, *Confidential*, enclosed in Clarendon to Stratford, Jan. 7/56, confidential (F.O. 195. 497). This memorandum embodied the views of Stratford (see p. 41 *infra*). The passage quoted above was deleted in the copy transmitted to the Austrian Government.

successful and well-directed energy. The Danube was rendered more navigable, its estuary channels were cleared and a lighthouse was built; roads were constructed; a telegraph system linked Bukarest and Jassy; whilst, stimulated by improved transport facilities, trade with Austria by way of the Danube and with the Allies in the Crimea prospered.[1] In general, the economic policy of Austria in the Principalities was part of a policy, based on imported ideas of *Laissez-Faire*, which had already in 1850 established free trade within the Austrian Empire.[2] It seems clear that Austria desired to retain economic unity with the Principalities and to obtain further some definite political relationship: to leave the native princes to rule under her protectorate[1]—a possibility which (as will be shown later) the Porte early foresaw and condemned. This, however, was not possible, for although Count Buol, the Austrian Foreign Minister, boasted significantly to Count Beust[1] in 1855: "Wir haben die Donaufürstentümer in der Tasche!", Austria had played such a negative and ineffective part during the Crimean War as to have earned no claim on the victors for a share in the spoils of victory. The possibility of handing over the Principalities to Austria was tentatively considered by the statesmen at Paris in 1856, but only on the basis of an exchange by which Sardinia should receive Lombardy and Venetia from Austria. Palmerston advocated such an exchange in 1854, when, at the Home Office, he took great pleasure in reconstructing the post-war map of Europe, on the assumption that victory would be won by a powerful European coalition.[3] Napoleon III proposed the exchange at the

[1] H. Friedjung, *Der Krimkrieg und die österreichische Politik*, pp. 182–187.

[2] Cp. "The Economic Aspects of Dualism in Austria-Hungary", by Ifor L. Evans, in *The Slavonic Review*, Mar./1928.

[3] *The Later Correspondence of Lord John Russell*, II, 160. Memorandum, Mar. 19/54.

Congress of Paris in 1856 as a solution of the Italian question, but it was rejected by Austria;[1] Cowley thought it theoretically desirable as an alternative to Austria's demand that Russia should cede Bessarabia to Turkey.[2] In short, any hopes of acquiring the Principalities, which Austria may secretly have cherished,[3] were not publicly stated as a political aim owing to the weakness of her position, and Sir George Seymour, British Ambassador at Vienna, was able to write (December 24, 1856) that "the idea of possessing themselves of these Provinces never, I am convinced, for one moment occupies the thoughts of the Emperor's Government".[4]

Austrian views, as advanced at the Conference of Vienna,[5] differed from those of Great Britain only in that they favoured a Collective Guarantee of the privileges which had been accorded to the Principalities by the Porte. These privileges—autonomy, and freedom of worship, commerce and navigation—should be examined by the Porte in concert with its Allies; they should be "carefully developed according to circumstances" and reissued in a "Solemn Hat" (i.e. Hatti-Sheriff), which the Five Powers should guarantee. If differences arose between the Porte and the Principalities, the guaranteeing Powers should consider the matter in conference; if the repose of the Principalities were threatened, no intervention by the Porte should take place except in the name of the guarantors. A "national armed force" should be raised in the Principalities to

[1] F. A. Simpson, *Louis Napoleon and the Recovery of France*, p. 358.
[2] Greville, *Memoirs*, VIII, 29.
[3] Austria's ambitions at the expense of Turkey took another form by 1860 when, in the undesired event of a partition of Turkey, she desired the country between the Adriatic and a line from Vidin to Salonica and thence to Scutari in Albania. See the note by Miss E. F. Malcolm-Smith in *The Cambridge Historical Journal*, I, no. 3.
[4] F.O. 195. 515, to Clarendon.
[5] Hertslet, *British and Foreign State Papers*, vol. XLV. Protoco of the Conference of Vienna, Mar.–June/55.

guard the frontiers and keep the peace. Such was the programme of Austria, as yet reticent about questions such as national representation and union, which she hoped would not arise. She showed a desire to share in the reform of the institutions of the Principalities and doubtless foresaw the chance of constant interference, as a guaranteeing Power, in disputes between the Principalities and the Porte.

Russia had reconciled herself by the spring of 1855 to relinquish her claims to protection of the Principalities. At the Conference of Vienna,[1] she urged the need for some examination of the *Règlement Organique* with a view to its reform. Russia maintained that it would be unwise to discuss reforms at the Conference since differences might arise, and suggested that the Treaty of Peace should contain four general principles, the details being subsequently evolved: the first two were the preservation of the existing privileges of the Principalities and an agreement by the Powers collectively to guarantee them; the third principle, interesting as the first public statement of a plan later adopted by the Congress of Paris, was that the Powers should agree

to consult the wishes of the country as to the maintenance or modification of the *Règlement* which constitutes the basis of its internal organisation[2];

finally, Russia suggested the adjournment of this question until the Powers might concert with the Ottoman Government. There was a further suggestion that, in cases of urgency, the army in the Principalities might be increased by an agreement between the Porte and the limitrophe Powers. It was already clear that, if Russia was to lose the exclusive influence she had secured by treaty, she wished to retain the goodwill of the inhabitants of

[1] Note 5, p. 33.　　　[2] Annex A to Protocol 2.

Moldavia and Wallachia. Her enunciation of the new and startling proposition to consult the wishes of the Principalities themselves, must be ascribed chiefly to this motive. Probably she desired also to embarrass Austria, who had signally succeeded thus far during the war in showing her ingratitude for the Czar's timely assistance during the Hungarian Revolution of 1849.

The question of the Principalities was of great importance to Turkey, which realised acutely that Russia had "reduced the Porte's right of ownership (*propriété*) of the Principalities to a purely nominal and formal thing, and gave to her (Russia's) claim to protection a strength which was more than a right of possession".[1] If Russia were beaten in the Crimean War, the Porte would be able to regain some of its former power over the Principalities.

"It is evident", wrote Lord Stratford de Redcliffe from Constantinople,[2] "that the Porte has strong opinions of its own on some of the points...to be debated there (*sc.* Vienna).

"An Austrian protectorate in the Principalities, however limited, would never meet with its cordial assent. The consolidation of the two provinces under a single chief, would also fail to receive its support. There is every disposition, I conceive, to improve the conditions of the country, to secure it administrative independence and to render the relations between the boyars and inhabitants in general less onerous to the latter. The Porte, I believe, is not insensible to the importance of calming the jealousy of Austria with respect to democratic institutions, and the advantages to which she looks for herself are less those of power than of increased revenue and surer defence against Russia. The Princes, I apprehend, will remain to be chosen among the native aristocracy, and if the Porte has its way the tribute will be reasonably augmented

---

[1] F.O. 78. 1075, Porte's Memorandum on the Principalities, enclosed in Stratford to Clarendon, Mar. 31/55.

[2] F.O. 78. 1075, to Clarendon, Mar. 23/55, confidential.

and the destroyed fortresses will be revived for the reception of Turkish garrisons."

Stratford's impressions were borne out by the Instructions[1] and the Memorandum[2] with which Ali Pasha was furnished when he set out for Vienna early in April, 1855. He came to replace, as Plenipotentiary, Aarif Effendi whose lack of official powers and personal incompetence made him an unsatisfactory representative.[3] He was too late, however, to join in the discussions on the Principalities. Ali was instructed to demand the termination of Russia's "protectorate" and a joint guarantee of the privileges accorded to the Principalities; the restoration of fortresses on the left bank of the Danube which had been held before 1829 (such as Braïla and Giurgiu, which commanded respectively the northern routes to Jassy and Bukarest) and the right to construct new ones; and, finally, the reform of the institutions of the Principalities at Constantinople where agents from those countries should take part. Ali's Memorandum indicated very clearly that Turkey's aim was not only to resume her old position before the war, but also to extend the limited rights which Russia had left her after the engagements of 1829, 1834 and 1849. The Porte wished to choose the prince for life from natives or other Christian subjects (but he was to be dismissed solely for treason against the Porte or violation of the privileges of his country); to bestow honours and the higher ranks in the army; to keep a Commissioner in each Principality charged to watch over the application of the reformed constitution and to act as the channel between the hospodar and the Porte and between the guaranteeing Powers and the Porte; and, finally, to send

---

[1] F.O. 78. 1075, enclosed in Stratford to Clarendon, Mar. 31/55.
[2] F.O. 78. 1075, to Clarendon, Mar. 23/55, confidential.
[3] L. Thouvenel, *op. cit.* p. 43.

troops to the Provinces to restore order in cases of sedition. The Porte's position was quite intelligible: in order to form a barrier against Russia, it was necessary, not to unite the Principalities under a foreign prince, but merely to tighten the bonds of suzerainty which connected them with the Porte.

It is obvious, then, that the Ottoman Government saw plainly the issues involved in the question of the Principalities. By preparing early, it hoped to disarm possible opponents, among whom the most powerful was its ally France. On April 10, 1855, Lord Cowley wrote:[1]

The Emperor (Napoleon III), I understand, is not at all inclined to enter into the Turkish view of the manner in which the Danubian Provinces should be administered.

At the Conference of Vienna, Baron Bourqueney, the French Plenipotentiary, alone suggested the possibility of uniting Moldavia and Wallachia:

ne voulant pas exclure la possibilité de réunir un jour les territoires des 2 Principautés en un seul, si jamais cette réunion était jugée de nature à faciliter leur administration et à favoriser leurs intérêts bien entendus.[2]

Union, according to Bourqueney, would create a natural barrier to Russia; it had been foreshadowed, as eventually desirable in the *Règlement*; moreover it was popularly desired in the Principalities, so that

le vœu des deux provinces à cet égard (*i.e.* Union) se présente conforme aux convenances des Gouvernements alliés.[3]

An hereditary prince would be desirable, and, as the recent history of Egypt and Serbia has shown, there need be no infringement of Turkish suzerainty; or perhaps a

[1] F.O. 195. 465, to Clarendon, confidential.
[2] Hertslet, *British and Foreign State Papers*, vol. XLV, Protocol 2.
[3] *Ibid.* vol. XLV, Annex to Protocol 6.

foreign prince from a European royal house might be a better choice. These were the French views stated at Vienna, remarkable in the way they combined the old principle of the "convenances" of Europe with the newer principle of consulting the wishes of the people.

Each Principality sent an agent to the Conference of Vienna but only in the unofficial capacity of advisers to the Porte on local affairs. Buol, the Austrian Foreign Minister, suggested the idea,[1] urging that the nomination of the agents should be made by the hospodars, whom, owing to the Austrian occupation, he effectively controlled. Clarendon doubted the expediency of the proposal and agreed with Drouyn de Lhuys that, if sent, the agents should be nominated by the Porte.[2] This plan was attempted: each hospodar was ordered to select his agent from a list of three candidates submitted by the Porte. Stirbey, the hospodar of Wallachia, refused to choose from the Porte's list[3] and Colquhoun, the British consul, reported[4] the utter worthlessness of the Porte's candidates; finally Stirbey secured the appointment of his son-in-law, M. Arsaky, a Greek.[3] The agents from the Principalities did not play even a minor part at the Conference of Vienna: they were selected early in June, but the important discussions on the 1st Point were concluded by the end of March.

The Conference of Vienna ended in June, 1855, without result. The Powers, with the exception of Turkey, whose Plenipotentiary, Aarif Effendi, had lacked sufficient instructions, agreed (March 19) that Russia's "protection" should be abolished, that the suzerainty of the Sultan and the privileges of the Principalities should be confirmed,

---

[1] Wiener Staatsarchiv (cited *infra* as V. S. A.). *Rapports de Constantinople*, XII, 52, Koller to Buol, Mar. 29/55.

[2] F.O. 195. 463, enclosures in Clarendon to Stratford, Mar. 8/55.

[3] F.O. 195. 468, Colquhoun to Westmorland, June 15/55.

[4] F.O. 195. 466, enclosure in Clarendon to Stratford, May 30/55

and that a Collective Guarantee should be instituted. It is clear, however, that considerable differences existed, especially on the issue raised by France, the union of the Principalities under an hereditary (and perhaps foreign) prince.

The question of the Principalities was reopened after the fall of Sebastopol. The initiative came from Great Britain. On September 15, 1855, Lord Clarendon, who was Foreign Secretary, wrote[1] to Stratford:

H(er) M(ajesty's) Government urge the Porte to propose to England and France a new organisation of the Government and constitution of Moldavia and Wallachia...so that the Sultan may of his own will establish good government in those provinces.

Clarendon's object was to safeguard the Sultan's right to deal with questions of internal policy, and to avoid by prompt action the necessity for a Collective Guarantee of the Powers, which would give to Russia and Austria jointly, "greater powers of interference in the Provinces than have hitherto been claimed and exercised by Russia alone".[1] Clarendon's scheme promised well. To effect an agreement between three Powers, Great Britain, France and Turkey, was a practical proposition. It had the merit of excluding Russia from the negotiations, and might checkmate Austria who sought some loop-hole for future interference in the Principalities. Finally, it avoided all danger of infringing the sovereign rights of the Sultan—rights which the Allies had engaged to defend in the Convention of London of 1854.

Count Walewski, who had succeeded Drouyn de Lhuys at the Foreign Office, supported the scheme which, it was agreed, should be worked out at Constantinople between the French and British Embassies and the Porte.[2] He seemed inclined to associate Austria with the scheme, but

[1] F.O. 195. 470.
[2] F.O. 195. 470, Cowley to Clarendon, Sept. 17/55.

Cowley effectively dissuaded him from this view.[1] The French Ambassador at Constantinople was to receive instructions similar to those sent to Stratford.[1] It seemed, then, that at Constantinople a committee of three would settle the question of Moldavia and Wallachia. Austria, however, refused to be ignored. She had acceded to the Convention of London in December, 1854, and in December, 1855, Great Britain and France assented to her peace ultimatum to Russia: she had, therefore, some basis to her claim to share in the negotiations on the 1st Point. In December, Count Colloredo handed to Clarendon a copy of the instructions which were to be addressed to the Internuncio at Constantinople, in order that he might discuss with the Ambassadors of England and France the 1st and 4th Points[2]—the future of the Principalities and the position of the Christians in Turkey respectively. These instructions—which contained principles to be observed in settling the 1st Point—might furnish (said Buol) a basis for a new arrangement and facilitate a speedy settlement. Clarendon objected to Austria's wish to participate because it made the settlement depend on the consent of four Powers;[3] nor was he pleased at the Austrian aim to place the new reforms under "the formal guarantee of Europe".[4] He was convinced of the "importance of immediately settling the future organisation of the Principalities as far as it may be practicable". He was equally convinced, however, that a European guarantee was dangerous, because it might create dissension among the Powers, and unnecessary, because Turkey was not hostile towards the Principalities.[4]

In December, 1855, the British Government drew up its views on the Principalities in a Memorandum[5] which was

[1] Note 2, p. 39.
[2] F.O. 195. 473, Clarendon to Seymour, Dec. 14/55.
[3] F.O. 195. 473, Clarendon to Seymour, Dec. 14/55.
[4] F.O. 120. 310, Clarendon to Seymour, Dec. 26/55.
[5] Note 3, p. 32.

actually (as Clarendon stated[1]) the work of Stratford. It showed that the question had two desiderata: it was necessary to provide for the future welfare of the inhabitants, and at the same time to strengthen the Turkish frontier. The Principalities had some claim on the goodwill of the Powers:

> It rests with them (the Allies) to atone for ages of military vexation and misgovernment to a people entitled on many accounts to a far better lot than they have hitherto enjoyed.

But where the interests of the Moldo-Wallachians conflicted with European interests, it was expedient to sacrifice the former to the latter. Clarendon, though undecided on the question, thought it unwise to attempt "so hazardous an innovation" as union, on the ground that the Principalities might aggressively seek full independence of the Sultan. He thought it desirable also to continue the practice of selecting hospodars from the native aristocracy:

> The native families offer few individuals worthy of the trust, but national feelings are enlisted in favour of a national choice, and the recurrence to strangers would no doubt be a cause of discontent.

A new constitution, "suited to national habits and wants" and emanating from the Porte, should replace the existing *Règlement*. No foreign protectorate should succeed that of Russia and instead

> there should be a constituent act emanating from the Sultan and seconded by his Allies, which would afford the best and most convenient security for the sovereign and for the people.

The exchange of views between the British and Austrian Governments was successful, for in January, 1856, Austria

[1] F.O. 195. 499, Clarendon to Stratford, Feb. 13/56.

announced her intention not to insist on a formal act of guarantee.[1] She thought, however, that the contracting Powers, in return for the reorganisation of the Principalities, would acquire "a just claim to the acceptance of their joint intervention".[1] "No material difference", wrote Clarendon,[1] "existed between them (*sc.* British Government) and the Austrian Government with respect to the arrangement for the future government of the Principalities." The French Government, however, felt that the British views were not entirely satisfactory: "The Imperial Government", said Walewski,[2] "would prefer, for instance, the union of the two Principalities in one Government", but if the British Government insisted on its views, he was not disposed to oppose them. He therefore agreed to the British plan, and the Conference of Constantinople began its work.

The Conference of Constantinople consisted of "friendly and confidential communications" between the Porte and the representatives of Great Britain, France and Austria. Sardinia did not take part: Layard asked in the Commons why Sardinia was excluded and was told that the Conference was not connected with the Treaty of Peace.[3] The aim of the statesmen was to reach some provisional agreement on the 1st and 4th Points, and thereby to simplify the work of the prospective Peace Conference. The questions raised by the 1st and 4th Points affected the sovereignty of the Porte and were, strictly speaking, the concern of the Sultan's government alone. To leave these questions to the future Congress was to invite differences and difficulties; to solve them beforehand was to eliminate the interference of Russia in their solution. Actually on the 4th Point an agreement was reached which, issued as a hatti-humayun

---

[1] F.O. 195. 497, Clarendon to Seymour, Jan. 17/56.
[2] F.O. 195. 498, Cowley to Clarendon, Jan. 23/56.
[3] Hansard, *op. cit.* vol. CXL, Feb. 12/56.

of the Porte, formed part of the final peace settlement. On the 1st Point the Allies drew up a Memorandum, known as the Protocol of Constantinople,[1] to which they all assented on February 11, 1856. The Protocol, however, was neither signed nor dated.[2] The instructions of Thouvenel, the French Ambassador, limited him to "officious (sic) interference unaccompanied by formalities"[2] and Stratford, though desirous of some formal engagement, "had no authority to insist upon a different course of proceeding".[2] Thouvenel wrote to Walewski, "Il n'y a donc, d'aucun côté, d'engagement sacramental",[3] and Buol emphasised the "*unofficial* character of these preliminary negotiations".[4]

The Protocol of Constantinople represented to some extent a compromise; its decisions, however, were bound to be transient because they excluded all points of controversy between the Powers. France withheld her plan for political union, and Austria her scheme for a Collective Guarantee. Stratford was hampered by a lack of instructions bearing on either the principles or details to be secured.[5] He considered at this time as *theoretically* desirable the extension of the frontier of Moldavia to the Dniester, the union of the Principalities under a foreign prince and thus the creation of a "material barrier" against Russia.[5] In order to reach some basis of agreement before the meeting of the Congress of Paris, he was compelled to abandon this proposal as well as an attempt to secure a representative system for the Principalities. The Porte failed to establish its previous claims to appoint resident

---

[1] Published in Sturdza, *op. cit.* II, 917.

[2] F.O. 78. 1172, Stratford to Clarendon, Feb. 12/56.

[3] Sturdza, *op. cit.* II, 949, Feb. 12/56.

[4] V. S. A. *Dépêches à Constantinople*, XII, 58, private letter to Prokesch, Mar. 2/56.

[5] F.O. 78. 1172, Stratford to Clarendon, Feb. 11/56, no. 160.

commissioners, and to gain for its Mohammedan subjects the right to reside, travel and trade north of the Danube. It obtained, however, the right to build and maintain fortresses even on the Pruth, to appoint hospodars, to elaborate at Constantinople a new constitution for the Principalities, and to nominate (in concert with its allies) kaïmakams in each Principality on the expiration of the official term of the ruling hospodars. Lord Stratford considered that the Protocol had the "salutary effect of substituting the Sultan's charter for Russian dictation",[1] but Liberals from the Principalities were disappointed at an arrangement which denied them union and enlarged the suzerainty of the Sultan.[2] Clarendon, writing from Paris on March 4, 1856, described the Protocol as "the groundwork for a good organisation of the Principalities",[3] but Napoleon III protested to Clarendon that union would be "an improvement upon the feeble attempt at reorganisation that had been proposed at Constantinople".[4] In two important respects the Protocol was inadequate: it made no provision for a Collective Guarantee, and it did not even consider the possibility of any form of union.

When the Congress of Paris[5] met on February 25, 1856 to conclude peace, the propositions agreed upon at Constantinople were ignored, the question of the Principalities was reopened, and the Powers took sides on the question of Moldo-Wallachian union. The Foreign Ministers of Great Britain, France, Austria and Sardinia attended the Congress as first plenipotentiaries, whilst Turkey was represented by her Grand Vizier. Russia was repre-

---

[1] F.O. 78. 1172, Stratford to Clarendon, Feb. 11/56, no. 160.
[2] Sturdza, *op. cit.* II, 965, Gr. Ghika to Walewski, Feb. 29/56.
[3] F.O. 195. 500, to Stratford, confidential.
[4] Martin, *The Life of the Prince Consort*, III, 465.
[5] For protocols of the Congress see Hertslet, *British and Foreign State Papers* (1856), vol. XLVI; see also Sir E. Satow, *International Congresses* (F.O. Handbook, no. 151).

sented by Count Orloff, a veteran of the Napoleonic wars,
and by Baron Brunnow, formerly Minister at London.
Prussia, although neither a belligerent nor even (as was
Austria) an inactive member of the Alliance against Russia,
claimed admittance to the Congress. Frederick William IV,
called "The Trimmer" because of his vacillating policy,
asserted that he had "an indubitable right" to be represented.[1] Prussia's claim to admittance rested upon two
grounds: first, as a signatory to the Convention of the
Straits of 1841 which was bound to come under review,
and second, as a Great Power.[2] Austria supported Prussia's
claim in order to prevent her from leading the pro-
Russian states in the German Diet.[3] It was believed
officially at Berlin and by the German Press that Great
Britain was the obstacle to Prussia's attendance, and that
France did not see eye to eye with her ally in this matter.
Manteuffel, the Prussian Foreign Minister, plainly intimated to the French *chargé d'affaires* his desire for
admission, and even expressed the hope of an eventual
alliance between France and Russia, which Prussia "might
be inclined to join"[4]; on another occasion he told the
Marquis de Moustier, the French Minister at Berlin, that
if represented at the Congress, Prussia "would be found
always on the side of the Allies and not with Russia".[5]
British feeling was certainly hostile to Prussia both in the
Cabinet and in the Press: Baron Bunsen, the Prussian
Minister, had been recalled from London in 1854 because
he had advocated an English alliance;[6] and the British
Ministers argued that by remaining passive during the war

---

[1] *The Bernstorff Papers*, I, 337.
[2] *The Bloomfield Papers*, F.O. 356. 12, Bloomfield to Clarendon,
Feb. 20/56, no. 92.
[3] *Ibid.* Bloomfield to Clarendon, Feb. 9/56, no. 75.
[4] *Ibid.* Bloomfield to Clarendon, Feb. 9/56, no. 74.
[5] *Ibid.* Bloomfield to Clarendon, Feb. 22/56, no. 94.
[6] *The Later Correspondence of Lord John Russell*, II, 165.

Prussia had forfeited her right to admission.[1] Moustier officially favoured Prussia's demand, and when finally on March 11 the Congress invited Prussia to send plenipotentiaries, Napoleon III expressed, in a private letter, a wish to become acquainted with Count Manteuffel.[2] The Prussian Government, flattered by this gesture, attributed their presence at the Congress to the efforts of French policy, but it was nevertheless true, as Clarendon sarcastically observed to Countess Bernstorff, that they "only arrived for dessert".[3]

The plenipotentiaries of Austria and Turkey, Count Buol and Ali Pasha, came to Paris with decided, though negative, views on the question of the Principalities. Neither would consent to political union nor to hereditary princes. In an interview with Cowley,[4] who was British Ambassador at Paris and second Plenipotentiary at the Congress, Ali declared that an hereditary prince would invoke Russian help in order to attain complete independence of the Porte, and that Russia would convert this independence into dependence upon herself—upon which Cowley observed: "I venture to think with considerable truth"; whilst to Buol union suggested a second Kingdom of Greece, and he did not think that "that creation had been a satisfactory experiment".[5] In Napoleon III the cause of union, loudly championed by "Rumanian" exiles at Paris, found an enthusiastic advocate. Already in July, 1853, after the Russian occupation of the Principalities, the French representative at Constantinople had "talked ...of looking forward to the independence of the Danubian Principalities", an idea which the British Ambassador,

---

[1] *The Bernstorff Papers*, I, 336.
[2] *The Bloomfield Papers*, F.O. 356. 12, Bloomfield to Clarendon, Mar. 13/56, no. 112.
[3] *The Bernstorff Papers*, II, 1.
[4] F.O. 195. 500, Cowley to Clarendon, Feb. 27/56, confidential.
[5] F.O. 195. 500, Cowley to Clarendon, Mar. 5/56, confidential.

Lord Stratford de Redcliffe, then criticised as "premature".[1] On March 4, Clarendon wrote from Paris that *émigrés* from the Principalities favoured union under a foreign prince and independence of the Porte, and that the Emperor was "not unfavourable to this arrangement".[2] Clarendon was informed on March 6 of a letter received by Walewski, the French Foreign Minister, from Napoleon III,

stating in strong terms that no peace would be solid or durable which did not provide for the union and the independence of the Principalities and urging that an instruction to that effect should be given to the Committee of the Conference which was to consider and report upon the form of government to be established.[3]

On the same day[4] Clarendon was given an audience of the Emperor at which the latter made an eloquent plea for union, to which Clarendon raised many objections. The opposition of Austria and Turkey was "insurmountable"; the religion of the foreign prince would cause numerous difficulties; and finally, the union of Moldavia and Wallachia would be tantamount to an "act of spoliation" of the Turkish Empire.

I did not see [said Clarendon] what answer could be given to the Sultan if he appealed to us as the defenders of the integrity of the Ottoman Empire against such an act of spoliation.[4]

[1] S. Lane-Poole, *The Life of Stratford Canning*, II, 283.
[2] Note 3, p. 44.
[3] F.O. 195. 500, Clarendon to Palmerston, Mar. 7/56, no. 39.
[4] The account of this interview is given in Clarendon's despatch to Palmerston on Mar. 7/56, no. 40, in F.O. 27. 1168; a published version of the despatch, with some small verbal differences, is to be found in Martin, *The Life of the Prince Consort*, III, 465-466. F. A. Simpson, *op. cit.* p. 363, appears in error in dating this despatch March 9; in the light of its contents the statement of Prof. T. W. Riker in the *English Historical Review*, XLII, 229: "Not, however, until the session of March 8, when Walewski formally proposed union, had Clarendon given a hint of his intentions", would seem to need modification.

On March 8, however, Clarendon wrote that he thought it "very desirable" that union should be discussed as "opinion is in favour of that arrangement"[1]; and at the session of the Congress that day, when Walewski urged the Congress "to admit and proclaim union" as essential to the true interests of the Principalities and as conformable with the popular desire, both he and Cowley supported the motion and emphasised the importance of consulting the freely expressed wishes of the inhabitants themselves.

Buol and Ali Pasha violently objected to Walewski's proposal, maintaining that the division between Moldavia and Wallachia was historic and indicative of real differences in manners and customs, and that popular opinion in those countries did not favour union. Moreover they were unauthorised[2] to consider that project. Clarendon instructed Stratford to demand full powers for the Ottoman Plenipotentiary to discuss union. Stratford executed his instruction by *demanding* these powers, but he made clear to the Porte his personal belief that union was undesirable and that his Government would not press it;[3] whilst Baron Prokesch, the Austrian Internuncio, expressed his opposition to a scheme which, if carried out, would threaten Austria (because of her Rumanian population) "in the marrow of her bones".[4] In consequence, despite the efforts of the French Ambassador, the Ottoman Council, after two sessions, refused to grant the desired instructions.[2]

Count Orloff supported the French project, stating that Russia, having had special opportunities of ascertaining the needs and wishes of the Moldo-Walla-

---

[1] F.O. 195. 500, to Stratford, Mar. 8/56.
[2] Note 5, p. 44, Protocol 6 of the Congress.
[3] Sturdza, *op. cit.* ii, 1090 and 1094, despatches from Thouvenel to Walewski.   [4] *Ibid.* ii, 1101.

chians, believed that union would promote their prosperity.[1] Count Cavour, on behalf of Sardinia, likewise
assented and referred to the *Règlement Organique* in which
the principle of eventual union is recorded.[1] The failure
of Ali Pasha to get instructions created a deadlock in
the Congress but in order not to delay peace beyond
the expiration of the armistice on March 31, the Powers
agreed to Walewski's proposal that the treaty of peace
should contain an article

laying down the principles (without prejudice to the question
of whether Wallachia and Moldavia should be united or not)
upon which the constitution was to be founded, and that the
development and application of those principles should be
embodied in a supplementary Convention.[2]

The Emperor failed then to carry out at Paris his scheme
for the political union of the Principalities, but it is incorrect to maintain that Great Britain opposed Napoleon's
unionist policy at the Congress and caused its defeat.[3]
It was the uncompromising attitude adopted by Austria
and Turkey which rendered agreement on union impossible.

The attitude adopted by Clarendon and Cowley was
certainly ambiguous, but their public utterances revealed,
if not enthusiasm for union, at least a desire that it should
be considered. Walewski interpreted Clarendon's position
as very favourable to union. In a letter[4] to Thouvenel on
March 29, 1856, he declared that the British Government
had shown itself scarcely less eager for union than the
French, and that Clarendon, at their last meeting, had
promised him warm support.

---

[1] Note 5, p. 44, Protocol 6 of the Congress.
[2] F.O. 195. 500, Clarendon to Palmerston, Mar. 11/56.
[3] F. A. Simpson, *op. cit.* p. 364.
[4] Sturdza, *op. cit.* II, 1105.

These words substantially describe Great Britain's policy at the Congress, although they exaggerate somewhat, since Walewski admitted[1] in May that Clarendon had never pronounced himself as strongly in favour of union as he himself had done. Greville, who was present during the Congress unofficially at Paris where he met the principal statesmen, noted[2] as late as August 17 that "France and England are in favour of it (*sc.* union)", and Cowley was forced to admit[1] to Walewski in May that Clarendon gave "a qualified approval" of union at Paris and determined to oppose the scheme only after his return to London.

The fact is that Clarendon had no strong views on the future of the Principalities in general or on the question of union in particular. At the Congress Great Britain's interest in union was essentially a secondary one.[3] Before his arrival in Paris Clarendon expressed a mild preference for the existing separation, and a similar aversion from a general guarantee, being impressed by the dangers of local feuds and foreign interference, which in January, 1856[4] he cited as objections to union. According to Hübner,[5] Cowley, by reason of knowledge of the Principalities gained at the Constantinople Embassy, privately opposed union at Paris but failed to influence Clarendon in this direction. He confessed to Stratford later that "we were not sufficiently circumspect on this question in the outset".[6] Even so, his official utterances were no less unionist than those of

[1] F.O. 195. 503, Cowley to Clarendon, May 29/56, confidential.

[2] Greville, *Memoirs*, VIII, 55.

[3] For an appreciation of Clarendon's work at the Congress of Paris, see Algernon Cecil, *British Foreign Secretaries, 1807–1916*, pp. 240–250.

[4] F.O. 195. 498, to Cowley, Jan. 24/56.

[5] V. S. A. *Rapports de Paris*, IX, 54, Hübner to Buol, Feb. 8/57, *réservé*.

[6] *The Stratford Papers*, F.O. 352. 44, to Stratford, Sept. 13/56, private.

Clarendon. Various factors contributed to modify Clarendon's views at the Congress. He came face to face with unionist propaganda encouraged by the Emperor and was assailed by Addresses, Memoirs and Appeals from Moldo-Wallachians who sought help in the cause of union.[1] He fell to some extent under the personal fascination of the Emperor, a fact which he himself admitted,[2] Greville[3] and the Prince Consort[4] observed, whilst Buol believed[5] that the British Cabinet favoured union "rather to comply with France than to satisfy convictions". Moreover, as a minister of a parliamentary state, Clarendon could not but encourage the plan of consulting the wishes of the Principalities expressed through representative Divans *ad hoc* and, indeed, he maintained that "any project should be well considered which was likely to find favour with the people",[6] a principle which Queen Victoria herself advanced, in a letter to Palmerston, in favour of uniting the Principalities.[7]

Peace was signed at Paris on March 30,[8] thanks to the agreement of the Powers to postpone the final solution of the question of the Principalities. The project of union was not defeated but merely withheld, until a Commission, composed of representatives of the Powers and appointed to meet in the Principalities and to ascertain the wishes of Divans *ad hoc*, should have reported to a future conference. The Divans *ad hoc* were to be freely elected assemblies representative of all classes in each Principality.

[1] Enclosures in F.O. 27. 1171.
[2] F. A. Simpson, *op. cit.* p. 359, footnote 1.
[3] *Memoirs*, VIII, 24 and 37.
[4] Vitzthum von Eckstaedt, *op. cit.* I, 215, "that man exercises a charm over our Ministers which I cannot understand".
[5] V. S. A. *Expédition, Varia,* XII, 58, to Prokesch, June 28/56, no. 2, *réservé.*
[6] F.O. 195. 500, Clarendon to Palmerston, Mar. 9/56.
[7] *Queen Victoria's Letters,* III, 229.
[8] Treaty of Paris: Hertslet, *The Map of Europe, etc.* II, 1250.

The suzerainty of the Porte was reaffirmed; Austria was to withdraw her troops from the Principalities; and the privileges formerly enjoyed by the Principalities were placed under the Collective Guarantee of the contracting Powers, without whose consent no armed intervention in the Principalities should take place. Finally, Russia agreed to return southern Bessarabia to Turkey, with the result that Moldavia recovered part of Bessarabia which it had held prior to 1812, and Russia was cut off from direct access to the Balkans and the mouth of the Danube.[1]

[1] See map *infra*, and maps in Hertslet, *op. cit.* vol. II.

CHAPTER THREE
NAPOLEON III AND UNION

"The agglomeration of people of the same race under one rule is a theme so consonant to the Emperor's ears, that His Majesty would be likely to listen with complacency to any scheme, the basis of which is the restoration of nationality." COWLEY to CLARENDON.[1]

[1] See Appendix III (a).

CHAPTER THREE

NAPOLEON III AND UNION

IT may well be asked: Why did Napoleon III assume the leadership of the unionist cause? Two plausible explanations of this policy were advanced by French statesmen at the Conference of Vienna and at the Congress of Paris: they were based on two principles, the Barrier principle and that of Nationality. According to the first, France aimed at uniting the Principalities under a foreign prince in order to strengthen Turkey against Russia. According to the second, her aim was to satisfy the alleged desire of the Moldo-Wallachians to form one national state, limited only in respect of Turkish suzerainty, and guaranteed collectively by the Great Powers. To what extent were these explanations of French policy indicative of the Emperor's motives in championing union?

If Napoleon III desired union in accordance with the Barrier principle, it follows that his intention was either to strengthen Turkey on her Danubian frontier or, what is not quite the same thing, to check Russian aggression towards the Balkans. Neither of these intentions can be proved from a consideration of the evidence, which, indeed, goes to prove that Napoleon III had no sincere interest in preserving or strengthening Turkey, and that during the years 1856–58, far from wishing to embarrass Russia, he made tentative efforts to gain Russian friendship.

Napoleon III actually undertook obligations towards the Ottoman Empire in two Treaties[1] of Paris on March 30 and April 15, 1856. In the first, he joined with the other contracting Powers in declaring that the violation of Ottoman integrity was "a question of general interest". In the second, concluded between France, Great Britain

---

[1] Hertslet, *op. cit.* II, 1250 and 1280.

and Austria, and quite obviously directed against Russia, he explicitly joined in a Collective Guarantee of the integrity of the Ottoman Empire, since the signatories agreed to regard as a *casus belli* any infraction of the Treaty of March 30.[1] Lord Stratford de Redcliffe commented on the Treaty of April 15 as "a good leaf taken out of the book of the Congress of Vienna".[2] The Prince of Prussia described it as "probably the most significant state document of recent times".[3] It certainly had significance but not in the way indicated by either of these critics, namely, as a defensive measure of the three Allies of the Crimean War against their former enemy. For Count Hübner, the Austrian Ambassador at Paris, was quick to observe[4] that Napoleon III would have preferred that this treaty had not been signed. The Emperor revealed its contents to Count Orloff, explaining that he was bound to conclude it owing to the Memorandum of November 14, 1855, which he had signed with Austria.[5] The treaty was published[6] in England shortly afterwards, and although there was momentary indignation at St Petersburg, it became clear that to Napoleon at least the treaty was merely, in Brunnow's words, an "œuvre posthume".[6]

Napoleon III's feelings towards Turkey were revealed more clearly in an interview with Cowley in December, 1856.[7] The Emperor, it appears, had discovered among the archives of the reign of Charles X the long and detailed scheme by which Prince Polignac had hoped to

[1] See the article entitled "Treaties of Guarantee" by J. W. Headlam-Morley in *The Cambridge Historical Journal*, II, no. 2, pp. 162–163.

[2] *The Stratford Papers*, F.O. 352. 44, to Clarendon, Apr. 24/56, private: the reference is doubtless to the Quadruple Treaty of Nov. 20/1815, which was directed against France.

[3] *The Bernstorff Papers*, II, 12.

[4] *Neuf ans de souvenirs d'un ambassadeur d'Autriche à Paris*, I, 417.

[5] F. Charles-Roux, *op. cit.* bk. III, p. 106.

[6] Vitzthum von Eckstaedt, *St Petersburg and London*, I, 200.

[7] Note 2, p. 11.

reconstruct the map of Europe and win laurels abroad for the restored Bourbon dynasty; in handing to Cowley a copy of this scheme the Emperor observed

that he was far from dreaming of such territorial changes... but that he could not help feeling that, when harmony was restored between the Two Governments,[1] it would be well to pass in review the different Questions which might present themselves,

and he added, alluding to French possessions in North Africa, that he wished to see the coasts of the Mediterranean in the hands of Christians alone, a view which was reminiscent to Clarendon[2] of the policy of partitioning the Turkish Empire which the Czar Nicholas had avowed to Sir George Seymour in 1853. In May, 1857, Cowley reported[3] that Napoleon III condemned sweepingly the Turkish system of government and had no sincere belief in the integrity of the Ottoman Empire.

The fact is [wrote Cowley[3]] that the Emperor, although he does not avow it, would not see with disfavor a separation of the Principalities from Turkey. His whole policy therefore, with regard to those Provinces, is actuated by other motives than those of Her Majesty's Government; or rather I should say that He does not feel the same necessity that exists, for preserving the Ottoman dominions intact.

Hübner noted as a significant fact[4] that, in his opening speech to the *Corps Législatif*, on March 3, 1856, the Emperor omitted all mention of his Turkish ally—an omission all the more remarkable in view of his interest in the Latin Christians of Turkey and in the "doctrine

[1] The allusion is to the Anglo-French differences over the Russo-Turkish boundary delimitation, see pp. 73–74.

[2] *Queen Victoria's Letters*, III, 281, Clarendon to the Queen, Dec. 22/56.

[3] See Appendix III (*b*).

[4] Hübner, *op. cit.* I, 399.

of nationality". Indeed, the Emperor made it an open secret that he fought in the Crimean War, not *for* the Turks but *against* Russia.[1]

To fortify the Sultan's dominions, then, can hardly have been Napoleon's motive in advocating Moldo-Wallachian union, and many statesmen during the years 1856 to 1858, unable to perceive any material motive in Napoleon III's conduct, believed that he intended to make the question of the Principalities a prelude to an attack on Austria's Italian lands. It is impossible to substantiate this arresting and plausible theory,[2] which was held by Thouvenel,[3] the French Ambassador at Constantinople, and by the Austrian Foreign Minister, Buol,[4] although it sketches an attractive contrast between two antagonists, France and Austria, the one pledged to the nationalism of 1848, and the other to the reaction of 1815. Stratford, indeed, asserted his belief to Prokesch, the Internuncio at the Porte, that the French policy of union was merely "the fragment of a scheme" and "part of a project which tends at first to isolate Austria".[5] Thouvenel thought Napoleon's zeal for union inexplicable and unjustifiable unless his aim was "to settle on the Po the question raised on the Danube".[6] The weakness of this theory is that it postulates in the mind of the Emperor *arrière-pensées* of which there is no definite proof, and that it excludes the possibility that Napoleon III could be innocent of Machiavelian designs. It is certainly true that he despised and disliked

---

[1] Vitzthum von Eckstaedt, *op. cit.* I, 278.
[2] L. Thouvenel, in his *Trois années de la question d'Orient*, p. 82, writes: "Pour nous, la lutte de 1859 a commencé dès 1857".
[3] *Ibid.* p. 99.
[4] Hübner, *op. cit.* II, 49.
[5] V. S. A. *Expédition, Varia*, XII, 60. Private letter, Prokesch to Buol, Apr. 8/57.
[6] L. Thouvenel, *op. cit.* p. 99.

Austria at the Congress of Paris, as indeed he personally disliked both Buol[1] and Hübner,[2] her plenipotentiaries. "I don't like Austria", His Majesty said with some warmth, "I detest her policy but I don't wish to quarrel with her".[3] And Hübner relates that Napoleon did not speak to him during the year 1857.[4] The question of the Principalities certainly embittered Austro-French relations during the years 1856 to 1858, but there is some evidence against the assumption that Napoleon was secretly planning a war with Austria during his advocacy of Moldo-Wallachian union. Hübner himself declares his disbelief in secret schemes of the Emperor.[5] Moreover, if Napoleon in the years 1856 to 1858 contemplated his Italian adventure, two excellent opportunities to break with Austria were ignored, one in August, 1857, after the rupture of relations with the Porte, the other in the summer of 1858 when Austria was almost isolated at the Conference of Paris.

There is little reason to believe, then, that Napoleon desired (as he officially intimated)[6] to strengthen the Turkish frontier; nor does it appear probable that he desired to weaken Russia by his policy of union, first, because Russia supported union, and second, because he consistently showed an inclination for Russian friendship, if not for a Russian alliance.[7]

---

[1] Sir E. Satow, *An Austrian Diplomatist in the Fifties*, p. 42.

[2] Vitzthum von Eckstaedt, *op. cit.* I, 293: "Je déteste Hübner, s'il me demande quelque chose, je suis toujours tenté de lui refuser".

[3] F.O. 27. 1169, Clarendon to Palmerston, Mar. 19/56, no. 65.

[4] Hübner, *op. cit.* II, 80.   [5] *Ibid.* II, 51.

[6] *E.g.* at Vienna (1855), at Paris (1856), and at Osborne (1857).

[7] F. A. Simpson, *op. cit.* pp. 363–365, gives due weight to Napoleon's dislike of the Turks and disbelief in the dogma of Ottoman integrity, but stresses the view that Napoleon sought to unite the Principalities in order to erect a barrier to Russian aggression. Contrast the view of Driault, *La Question d'Orient* (8th ed.), p. 193, that *Russia* supported union with the idea of creating a strong barrier against Austria and Turkey.

Russia was not wholly opposed to the political union of the Principalities. During her occupation from 1806 until 1812 she countenanced the temporary union of the Principalities under Prince Constantin Ypsilanti. She considered uniting them in 1830, and the fact that union was stated as eventually desirable in the *Règlement* indicated her theoretical approval. At the Conference of Vienna it was she who suggested the consultation of local feeling with a view to constitutional reform; at the Congress of Paris she assented to the consideration of union. By the Treaty of Paris Russia lost her exclusive guarantee and became merely one of seven guarantors. She favoured union in order to cultivate good relations with Napoleon III and with the Principalities themselves, knowing full well from the personal experience of her statesmen that the policy of union was fraught with numerous difficulties and was by no means objectionable even if achieved. Baron Brunnow did not think that the unionist project would be realised:

he had resided too long a time in the Principalities not to feel convinced that the Congress was undertaking a task of far greater magnitude and difficulty than they seemed to be aware of or than, he was afraid, they would be able to carry out.

. . . .

Russia had no objection (to union), but he considered the scheme all but impracticable. Even if the principle were sanctioned by the Divans, it would break down in the details, unless a foreign Prince was placed at the head of the new Government and then what became of the integrity of the Sultan's Dominions?[1]

And Count Kisseleff, who was reappointed Russian Ambassador to Paris in November, 1856, and whose knowledge of the Principalities—since he had ruled them during the period 1829 to 1834—was unrivalled, believed that

[1] F.O. 195. 504, Cowley to Clarendon, June 9/56, no. 602.

union was practically possible only under a foreign prince:

> There exists one reason, Count Kisseleff used to say, why the Principalities should not be united and that is a conclusive one. I do not know a single Moldavian who would choose to be under a Moldavian (*sic*) prince or a single Wallachian who would submit to being placed under a Moldavian prince.[1]

Count Nesselrode prophesied great difficulties ahead,[2] and Prince Gortchakoff, who was to be called from the Russian Embassy at Vienna to succeed him at the Foreign Office in 1856, avowed Russia's willingness for union, if it satisfied the wishes of the Moldo-Wallachians, although on the question of a foreign prince Russia made one reservation:

> Upon that point (*sc.* Foreign Prince), we have no very settled notions. We consider this very remote. Upon one point, however, you would find us very resolute, we could not admit of such a Prince being a Protestant or a Catholic. He must be of the religion of the country. The inconvenience of a disregard of this principle has been seen in Greece.[3]

It is clear, therefore, that Russia was not averse in theory from a policy the execution of which would embarrass her former enemies; and although opposed to a foreign prince of non-Orthodox religion, she voiced no objection to union as constituting a political barrier to her arms. She knew enough about the Principalities to know that, united or separated, they were likely to become a sphere of influence to Russian policy. The Porte itself did not believe that union would create a barrier, although Napoleon III refused to admit that it was the best judge of its own

---

[1] F.O. 195. 511, Seymour to Clarendon, Sept. 30/56.
[2] F.O. 195. 504, Bloomfield to Clarendon, May 31/56, confidential.
[3] F.O. 195. 504, Seymour to Clarendon, June 15/56, secret and confidential.

interests.[1] Stratford thought that the principle of barrier would justify union under a foreign prince—"but then", he wrote,[2] "you must get the barrier". Few statesmen outside France were inclined to endorse Gladstone's view that, by union, "between Russia and Turkey there would be opposed a living barrier".[3]

The project of uniting the Principalities was hardly, then, directed against Russian power; rather it provided one of several grounds for Franco-Russian friendship—a sudden and curious phenomenon which attracted the notice of statesmen soon after the Crimean War. Palmerston wrote[4] to Walewski in September, 1856: "France appears to change and associate herself in everything with Russia. Reflect a little, I beg of you, on the effect all this must produce on the alliance between the two countries". According to Greville,[5] Clarendon believed in February, 1857, that "if any serious dispute arose, France and Russia would probably become allied against us.... Russia pays the most unceasing and the most abject court to Louis Napoleon, and not without success". Moreover, Buol continually asserted that France was playing Russia's game, which was to wreck the alliances of the Crimean War, and it was the constant complaint of Thouvenel that Napoleon was sacrificing French prestige at Constantinople by associating with his late enemy. Nor were signs lacking to indicate the growth of a Franco-Russian understanding. It was largely Napoleon's work, by secret diplomatic intercourse with Russia, that peace was made as early as the spring of 1856, at a time when public opinion in England desired to prolong the war;[6] a new

[1] Martin, *op. cit.* IV, 103.
[2] *The Stratford Papers*, F.O. 352. 44, to Clarendon, Mar. 6/56, private.   [3] Hansard, *op. cit.* CL, 43.
[4] Sturdza, *op. cit.* V, 882.   [5] *Memoirs*, VIII, 88.
[6] For a study of British public opinion just *before* the Crimean War, see B. Kingsley Martin, *The Triumph of Lord Palmerston, passim.*

Czar—Alexander II—and a new Foreign Minister—
Gortchakoff—made possible better relations between
France and Russia. Napoleon supported Russia's frontier
claims at the Congress so that Clarendon wrote, "Upon
the Bessarabian frontier we had to choose between a concession to Russia or something very like a rupture with
France".[1] Count Orloff, the first Russian Plenipotentiary,
was lionised at Paris;[2] the Duc de Morny, sent to
St Petersburg to attend the coronation of Alexander II,
endeavoured to conclude a secret Franco-Russian convention;[3] whilst at Paris, during the Congress, there
was a disposition to regard the fall of Sebastopol as satisfaction for 1812 and to look forward to a renewal of the
Franco-Russian relations of 1807.[2] Certainly, as will be
noticed later, in the boundary dispute which arose out of
the Treaty of Paris, Napoleon supported Russia to the
extent of incurring a diplomatic check; and the question
of the Principalities led to the common action of France
and Russia at Constantinople in August, 1857, and to the
Stuttgart Interview between the Emperor and the Czar.

In Napoleon's belief that separate nationalities should
form separate political entities, is found an important clue
to his policy of Moldo-Wallachian union. The degree to
which he was sincere in his desire for a united Moldo-
Wallachia may well be questioned. It has already been
noted that he considered the possibility of giving the
Principalities to Austria in exchange for Lombardy and
Venetia; and again in 1866 he appears to have contemplated Austria's exchanging Venetia for the Principalities.[4]
There is no doubt, however, that this policy was essentially
his own. Thouvenel, who complained continually that by

[1] S. Lane-Poole, *op. cit.* II, 435 and Greville, *op. cit.* VIII, 31.
[2] F. Charles-Roux, *op. cit.* bk. I, ch. VII.
[3] Duc de Morny, *Extraits des Mémoires: une Ambassade en Russie*,
p. 141.
[4] N. Iorga, *Correspondance diplomatique sous le roi Charles Ier*, p. v.

her advocacy of the union of Moldavia and Wallachia France was losing at Constantinople the prestige gained by her victories in the Crimea, was informed by Benedetti, *Chef de Département* at the Foreign Office, in November, 1856, that despite ministerial opposition the Emperor would not abandon his policy of union: " L'Empereur veut que nous tenions bon, quelles que soient les chances et même les inconvénients ".[1] And, in his speech to the Senate and the *Corps Législatif*,[2] on February 16, 1857, the Emperor admitted his personal interest in the question of union (and by inference the opposition of his ministers) when he said:

with reference to the views of the French Government—or rather the French Emperor—respecting the policy to be adopted in the case of the Danubian Principalities....

The dismissal of Drouyn de Lhuys, on his return from the Conference of Vienna in 1855, marked a significant change in French foreign policy. Drouyn was a man of independent character who believed in a pro-Austrian policy, so much so that it has been suggested by Vandal[3] that, had he remained in power, he might have counteracted the Emperor's enthusiasm for the subject nationalities. Walewski, however, who came from the Embassy of St James to the Foreign Office, was by no means an able statesman:[4] although he tried to influence the Emperor in a pro-Russian direction, his rôle became rather that of servant[5] to a monarch who was free, regardless of ministerial opposition, to pursue whatever course his restless and Quixotic ambition might suggest. In

---

[1] L. Thouvenel, *op. cit.* p. 63.
[2] *Annual Register*, XCIX, 226.
[3] Preface to L. Thouvenel's *Pages de l'histoire du Second Empire*.
[4] Cp. Vitzthum von Eckstaedt, *op. cit.* I, 195.
[5] *The Bernstorff Papers*, I, 296.

conversation with Clarendon at Paris, the Emperor revealed the bent of his mind.

> He [the Emperor] said that the great fault of the Congress of Vienna [1814–15] was that the interests of the sovereigns were only consulted, while the interests of their subjects were wholly neglected, and that the present congress [Paris, 1856] should not fall into a similar error.

. . . .

> It would be disgraceful to England and France if they had not the will or the power to establish a better state of things.[1]

These words throw much light on Napoleon III's unionist policy. He alone of the great European monarchs of 1856 owed his throne to a reversal of the Treaties of Vienna. He represented ideas which were still suspect in a Europe not yet free from the trammels of 1815. And, as heir to the Napoleonic system, he realised the importance of successful foreign adventure.

> He is convinced [wrote Cowley[2]] that the Governments which preceded him fell because they neglected to uphold the dignity of France, and he is resolved to recover for her that position in the Councils of Europe which had been lost through the feebleness of others.

Hübner endorsed this view[3] when he declared to the Emperor Francis Joseph that

> Il [Napoléon III] ne la [sa situation en France] croit forte qu'autant qu'il joue un grand rôle, parfois le premier, à l'étranger;

and Stratford thought that the Emperor's motives, in championing union, were "the inclination and calculation to regain for his country the importance of the First Empire, and to show himself the leading will on the

---

[1] Note 4, p. 47.　　　　　[2] See Appendix III (a).
[3] Hübner, op. cit. II, 51.

continent".[1] In supporting the union of the Principalities,
Napoleon was not in the least deterred by the opposition
of Austria whom he detested, or by that of Turkey whom
he despised. He was incited to this cause by his often
expressed interest in the doctrine of nationality, "a theme
so consonant to the Emperor's ears".[2] In despite of the
reactionary principles of the Congress of Vienna, Napoleon
wished to appeal to the wishes of subjects, not of rulers.
In the peace negotiations of 1855–56, in order to pacify
the militant spirit in England and to bring Russia to
terms, he had spoken about prolonging the war, by ap-
pealing to national feeling in Poland, Italy and the Rhine-
land.[3] Although it is not certain that he was a Carbonero,[4]
he had certainly avowed to Cavour Pan-Italian sentiments
at the Congress of Paris.[5] Napoleon was moved, too, by a
sincere philanthropy: "for on this question at least",
wrote Cowley, "his philanthropy far exceeds his respect
for Treaties".[6] Certainly, if his policy of union succeeded,
he would achieve some reward in prestige and self-esteem
and, although the assertion attributed to him by Stratford,
that he wished to achieve in peace what his uncle had
achieved by war,[7] may not have been a statement of public
policy, it is nevertheless true that the Emperor of the
French set much store by personal and diplomatic
success.

   During the last weeks of the Congress there had seemed
some hope of securing an eventual decision by the Powers
on the question of union. This project had received the

---

[1] V. S. A. *Expédition, Varia*, XII, 60, private letter, Prokesch to Buol,
Mar. 25/57.   [2] See Appendix III (*a*).
[3] La Gorce, *Histoire du second Empire*, I, 453.
[4] F. A. Simpson, *The Rise of Louis Napoleon* (New edition), p. 64.
[5] F. A. Simpson, *Louis Napoleon and the Recovery of France*, p. 358.
[6] See Appendix III (*b*).
[7] V. S. A. *Expédition, Varia*, XII, 60, private letter, Prokesch to Buol,
Apr. 8/57.

approval of France, Great Britain, Russia and Sardinia, and even Prussia showed herself equally favourable. It would seem that her favourable attitude to union sprang from the known aversion from union at Vienna and the knowledge that both Russia and France encouraged the idea.[1] On April 26 Walewski wrote[2] that Manteuffel was firmly resolved to follow the French line, and accordingly instructions in this sense were sent to the Prussian Minister at Constantinople at the end of June.[3] The French Government realised that the support of Great Britain was essential to the success of the union, a view which Thouvenel,[4] striving for union at the Porte against the official neutrality of Stratford, warmly confirmed. In Great Britain, however, Napoleon III did not find the keen support which he expected but a disposition towards neutrality which later changed to one of avowed opposition. On his return to London, Clarendon, in concert with Palmerston, investigated the question further, and announced to Walewski that Great Britain would send her Commissioner to the Principalities "unfettered by any previous decision on the part of the British Government"[5]:

for Her Majesty's Government concur in the justness of the principle...that on the important question of union or continued separation of the Provinces, the wishes of the Provinces themselves should materially influence the decision of the Allied Powers.[5]

In May, 1856, Persigny was instructed to invite Clarendon to join France in active support of union at Constantinople.

---

[1] F.O. 195. 509, Bloomfield to Clarendon, Aug. 30/56, and F.O. 195. 505, Seymour to Clarendon, July 2/56, secret and confidential.
[2] Sturdza, *op. cit.* III, 447.
[3] *Ibid.* III, 587.
[4] To Walewski, June 30/56, Sturdza, *op. cit.* III, 585.
[5] F.O. 195. 503, to Cowley, May 26/56.

The overture resulted in an important interview between Cowley and Walewski in which the intentions of the French Government were revealed.[1] Walewski was convinced that to consult the wishes of the inhabitants was merely to confirm the desire for union. He believed that Austria and the Porte would exert all their influence to prevent union by pressure at the elections. He had therefore instructed Thouvenel "to do all in his power to attain the union", and now desired Clarendon to send similar instructions to Stratford. Clarendon refused[2] to infringe the Treaty of Paris by thus "prejudging" the issue. Walewski was surprised to learn (through Persigny) that the British Government was "less anxious for this union than he had been led to expect", and accused Clarendon of having changed his views on the question of union.[1] Cowley insisted that Clarendon had given only "a qualified approval" of union at Paris.[1] Clarendon himself was still willing to support union gladly, if (as he doubted) it were likely to produce a government stronger than had hitherto existed and immune from the interference of Russia and Austria.[2] On June 7, Walewski wrote[3] that he found himself in perfect accord with England, who objected merely to encouraging unionist feeling. Actually Clarendon went only so far as to instruct Stratford[2] to obtain a liberal basis for the electoral firman, so that a free consultation of local feeling could be assured.

If the British government was determined not to "prejudge" union, the Austrian was no less resolved to prevent it. Buol, outspoken and irascible,[4] whom Palmerston in a generous moment declared to be "as honest

---

[1] F.O. 195. 503, Cowley to Clarendon, May 29/56, confidential.
[2] F.O. 195. 504, Clarendon to Cowley, June 2/56.
[3] To Thouvenel, Sturdza, *op. cit.* III, 524.
[4] Sir E. Satow, *op. cit.* p. 21.

as an Austrian Minister can be ",[1] had never ceased to oppose union, and after the Congress had ended formulated his opposition in vigorous terms. Indeed, Austria's opposition to union was more Turkish than that of the Turks.[2] Buol desired that there should be no "vainqueurs" and "vaincus" on the question of union,[3] but the extremist position he maintained did not conduce to compromise. He had been compelled at Paris to assent to the plan of consulting Divans *ad hoc*, for how could he object to it when he had already stated at the Congress that the wishes of the Moldo-Wallachians were in favour of separate governments? Even so, Buol had no intention that union should be achieved. He could not face the possibility[4] of a Rumanian-speaking state of some five million inhabitants, endowed with parliamentary institutions and governed by a foreign prince, as a neighbour to Austria, who in Transylvania and Bukovina[5] ruled a considerable Rumanian population. He determined to delay the withdrawal of Austrian troops from the Principalities,[6] which to his great annoyance the Congress had decided he should do. In this determination he received some support, even from Turkey, since Fuad Pasha promised him in April, 1856 "complete apathy" on the subject of evacuation.[7] Buol probably realised, although he never

[1] *The Later Correspondence of Lord John Russell*, II, 198, letter from Palmerston, Mar. 15/55.

[2] Buol underlined those parts of despatches from Constantinople which dealt with the Principalities.

[3] F.O. 195. 542, Seymour to Clarendon, May 26/57, confidential.

[4] F.O. 195. 504, Seymour to Clarendon, June 11/56, secret and confidential.

[5] According to figures given in *A Handbook of Roumania*, p. 88, taken from the 1910 census, the Rumanian population of Bukovina, which occupies the south-east and south-west, forms rather more than one-third of its total population.

[6] V. S. A. *Expédition, Varia*, XII, 58, Buol to Prokesch, Mar. 30/56.

[7] V. S. A. *Rapports de Constantinople*, XII, 55, Prokesch to Buol, Apr. 10/56.

admitted it, that the Divans *ad hoc*, if elected freely in accordance with the Treaty of Paris, would vote in favour of union.[1] He therefore questioned "the right of any Power to interfere with the separate existence of the two provinces as contemplated by Turkey", and maintained the Sultan's absolute right of dealing with the Principalities.[1] He continually reminded the Powers of the case of Greek independence and asked if that experiment had proved worth while; he cited the union of Belgium and Holland to show the futility of such unions; and finally, he demanded, pointedly enough, whether Russia would support union unless it were to her advantage, and urged his belief that Russia was sowing disunion among her former enemies over this question, a belief which both Seymour and Cowley shared.[2] On his return from Paris in June, 1856, Ali Pasha spent a week in Vienna. The result of his visit was that Buol's opposition to union became "more decided than before".[2] He now asserted that union lay outside the competence of the Divans,[2] and instructed Baron Prokesch at Constantinople to urge the Porte to declare, when the European Commissioners met, the exact scope of the Divans.[3] Clarendon was asked to send instructions to Stratford similar to those sent to Prokesch; he firmly refused co-operation,[3] however, whilst Walewski protested[4] against Buol's attempt to violate the Treaty of Paris by restricting the scope of the Divans.

On July 31, 1856, the Porte issued a circular despatch,[5] which was important in its effect on the British attitude to the union of the Principalities. The despatch was an able though exaggerated statement of the Porte's case

---

[1] F.O. 195. 504, Seymour to Clarendon, June 11/56, secret and confidential.
[2] F.O. 195. 505, Seymour to Clarendon, July 2/56.
[3] F.O. 195. 505, Clarendon to Seymour, July 8/56.
[4] F.O. 195. 507, Cowley to Clarendon, Aug. 8/56.
[5] Sturdza, *op. cit.* III, 729.

against union, drawn up at the request of Austria.[1] The Sultan stressed both "his views and his rights", expressed his willingness to grant reforms including representative assemblies, and stated his positive objections to union. Clarendon listened with great attention to the Turkish Ambassador, Musurus, whose arguments, he admitted, distinctly impressed him.[2] He ignored, however, the Porte's[1] unjustifiable use of the term "sovereign rights" to describe its relations with the Principalities, to which, however, Manteuffel, the Prussian Foreign Minister, objected.[3] He was now convinced that the union of the Principalities would encourage a desire for complete independence and thus jeopardise the integrity of the Ottoman Empire, which Great Britain had recently guaranteed in the treaties of March 30 and April 15. In an important despatch to Cowley, dated August 22, 1856, he therefore stated[2] his determination to maintain the existing separation:

I have now to instruct Your Excellency to inform Count Walewski that the arguments and reasonings of the Turkish Government seem to Her Majesty's Government to have great weight and that, although the plan of union appeared at first sight plausible and likely to be attended with some advantages, a more full and deliberate examination and consideration of the matter has led them to the conclusion that the injurious consequences which would follow from it, would greatly counterbalance any advantages which it might produce, and that it seems therefore to be highly desirable for the general interests of Europe that the separate condition of the Principalities should be maintained.

Here was indicated decisively for the first time a clear divergence between the views of Great Britain and those

[1] V. S. A. *Rapports de Constantinople*, XII, 57, Prokesch to Buol, July 23/56.
[2] F.O. 195. 508, Clarendon to Cowley, Aug. 22/56, no. 862.
[3] F.O. 195. 509, Bloomfield to Clarendon, Aug. 23/56.

of her French ally. Although Napoleon had guaranteed the integrity of Turkey, he was far more interested in the future of the Moldo-Wallachians than in the preservation of Turkey; and Great Britain, anxious to maintain the balance of power in the Near East, preferred the interests of the Porte to the aspirations of the Moldo-Wallachians.

Meanwhile the Powers were preparing for the European Commission which was to meet in the Principalities and learn the views of representative Divans *ad hoc* on the question of definitive organisation. It had not been the intention of the Congress of Paris to include Prussia and Sardinia in the Commission. Both states, however, desired admittance. Prussia, encouraged by the French Minister at Berlin,[2] appointed Baron de Richthofen as Commissioner.[2] Clarendon argued that, if Prussia was to have a member on the Commission, Sardinia should be equally represented,[3] and Buol, though unwilling, assented to Sardinia's inclusion.[4] This increase, by the addition of two unionist supporters, was favourable to France; for Great Britain, however, the change (which Sir Henry Bulwer, the British Commissioner much deplored) was unfortunate. Had the membership of the Commission been limited to five, Great Britain might have acted, Bulwer maintained,[5] as a mediator between two equal groups: France and Russia in favour of union, Austria and Turkey against it. The enlargement of the Commission was to render this impossible and, instead of mediating, Great Britain was forced into the ranks of the anti-unionist minority group.

[1] F.O. 195. 502, Bloomfield to Clarendon, May 10/56, confidential.
[2] Sturdza, *op. cit.* III, 585, Thouvenel to Walewski, June 30/56.
[3] F.O. 195. 502, to Bloomfield, May 13/56.
[4] F.O. 195. 506, Seymour to Clarendon, July 16/56.
[5] F.O. 195. 508, to Clarendon, Aug. 17/56, private and confidential.

In the autumn of 1856 interest centred on the electoral firman which, in accordance with the Treaty of Paris, was to summon Divans *ad hoc* in Moldavia and Wallachia. It had been agreed that the Sultan, as suzerain, should issue this firman in concert with the other signatories to the treaty. Austria desired that the firman should expressly preclude the consideration of union by the Divans, although the Congress of Paris had not contemplated any such restriction. On September 15, 1856, Musurus asked the advice of the British Government on the course to be adopted by the Porte: should the Sultan in his firman reserve the consideration of union from the competency of the Divans, or alternatively, should he make no reservation in the firman, but publish simultaneously a separate Note to the Powers to the effect that he would never allow union to be realised? Musurus discussed this question in an interview with Palmerston, who, without advising the Porte, gave a personal opinion in favour of the latter course on the clear understanding that it was unofficial; Clarendon endorsed Palmerston's view, urged that the Note should be courteously worded and emphasised the strictly confidential nature of the advice.[1] A Note[2] was accordingly sent on October 14, stating that, even if the Divans voted for union, the Porte reserved its right to reject it. With strange inconsistency Clarendon criticised the Note as "ill-advised" and "at variance with the Treaty of Paris",[3] whilst Walewski informed the Turkish Ambassador that he regarded it as "non-avenue".[3]

The seven Powers signatory to the Treaty of Paris selected their representatives for the Commission in the summer of 1856, but it was not until April, 1857, that

[1] F.O. 195. 510, "Private Memorandum to M. Musurus, Sept. 20/56, by Lord Clarendon's desire, in answer to his private letter of Sept. 15/56".

[2] Sturdza, *op. cit.* III, 879.

[3] F.O. 195. 513, Clarendon to Cowley, Nov. 17/56.

the Commission met at Bukarest: the delay was occasioned
by a boundary dispute which arose after the peace. This
dispute, which concerned the possession of Bolgrad and
Serpent's Isle, indirectly influenced the question of the
Principalities. The discovery of two places with the name
Bolgrad, presented to Russia an opportunity to claim a
better frontier. The Treaty of Paris, which aimed to
exclude Russia from the Danube, had stipulated that the
Russo-Turkish frontier should pass to the south of
Bolgrad. Russia maintained that the Bolgrad there referred to was the thriving town of Bolgrad adjacent to
Lake Yalpukh from which there was direct access to the
Danube delta. The British contention was that the Bolgrad
of the treaty was Bolgrad (Tabak), an almost deserted
village a little to the north, the only Bolgrad marked on
the old maps consulted by the Congress. Further, Russia
laid claim to Serpent's Isle off the mouth of the Danube:
important merely for its lighthouse, it had been held
by Russia after 1829 but had never been ceded to
her by Turkey.[1] Napoleon III supported Russia's pretensions, which were forcibly encouraged by the Duc
de Morny at St Petersburg.[2] But Great Britain stood out
firmly for no concession to what she considered Russian
sharp practice, whilst Austria and Turkey followed her
lead. Buol's view was that "delimitation must precede
evacuation", and with British concurrence he refused to
withdraw Austrian troops from the Principalities.[3] Moreover a British fleet was sent to the Black Sea.[4] Queen
Victoria wrote a stern letter to the Empress in September,
which Clarendon toned down lest it might appear "rather

[1] Sturdza, *op. cit.* III, 951–959. Memoir by the Prussian Government.
[2] See F. Charles-Roux, *op. cit.* pp. 154–169 and Duc de Morny, *op.
cit.* p. 133.
[3] F.O. 195. 509, Seymour to Clarendon, Aug. 19/56.
[4] F.O. 195. 512, Clarendon to Cowley, Oct. 20/56, no. 1275.

too severe".[1] According to Lord Lyons, the Czar was trying to isolate England,[2] and certainly the dispute threatened to some extent the Anglo-French alliance. Finally, Clarendon agreed to a Conference, when it was known that Great Britain would have a majority of votes,[3] and this "got-up comedy with a foregone conclusion"[4] resulted in the Protocol of Paris[5] of January 6, 1857, which settled the boundary questions in favour of Great Britain, whilst it directed that Austria should evacuate the Principalities by the end of March. The importance of the Protocol was that it registered Napoleon's defeat in the first clash of post-war diplomacy, and revealed his weakness when pursuing a line opposed to that of his English ally. Moreover, it made him all the more anxious to win a victory in the next diplomatic struggle, the union of the Principalities. The union question was now identified with the Emperor's *amour-propre*, and it was the opinion of Cowley (which Hübner shared)[6] that "more particularly as a set off against the check which France had received in the question of Bolgrad and Serpent's Isle, (the Emperor) determined on carrying the question of the Union".[7] Napoleon III could not retrace his steps and allow another Austrian triumph, however much he might desire to retreat from an embarrassing position.

His success at the Conference of Paris encouraged Buol in his opposition to the union of the Principalities. In December, 1856, he had hinted that Austria would be

[1] *Queen Victoria's Letters*, III, 264–265.
[2] V. S. A. *Rapports de Constantinople*, XII, 57, Prokesch to Buol, Nov. 7/56, confidential.
[3] F.O. 195. 514, Clarendon to Stratford, Dec. 2/56.
[4] Greville, *op. cit.* VIII, 70.
[5] Hertslet, *op. cit.* II, 1298.
[6] V. S. A. *Rapports de Paris*, IX, 54, Hübner to Buol, Feb. 8/56, no. 12, *réservé*.
[7] F.O. 146. 794, Cowley to Malmesbury, June 4/58, secret and confidential.

willing to fight to prevent the erection of a united Moldo-Wallachia, adding "c'est pour nous une question de vie ou de mort".[1] Napoleon, after the Bolgrad affair, determined not to abate one jot his unionist aims. An article,[2] outlining and defending union, was published in the *Moniteur*, on February 5, 1857, which expressed the Emperor's ideas, since he referred to it, as an indication of his policy, in his speech to the *Corps Législatif* on February 16.[3] Cowley objected that the question of union should not be "prejudged" before the meeting of the Divans,[4] whilst Clarendon read the article "with some surprise" and virtually condemned the views it expressed in reply on February 9 to a question of Lord Lyndhurst in the House of Lords.[5] The Sultan's ministers, somewhat alarmed, demanded an understanding between the anti-unionist Powers,[6] whilst Buol intimated[7] that Austria "would resist union even if left to struggle alone". Napoleon, however, was unmoved by this hostile reception of his views, for he wrote[8] in the margin of a despatch from Thouvenel to Walewski, dated April 2: "Appuyez fortement pour obtenir le concours de Reschid-Pacha à l'union. Ne rien ménager pour obtenir ce résultat". In view of the growing divergence between the Powers, Cowley made a strenuous effort in May, 1857, to reconcile the conflicting views of the French and British Governments. In an interview with Walewski he expressed his desire to secure an amicable arrangement on a question "which interested neither except in a general point of

---

[1] F.O. 195. 537, Seymour to Clarendon, Dec. 31/56.
[2] Sturdza, *op. cit.* III, 1111.
[3] Note 2, p. 63.
[4] F.O. 195. 538, Cowley to Clarendon, Feb. 10/57.
[5] Hansard, *op. cit.* CXLIV, 332.
[6] F.O. 195. 538, Stratford to Clarendon, Feb. 28/57.
[7] F.O. 195. 539, Seymour to Clarendon, Mar. 18/57, confidential.
[8] Sturdza, *op. cit.* IV, 214.

view ".[1] Walewski declared, what was probably untrue,[2] that his Government was originally indifferent on the question of union, that they had been determined not to insist on it at Paris if it met with the opposition of the British Cabinet,

but that Your Lordship (Clarendon) having signified both to the Emperor and to himself, your acquiescence in it on your arrival in Paris, it had been warmly taken up by the French Government both during the sitting of the Congress and since: that under these circumstances, some indulgence was due to the French Government on the part of that of Her Majesty, since the interest of the former in this question originated in the supposition that they were acting in complete unison with the sentiments of Her Majesty's Government.[1]

He explained that his Government had been driven to make a public demonstration of its opinion in favour of union owing to the "covert steps taken by Austria and Turkey to prevent its realisation". Cowley claimed "frank conduct" on the part of his Government, but admitted that they had determined to oppose union only in August, 1856. Walewski further maintained that if Great Britain would support union, that measure would no longer be opposed by the Porte; that even the neutrality of the British Government would encourage Turkish opposition,

and if the Sultan were to place his veto upon the project, the question would arise as to his right to do so, a question which he should be sorry to see discussed by a conference.[1]

In one respect, however, France was willing to compromise: "the reins of government must not (said Walewski)

[1] Appendix III (b).
[2] It is certainly untrue that the French Government were "originally indifferent" to union. See their views expressed in 1853 (p. 46 supra) and in 1855 (pp. 37–38 supra). Clarendon acquiesced in the union proposal at Paris, but not before the 8th of March, and he did express some opposition (v. pp. 47–48 supra).

be confided to the hands of a Foreign Prince".[1] In other respects the discussion had served rather to define differences than to produce agreement.

Nor was an interview with the Emperor on the same day more satisfactory.

He (Napoleon) dwelt long, and with considerable animation upon the fact that the Great Powers of Europe having invited the people of Moldavia and Wallachia to express their wishes in respect to their future Government, could not with consistency or honor, turn a deaf ear to their aspirations.[1]

"But what", replied Cowley, "if those aspirations went far beyond an administration in common of the two Principalities, if under the term 'union', the word 'independence' was concealed; if the Government of a single chief meant separation from Turkey?"[1] The interview left Cowley convinced that, without actually avowing it, the Emperor was indifferent to the integrity of the Ottoman Empire and to the possible secession of the Principalities:

Such being the case it is difficult to argue with His Majesty, for, on this question at least, his philanthropy far exceeds his respect for Treaties.[1]

Cowley believed that, apart from his views on Turkey and his enthusiasm for the nationality idea, Napoleon was influenced by a desire not to submit to England on all points. "The choice", he wrote, "must be first made between concession and resistance", and he observed that the French Government looked to English public opinion and to Russian co-operation for support of their union policy.[1] Indeed, the Emperor was relying on doubtful allies. Kisseleff asserted that union under a native prince was impracticable, and Walewski himself had begun to doubt whether Russia would ultimately support union;[2] whilst

[1] Appendix III (b). Cited by F. A. Simpson in his *Louis Napoleon and the Recovery of France*, p. 365.
[2] F.O. 195. 538, Cowley to Clarendon, Feb. 10/57.

public opinion in England was almost indifferent, as the rejection of Gladstone's motion[1] in favour of union on May 4, 1858 to some extent indicated.

In an overture[2] to Buol in May, 1857, Walewski offered to withdraw the proposal of a foreign prince for the Principalities. Walewski told Hübner in confidence that Baron Bourqueney at Vienna had been ordered to make advances to Austria, and added:

Concede to us the principle of union and in practice we are ready for all kinds of transactions....We have abandoned the idea of a foreign prince—perhaps we shall be able to make other concessions.[3]

Walewski omitted, however, to define those further concessions. The French overture was received by Buol with suspicion: "This is *the old story of Bolgrad over again*, the Emperor Napoleon is beginning to find out that his Minister has gone too far and he wants to fall back a little".[2] Buol protested, too, against Walewski's assertion that Austria was mistaken in anticipating danger from union:

He (Napoleon III) is very kind, but we beg not to be treated like a sick state, we know our own case, and do not stand in need of prescriptions.[2]

In a counter-proposal[2] Buol urged that France should state publicly her withdrawal of a foreign prince and abstain from intrigues in favour of union; then, he argued, union would break down, either by the disagreement of the Divans *ad hoc* or by the refusal of the Sultan, supported by Austria, to consent to union. Only "*in an extreme case*", and with the sanction of the Sultan, would Buol

---

[1] Note 3, p. 61.
[2] F.O. 195. 542, Seymour to Clarendon, May 19/57, confidential.
[3] V. S. A. *Rapports de Paris*, IX, 54, Hübner to Buol, May 13/57, no. 42, *réservé*.

consider any concession; in such a case he was willing to admit a plan which,

> leaving the two Autonomies as they are at present, under the government of two native Hospodars, might bring about a fusion of their forces and systems and form a kind of Confederation composed of the two Provinces.[1]

Buol then drew up a Memorandum[1] outlining his scheme. The only unionist features it countenanced were common laws, army, currency and customs, and of these the last had been introduced since 1847.[2] Although Bourqueney "laboured conscientiously and boldly to wean his Government from the plan which they have so unfortunately taken upon themselves to advocate",[3] there was, as Seymour maintained,[4] no real hope of compromise. France desired, at the least, political union under a native prince; Austria's maximum concession was a "quasi-union" which was indeed no union at all. Diplomatic negotiation had failed to dispel the differences between the Great Powers over the question of uniting the Principalities. Nor did the situation lack a certain gravity, as Napoleon III's language[5] to the Turkish Ambassador at Paris indicated: "Je serais fâché que nous dussions nous brouiller sur cette question".

[1] Note 2, p. 78.
[2] See A. A. C. Sturdza, *Règne de Michel Sturdza*, p. 75.
[3] F.O. 195. 541, Seymour to Clarendon, Apr. 19/57.
[4] F.O. 195. 542, Seymour to Clarendon, June 1/57, confidential.
[5] L. Thouvenel, *op. cit.* p. 106, Benedetti to Thouvenel, May 31/57.

CHAPTER FOUR

THE COMMISSION AND THE MOLDAVIAN ELECTIONS OF JULY, 1857

"The Porte would have acted more discreetly in purchasing the elected instead of meddling with the elections." ALISON.[1]

[1] F.O. 195. 547, quoted in Bulwer to Clarendon, Sept. 17/57.

CHAPTER FOUR

THE COMMISSION AND THE MOLDAVIAN
ELECTIONS OF JULY, 1857

MEANWHILE, at Constantinople, the Porte was engaged in appointing kaïmakams or temporary rulers in the Principalities, and in elaborating, in concert with the representatives of the Powers signatory to the Treaty of Paris of March 30, 1856, the convocation firman for the Divans *ad hoc*. The existing hospodars of Moldavia and Wallachia, appointed in accordance with the *Acte* of Balta-Liman for a term of seven years, terminated office in the summer of 1856. In nominating kaïmakams the Sultan was applying the principle laid down by the Congress of Paris that, when the duties of the hospodars expired, he should secure "order and respect for the legal state of things".[1] Loud protests were raised by Rumanian national leaders, and, in particular, by John Bratianu,[2] at this assumption of power by the suzerain Court; and it is true that in appointing kaïmakams the Porte violated a local privilege, guaranteed by the Treaty of Paris, of instituting, in accordance with the *Règlement Organique*, a kaïmakamie of three, namely, the President of the Divan, the Minister of Justice and the Minister of the Interior.[3] Nevertheless, in July, 1856, the Porte nominated Alexander Ghika and Theodore Balş, as kaïmakams respectively of Wallachia and Moldavia. The former, who had been hospodar of Wallachia from 1834 until 1842, was Stratford's candidate. M. Béclard, French consul at Bukarest, described Ghika, who was sixty-two, as "un vieillard, usé, aigri, presque tombé en enfance".[3] Prokesch and Ali Pasha regretted his appointment but consoled themselves with the reflexion that it was wise to humour Stratford in

---

[1] Hertslet, *British and Foreign State Papers*, vol. XLVI, Protocol 22.
[2] See his *Mémoire* in Sturdza, *Actes et documents, etc.* III, 149.
[3] Damé, *op. cit.* p. 98.

order to secure British aid against the union.[1] The Moldavian kaïmakam, Balș, was Austria's candidate, eminently suitable, since he had been "openly at the head of a party who, in an address to the Sultan, had protested against the union".[1] M. Béclard estimated that the two appointments involved Balș and Ghika in a joint expenditure at the Porte of 60,000 ducats.[2] There would seem to be no ground for the statement[3] that, in defiance of his instructions, Stratford approved of these nominations, since Clarendon considered them "unexceptional men".[4] On the death of Balș in March, 1857, Nicholas Vogorides, his Minister of Finance, was made kaïmakam. Vogorides, a Bulgarian, and the son of the kaïmakam of Moldavia in 1821, was destined to become the determined opponent to the union of the Principalities. At his election, however, both French and Austrian statesmen badly misjudged his character and political views. M. Place, French consul at Jassy, himself a zealously active unionist, seems to have believed Vogorides' confession that he was "très partisan de la réunion",[5] whilst Count Buol objected to Vogorides on the ground that he was deficient in energy and was not a native.[6] Stratford, who had no share in his nomination, believed him lacking in the experience and capacity necessary for governing at such a difficult time[7]; both he and Reshid Pasha, the Grand Vizier, were right, however, in judging Vogorides as "most fit for the Porte's interest".[8]

[1] V. S. A. *Rapports de Constantinople*, XII, 57, Prokesch to Buol, July 2/56 and July 9/56.
[2] L. Thouvenel, *op. cit.* p. 74.
[3] E. Bourgeois, *Manuel historique de Politique Étrangère*, III, 426.
[4] F.O. 195. 506, to Stratford, July 23/56.
[5] L. Thouvenel, *op. cit.* p. 85.
[6] V. S. A. *Dépêches à Constantinople*, XII, 61, Buol to Prokesch, Mar. 28/57, no. 1.
[7] F.O. 78. 1260, Stratford to Clarendon, Apr. 6/57.
[8] *The Stratford Papers*, F.O. 352. 45, Pisani to Stratford, Mar. 5/57 and F.O. 352. 46, Stratford to Gardner, Mar. 11/57, private.

Having appointed the kaïmakams, the Porte, together with the representatives, proceeded to elaborate the convocation firman. The Commissioners to the Principalities, who were awaiting at Constantinople the drafting of the firman and the withdrawal of the Austrian army of occupation before beginning their work, were excluded from the preliminary meetings at which the firman was discussed and drafted. This exclusion caused a personal quarrel between Lord Stratford and Sir Henry Bulwer. Their relations had never been cordial, and Thouvenel, who compared the one to a lion and the other to a serpent, prophesied "un esclandre" as the result of their association.[1] Bulwer was an experienced diplomatist who had served under Palmerston in Belgium in 1830 and in Spain, from which country he had been summarily expelled in 1848 by General Narvaez.[2] Queen Victoria, judging from his career in Spain, alleged that he "has...almost been sporting with political intrigues" and was imprudent in his choice of company.[3] He seems to have had ambitions early to serve as Ambassador to Turkey, where he was Secretary to the Embassy in 1837. In 1849 his appointment as Ambassador was rumoured at Constantinople.[4] He resigned his post as Minister to Florence in 1855, possibly with an eye to promotion to Constantinople, for at that time Stratford was being attacked in the Press and there was question of recalling him in favour of Bulwer.[5] The change, however, did not take place.

[1] L. Thouvenel, *op. cit.* p. 65.

[2] He was expelled for recommending to the Spanish Government a more constitutional administration.

[3] *Queen Victoria's Letters*, II, 207.

[4] *The Layard Papers*, Add. MS. 38,987, Alison to Layard, Apr. 18/48.

[5] *The Quarterly Review*, Dec./1855, Art. viii, and Sir H. Maxwell, *The Life and Letters of...the fourth Earl of Clarendon*, II, 83. *The Quarterly Review* objected to the proposed change, chiefly on the ground of Bulwer's inexperience in Eastern affairs, a view which Austen Layard strongly endorsed. See *The Layard Papers*, Add. MS.

It has been held that Stratford and Bulwer differed dia-
metrically on every question, moral, political and religious.[1]
Certainly their relations over the Principalities is a record of
continual disagreement. Already in October, 1856, Bulwer
protested that Stratford was not co-operating with him sufficiently in the object of his mission by supplying him with
all the information he desired, and further, that Stratford
had insulted him, on the occasion of their visit to the
Sultan, by whispered conversations with an Ottoman
Minister.[2] Whatever the merits of this quarrel, Bulwer
had a valid grievance over the firman negotiations. On
November 19, 1856, Clarendon instructed[3] Stratford to
arrange a meeting between the Commissioners and the
representatives *before* the draft of the firman was completed; on December 12 he explained[4] that this meeting
would allow the Commissioners to suggest amendments
and to exchange views with the representatives on their
work in the Principalities; finally, on December 26 he
repeated[5] to Stratford that the proposed meeting should
precede the settlement of the firman. Stratford, however,
ignoring these instructions, reported[5] on January 8 that
the firman was drawn up. It was not until the 13th[6]
that the Commissioners attended a joint conference with
the representatives. The conference proved unfriendly
and even stormy. Bulwer's request[7] for an exposition of
what had passed at previous conferences was met by

38,984, letters to Layard from the Editor of *The Quarterly Review*,
Jan. 24 and Jan. 29/56.
   [1] S. Lane-Poole, *op. cit.* II, 449.
   [2] Private letters of Oct. 15 and Oct. 18/56 from Stratford to
Bulwer, and one of Oct. 16 from Bulwer to Stratford in *The Stratford
Papers*, F.O. 352. 48.
   [3] F.O. 195. 513.   [4] F.O. 195. 515.
   [5] F.O. 195. 537, to Clarendon. For a' copy of the firman see
S. Wambaugh, *A Monograph on Plebiscites*, p. 749.
   [6] Not the 7th as given by L. Thouvenel, *op. cit.* p. 65.
   [7] F.O. 195. 538, Bulwer to Clarendon, Jan. 19/57.

general opposition, especially from Stratford and Thouvenel. He then protested against the treatment he had
received from Stratford, who had, he declared, kept him in
entire ignorance of the discussions on the firman. Stratford,
"stung by Sir H. Bulwer's remarks, forgot himself as usual",
and an unseemly altercation ensued which was settled only
by the interposition of the Grand Vizier.[1] The foreign press
described this singular scene and *The Times* on January
29, 1857, printed some paragraphs from the *Indépendance
Belge*. In a private letter of explanation to Clarendon,
Stratford hinted that Bulwer's "outbreak" was "pre-
arranged for a report", and he denied that he had kept
Bulwer in the dark over the Principalities. Further, he revealed unmistakably the reason for his antipathy towards
Bulwer, since the latter "came with the rumour trumpeted
by his own nephew of being my successor elect, and he has
shown no care to discountenance a supposition which at one
time, taken with other things, was calculated to disparage
me with some people and to lower my official influence".[2]
He admitted in a later private letter that he had not reported
to Bulwer on the progress of the firman: "If he (Bulwer)
were sent out to divide the functions of the Embassy with
me, I was not apprized of it, and if I had been, I should
have known how to act".[3] In a despatch of January 14
he stated his only valid excuse for not holding the joint conference, namely "the lack and variety" (*sic*) of instructions
about the joint conference. The Russian, Prussian, and Sardinian Ministers had no instructions to meet the Commissioners, whilst the instructions of the Austrian and French
representatives stipulated only an explanatory interview.[4]
Further, he asserted—incorrectly at least as regards

---

[1] *The Times*, Jan. 29/57, p. 10.
[2] *The Stratford Papers*, F.O. 352. 46, to Clarendon, Jan. 19/57.
[3] *Ibid*. F.O. 352. 46, to Clarendon, Feb. 16/57.
[4] F.O. 195. 538, to Clarendon.

Bulwer—that the business of the Commissioners began with receiving the wishes of the Divans. Bulwer complained to Clarendon that "they (the Commissioners) were limited to textual criticism without right of amendment".[1] On two points, however, he received definite information at the joint meeting: first, that the discussion of union was not to be excluded from the competence of the Divans and second, that the authorities of the country would be responsible for the elections, although it was suggested that the presence of the Commissioners might exert a moral influence.

Bulwer's instructions,[2] dated July, 1856, ordered him to enquire and ascertain the wishes of the Divans *ad hoc* on all matters of internal administration, about which the British Government had "no preconceived opinion":

They (Her Majesty's Government) desire that the relations between the Principalities and the Porte should be placed on such a footing as may reconcile the interests of the former and the Sovereign rights of the latter, without, on the one hand, giving an opening to the Porte to interfere in the internal administration of the Provinces, or, on the other hand, encouraging the Provinces to shake off their allegiance to the Sultan.

The instructions further maintained that as yet no certain indication had been given of the wishes of the Principalities. At Paris Cowley tried, but failed, to obtain identical instructions for Baron de Talleyrand, the French Commissioner. Walewski "rather evaded than refused compliance".[3] Indeed, at the beginning of May Walewski had admitted that Talleyrand and Thouvenel had both been instructed to do all in their power to attain the union.[4] Bulwer demanded in an interview with Walewski on

[1] F.O. 195. 538, Jan. 19/57.
[2] F.O. 195. 506, enclosed in Clarendon to Stratford, July 23/56.
[3] F.O. 195. 507, Cowley to Clarendon, Aug. 14/56.
[4] Note 1, p. 67.

August 12 why Talleyrand had been received at Bukarest as a representative of the unionist party, to which Walewski lamely replied that he was making private arrangements there.[1] Since in August, 1856, the British Government decided in favour of the existing political separation in the Principalities, Bulwer demanded supplementary instructions.[2] In effect his original instructions remained unchanged. He was informed of his Government's new attitude towards union, and although it was not necessary to conceal their opposition to union, he was to maintain a strictly impartial attitude in his official duties.

In accordance with the Protocol of Paris of January 6, 1857, Austria withdrew her troops by the end of March, and Turkey the garrison which had remained at Bukarest. There was now no basis for Gortchakoff's declaration[3] that he would not send his Commissioner to the Principalities until foreign bayonets had been removed. The Porte now sent its electoral firman to the kaïmakams. The Commissioners after tedious delays finally met at Bukarest in April, 1857, to receive the views of the Divans—"one of the oddest expedients", observed *The Times* not inaptly, "recorded in the makeshift history of diplomacy".[4] Certainly this novel task was entrusted to a strange assemblage of diplomats, differing in political views and interests no less than in nationality and religion. Baron de Talleyrand, dressed in the uniform of a Colonel of the National Guard, was received with acclamation at Bukarest and Jassy as the advocate of union.[5] Sir Henry Bulwer strove continually to be judicious and impartial in a world

---

[1] F.O. 195. 507, Bulwer to Clarendon, Aug. 12/56.
[2] F.O. 78. 1195, Clarendon to Bulwer, Sept. 30/56.
[3] F.O. 195, 539, Seymour to Clarendon, Mar. 18/56, no. 292.
[4] Aug. 11/57, p. 7. Cp. S. Wambaugh, who writes in her preface to *A Monograph on Plebiscites* (1920), "It represents the first, and so far the only, instance of an international commission to administer a vote" (*i.e.* a popular vote).   [5] L. Thouvenel, *op. cit.* pp. 95–96.

of "foreign excitement and Ottoman compulsion". Basili, the Greek Commissioner of Russia, acquired considerable influence with the Wallachian kaïmakam and nobility, since Russia allowed it to be known that he would remain in the Principalities as consul.[1] In addresses to the local clergy he lost no chance of stressing the religious bonds which united the Principalities and Russia.[2] Baron Richthofen, the Prussian Commissioner, was an eager critic throughout of Vogorides' electioneering, rather with a view (believed Bulwer) to attacking Austrian policy.[3] Liehmann, who succeeded M. d'Eichmann as Austrian Commissioner, was "a sensible and practical man"[3]; Benzi, the Sardinian, was a consistent follower of Talleyrand. Finally, Safvet Effendi, although on the whole "an upright and well-meaning man",[3] was, like Liehmann, not above intriguing at the expense of his fellow Commissioners; he availed himself with alacrity of the offer of the local governments to defray his household expenses[4]; later on he fell ill, as did almost all of the Commissioners.[5]

The aim of the Congress of Paris was that the Commissioners, as its servants, should impartially ascertain certain local facts; what actually happened was, as Bulwer anticipated, that the Commissioners went to the Principalities, "less to furnish their governments with opinions than to maintain those which their governments had already declared".[6] The French attitude was perfectly clear from the *Moniteur* article and the official impor-

[1] *The Stratford Papers*, F.O. 352. 45, Colquhoun to Stratford, Feb. 28, May 29 and July 14/57, all private.

[2] L. Thouvenel, *op. cit.* p. 183.

[3] *The Stratford Papers*, F.O. 352.48, Bulwer to Stratford, June 23/57, private and confidential, and Bulwer to Clarendon, July 7/57, private.

[4] See S. Wambaugh, *op. cit.* p. 107, n. 1. This work contains a valuable collection of documents relating to the Commission and the elections generally, *e.g.* some of the protocols of the Commission.

[5] L. Thouvenel, *op. cit.* p. 159 and pp. 214–215.

[6] Note 5, p. 71.

tunities of their agents in the Principalities and at Constantinople. Russia's policy, wrote Lord Wodehouse,[1] was "strict neutrality": "nous ne sommes pas énoncés en aucun sens", declared Gortchakoff[2] in May, "ni engagés vis à vis de personne". Actually this politic neutrality was to some extent observed, since Gortchakoff refused[3] to agree to Walewski's proposal that the consideration of a foreign prince should be excluded from the scope of the Divans, although there is every reason to believe that Russia objected to a foreign prince.[4] Basili received instructions strictly to observe the Treaty of Paris—"nothing more, nothing less".[5] Even so, Russia was potentially a supporter of union. The year 1856–57 had witnessed a Franco-Russian liaison; moreover, the wishes of the Principalities, which she wished to satisfy, seemed to turn more and more towards union. The attitude of Austria and Turkey was avowedly and vehemently separatist. The two lesser Powers were, on the other hand, disposed to favour union. Prussian policy, wrote Loftus, was based on hostility to Austria and support of Russia.[6] The appointment of Richthofen, known to hold unionist views, owed much to the efforts of the Marquis de Moustier, the French Minister at Berlin. And although Manteuffel spoke continually about "strict neutrality",[7] this probably indicated less Prussia's real attitude than her desire not to compromise herself by any more open avowal, for Clarendon protested[8] to Bernstorff that Richthofen was

---

[1] F.O. 195. 543, to Clarendon, June 5/57.

[2] V. S. A. *Rapports de Paris*, ix, 54, quoted in Hübner to Buol, May 13/57, no. 42, *réservé*.

[3] F.O. 195. 543, Wodehouse to Clarendon, June 15/57.

[4] Cp. the Russian views at Stuttgart given in Appendix ii.

[5] Sturdza, *op. cit.* iii, 828, Talleyrand to Walewski, Sept. 18/56.

[6] F.O. 195. 543, to Clarendon, June 12/57, confidential.

[7] F.O. 195. 543, Loftus to Clarendon, June 19/57, confidential.

[8] F.O. 195. 543, Clarendon to Loftus, June 23/57, confidential.

concerting with his unionist colleagues, and suggested that he should imitate Bulwer's impartiality. Sir James Hudson, British Minister at Turin, reported[1] (June 2, 1857) that the Sardinian Government supported union and that their Commissioner would be guided by France; whilst the Marquis de Villa Marina at Paris, in affirming Sardinia's support of union, said[2]: "When they stood up for nationalities (sic) in Italy, how could they repudiate them elsewhere?"—a remark which Clarendon criticised "as a Jingle of words without any foundation of reason in ideas".[3] In adopting a pro-unionist policy Sardinia could champion the nationalist principle and at the same time co-operate with France with the hope of future reward. A further inducement, doubtless, was that the attainment of union would (as Manin believed[4]) be "mischievous to Austria".

The difficulties encountered by the Commission in the execution of its task were due not only to its internal differences but to its limited authority. It was the business of the kaïmakams to interpret the electoral firman and hold the elections, and the kaïmakams, as nominees of the Porte, were unlikely to be impartial officials. In fact, there was every likelihood that the Divans would reflect not the will of the country but that of the authorities who convoked them. It had been clearly stated, as the opinion of the Porte and the representatives at Constantinople, that the Commissioners should not interfere in the local government: "We have a right", wrote Bulwer,[5] "to

---

[1] F.O. 195. 542, to Clarendon.
[2] F.O. 195. 544, Cowley to Clarendon, July 15/57, confidential.
[3] F.O. 195. 544, Clarendon to Cowley, July 21/57.
[4] N. Senior, Conversations with M. Thiers, M. Guizot, and other distinguished persons, during the Second Empire, ii, 133: "I wish them to be united, not because I think that when united they will be a barrier against Russia, but because they will be mischievous to Austria".
[5] F.O. 195. 542, to Clarendon, May 28/57, private.

give counsel and raise objections, but no right to decide
or enforce our own opinion ". The Commission's duties,
as defined by the Treaty of Paris, were to collect information, to receive the views of the Divans, and to report on
the merits of these views. Any moral influence the Commission might have exerted was impaired by its own dissensions and by the propaganda encouraged by the agents
of certain Powers, in particular Austria and France.

In April, 1857, Ghika, kaïmakam of Wallachia, requested the Commission's decision on certain points of
the electoral firman.[1] His object in so doing was probably
to gain time in which to strengthen his personal party for
the future elections, since the main issue in Wallachia was
tending to become, not whether union or separation should
be demanded of the Powers, but whether Ghika's party
should dominate in the Divan over that of the ex-hospodar
Bibesco and his brother Stirbey.[2] Ghika was not a unionist
by conviction since union under a foreign prince would be
fatal to his own pretensions, whereas, if the Principalities
remained separate, he would have good prospects of
becoming hospodar of Wallachia. He was not, however, an anti-unionist in policy: union under a foreign
prince was such a popular cry in Wallachia and his
support depended so much on the lower and middle
classes that he was inclined to favour unionist hopes,
the more so since he was convinced that union could
never be achieved.[3] The Commission, believing that
it had no power to interpret the firman, applied to the
Porte through Safvet Effendi for authority to deal with
Ghika's questions, and suggested that the solution of those

[1] F.O. 195. 543, Bulwer to Clarendon, June 18/57, no. 82.
[2] F.O. 78. 1263, Colquhoun to Stratford, May 13/57.
[3] *The Stratford Papers*, F.O. 352. 48, Bulwer to Stratford, June
23/57, private and confidential; and F.O. 195. 546, Bulwer to Clarendon,
Aug. 13/57, no. 171.

questions should apply equally to Moldavia. No reply to this application reached the Commission during May, although Bulwer learnt from Stratford at the end of April that the Porte and the representatives were in general agreement as to the reply.[1] Whilst the Commission was awaiting the Porte's reply, Vogorides, at Jassy, who maintained a correspondence both "ostensible and secret"[2] with the Porte, was hurrying on the electoral arrangements in an anti-unionist spirit. The Commissioners of France, Prussia and Sardinia, acting as a separate group, called upon him to suspend his electoral proceedings until the Wallachian questions had been solved, so that the solutions could be applied equally in Moldavia.[3] At Constantinople, in consequence, the representatives of France, Prussia, Sardinia and Russia, without consulting Stratford or Prokesch, demanded of the Porte that Vogorides should delay the elections until the Wallachian difficulties had been settled.[4] Stratford objected strongly to this action, on the ground that the four Powers were interfering with the Sultan's independence, since the Treaty of Paris had not empowered the representatives either collectively or separately to interfere between the Porte and the kaïmakams,[4] a view which Clarendon endorsed. Further, Stratford did not believe that the reason for the action of the Four, namely, the alleged improper behaviour of Vogorides, was substantially proved. The Ottoman Council now turned to Stratford and Prokesch and, doubtless with a view to strengthening its position, asked for their opinions in writing.[5] To this they acceded, Stratford asserting, with the ready concurrence of Prokesch, "the

---

[1] F.O. 78. 1261, Apr. 27/57, no. 3.
[2] F.O. 78. 1269, Alison to Stratford, July 15/57, no. 16.
[3] F.O. 78. 1262, Stratford to Clarendon, May 11/57.
[4] F.O. 78. 1262, Stratford to Clarendon, May 18/57, no. 436.
[5] F.O. 78. 1262, Stratford to Clarendon, May 22/57.

importance of making a stand against unreasonable requisitions founded on mistaken views, and tending to realise a foregone conclusion ".[1] After an all-night sitting on the 20th of May the Ottoman Council determined to resist Thouvenel's demand, but compromised to the extent of proposing a conference with the representatives. With this Stratford unwillingly complied, and a conference was held on the 30th of May, resulting in an instruction to Safvet Effendi for the Commission dated May 31. According to both Stratford's and Thouvenel's versions of this instruction, the Commission's interpretation of the firman for Wallachia was to be applied also to Moldavia, "aussi exactement que possible sauf les cas exceptionnels qui seraient particuliers à la Moldavie ".[2]

The Commission now fell a victim to an Austro-Turkish intrigue. Although the Russian, Prussian and French Commissioners were informed[3] that instructions relating to the Wallachian questions had been sent, no reply reached them from Safvet Effendi until June 2. On that day, however, in response to an enquiry whether he had received any instructions relating to Moldavia, Safvet Effendi read the following telegraphic despatch, dated May 31:[4]

As the Porte hopes that now difficulties raised in Wallachia have been settled, you are to bring this to the knowledge of the kaïmakam of Moldavia so that the firman may be equally applied.

The other Commissioners demanded how they could have solved the Wallachian questions without the necessary authority, whereupon Safvet Effendi produced from his pocket another despatch from the Porte, which he had

[1] F.O. 78. 1262, Stratford to Clarendon, May 22/57.
[2] F.O. 78. 1263, a copy of this instruction is enclosed in Stratford to Clarendon, May 30/57, no. 473. Thouvenel's instruction is quoted in S. Wambaugh, *op. cit.* p. 114.
[3] See note 1, p. 92.
[4] F.O. 195. 543, Bulwer to Clarendon, June 18/57, no. 83.

received on May 1. He had withheld it, he explained, on the advice of M. d'Eichmann, the Austrian Commissioner, who declared that it did not represent the concerted views of the representatives and the Porte.[1] This despatch read thus:

As the Commission is in agreement on the subject of information asked on certain points of the Firman, the Porte, in concert with Contracting Powers, refers these matters to the Commission.

Bulwer protested to Clarendon against this "unworthy and threadbare stratagem". Talleyrand declared[2] that the aim of Austria and Turkey was to delay the Wallachian elections until those of Moldavia, which Vogorides was engineering in an anti-unionist direction, were hurried through. "No blame can attach to the Commission for the delay", wrote Clarendon, "the conduct of Safvet Effendi...was reprehensible and...his explanation was not satisfactory".[3]

Meanwhile, in Moldavia, Vogorides, untroubled in his interpretation of the firman by the nice scruples of Ghika, and undeterred by the request of the three Commissioners that he should delay his electoral arrangements, proceeded with the drafting of the electoral lists. It should be admitted, however, that as early as March he had raised questions relating to the firman, namely, whether mortgages on property and the property of a wife should affect a landowner's right to vote—questions which the Porte had promptly solved.[4] In adopting the Turkish attitude of opposition to unionists and unionist propaganda, Vogorides was only continuing the policy of his predecessor Bals, whose Ministry had been derisively called the

[1] Note 4, p. 94.
[2] F.O. 195. 543, Bulwer to Clarendon, June 18/57, confidential.
[3] F.O. 195. 543, to Bulwer, June 30/57.
[4] F.O. 78. 1260, enclosures in Stratford to Clarendon, Apr. 6/57.

" Gödel Ministry " owing to the powerful influence exerted by Gödel, the Austrian consul.[1] The probable explanation of Vogorides' anti-unionist policy is that, desirous to become hospodar of Moldavia, he sought by preventing union to win the goodwill of the Porte.[2] The nature of his secret correspondence with the Porte can be gauged by a letter[3] which Place, the French consul at Jassy, obtained by devious ways from the kaïmakam's private archives. Various accounts were current as to the means by which this incriminating document was procured, but, after a careful enquiry, Stratford inclined to the view that a sister of Vogorides, who was a friend of Place and had access to the kaïmakam's clothes and cabinet, was bribed by the Unionist Club at Jassy to abstract it.[4] The contents of the letter are clear enough and go far to explain the increased vigour and even violence of the French agents at Bukarest and Constantinople in fighting the Porte over the Moldavian elections. The letter, dated May 8/20, 1857, and addressed to Vogorides by Photiades, his official agent at the Porte, conveyed the Porte's approval of his anti-unionist measures and the instruction to persist energetically in opposition to the union, since the support of Stratford and Prokesch was assured. In the Austrian consul Vogorides had a zealous and active, though injudicious, ally; the British consul, Gardner, was "worthy and honest" but did not give him "enough moral support".[5] Certainly the kaïmakam's activities betrayed the full measure of his political predilections. He dismissed unionists[6] from the militia and

[1] L. Thouvenel, *op. cit.* p. 79.
[2] F.O. 78. 1269, Alison to Stratford, July 15/57, no. 15.
[3] L. Thouvenel, *op. cit.* pp. 112–114 contains a copy of the letter.
[4] F.O. 78. 1272, Stratford to Clarendon, Oct. 14/57. Prof. Iorga states in *A History of Roumania*, p. 233, that Vogorides' *wife* provided his enemies with proofs of his intrigues with Austria and Turkey.
[5] *The Stratford Papers*, F.O. 352. 46, Alison to Stratford, July 13/57.
[6] The dismissal of public servants except for a proved offence constituted an illegal act, since the powers of the kaïmakam, as defined by the *Règlement Organique*, were expressly limited in this respect. See

the civil service, appointing men of the opposite view;
he interpreted the firman so as to exclude large numbers
of unionist voters; he rigidly controlled the Press;[1] and
withheld the franchise from the Greek monasteries and
from many unionist priests with the result that the Metropolitan addressed a protest to the Commission.[2] Without
waiting to learn from the Commission the solutions they
were drawing up for Ghika on the interpretation of the
firman, Vogorides published his lists. Bulwer, who always
strove to be impartial but was inclined to support Vogorides
and to explain away his misdeeds, characterised this hasty
action as an "immense blunder".[3] He admitted, too, in
June, that Vogorides was "guilty of some attempts to
influence opinion", although he urged in extenuation the
unionist propaganda encouraged by the French agents.[4]
Actually, Vogorides' manipulation of the Moldavian elections was more flagrantly partisan than the British Commissioner then acknowledged. Later in the year—in October—
Vogorides ingenuously confessed to Bulwer that "many
voted last time for a separatist (I speak to you frankly)
because I gave them money or promised them places".[5]

The Commissioners, dissentient and embarrassed owing
to the activities of Vogorides, were powerless to restrain
him. Their instruction of May 31 from the Porte did

*Documents pour servir à l'histoire de l'application de l'article 24 du Traité
de Paris en Moldavie*, London (1857), p. 19.
   [1] At the direct command of the Porte, Balş had suspended the law of
May 12/56, which allowed a modified freedom of the Press, and revived
the censorship of 1848. See *Documents pour servir...Moldavie*, p. 67.
   [2] A copy of the protest is enclosed in Stratford to Clarendon,
June 15/57, F.O. 78. 1264.
   [3] *The Stratford Papers*, F.O. 352. 48, to Stratford, July 7/57, private.
   [4] F.O. 195. 543, to Clarendon, June 18/57, private and confidential.
   [5] F.O. 195. 548, Bulwer to Clarendon, Oct. 7/57. See the *Mémoire*
embodying charges against Vogorides, written by Moldavian boyars
and the Metropolitan, and dated May, 1857, in *Documents pour servir...
Moldavie*, pp. 17-54.

not indicate clearly whether they were authorised to *command* or merely to *advise* Vogorides to adopt their interpretation of the firman. Bulwer expressed himself to Clarendon as annoyed at the despatch of May 31 "which its very authors do not appear, at this day, in anywise agreed as to the meaning which their words were intended to convey. . . a difficulty, in short, was shoved off from one set of shoulders on to another, and this was called an adjustment".[1] To his enquiry as to the meaning of the instruction, Stratford replied[2] that it was intended "to afford the kaïmakam of Moldavia an opportunity of adopting the Wallachian decisions, in so far as circumstances allowed". The Commissioners of the unionist Powers, however, understood that the decisions were obligatory, not discretional. The Commissioners, placed in this perplexing position and duped once more, this time by Constantinopolitan diplomacy, began to range themselves more sharply into rival groups. The situation was peculiarly embarrassing for Bulwer: as an impartial Commissioner and as an honest man (he claimed to be both), he could not but admit the justification of his unionist opponents in protesting against the electioneering methods of Vogorides whose separatist aim, after all, was that of his Government. In a telegraphic despatch home on July 6 he reviewed the situation and predicted an approaching crisis[3]:

Having read various documents and acquired all the information in my power, I have reason to think that, if the elections are persevered with in Moldavia without attention to the suggestions made by the Commission, and without some rectification of the abuse alleged to have taken place, they, the Russian, Prussian, Sardinian and French Governments will not recognise a divan being constituted: and, though it is

[1] F.O. 195. 544, July 9/57.
[2] F.O. 195. 544, July 6/57 (telegram).
[3] F.O. 195. 543, to Clarendon.

difficult amidst conflicting testimony to give a decided opinion on this subject, I am afraid these governments will be able to produce some very plausible ground for their conduct.

He added that in the event of his Government deciding to face this situation, the Moldavian Divan would be unanimous against union. Clarendon replied[1] on the 8th that it would be difficult to remedy the irregularities committed, and that "there might be some advantage in a vote of the Moldavian Divan against union, even though there had been some irregularity in the Elections". Bulwer's prediction proved correct: the four unionist Commissioners, whom Buol styled the "Inseparables",[2] denounced the election proceedings and sought permission from their Governments to refuse recognition of the Divan if the elections were held.[3]

The crisis at Bukarest reflected a similar situation at Constantinople, where the union question had been acutely contested since the Treaty of Paris, and where, in consequence, began a train of events which culminated in the diplomatic rupture of August, 1857. The diplomatists who were principally interested in the future of the Principalities and sought to win over the Porte each to his particular point of view were Lord Stratford de Redcliffe, Thouvenel, the French Ambassador, and Baron Prokesch-Osten, the Austrian Internuncio. Stratford has been called the last of the great English Ambassadors,[4] and great indeed he was if measured merely by the authority he wielded in Turkey at intervals during half a century.

---

[1] F.O. 195. 543.

[2] F.O. 195. 544, Seymour to Clarendon, July 20/57, confidential.

[3] F.O. 195. 544, Cowley to Clarendon, July 15/57.

[4] Cp. F. A. Simpson, *op. cit.* p. 225, who makes the point that telegraphy had not yet succeeded in subordinating representatives abroad to the centralised control of the Foreign Office. Vivid glimpses of Stratford's character and personal relations are afforded by Sir A. H. Layard's *Autobiography and Letters*, 2 vols., *passim*.

A long official career at Constantinople (he was secretary
to a commission sent there in 1808 and Ambassador as
early as 1825) allowed him ample scope to indulge his
naturally autocratic inclinations; advancing age (for he
was seventy in 1856) seemed only to increase his energy
and industry; whilst his sense of honour in dealing with
the Turks, together with his customary practice of com-
bining personal feeling with official business, won from
the Turkish Ministers a respectful deference not un-
coupled with fear. His long ascendancy at the Porte must
be attributed largely to his gifts and faults of character
and personality: a fine physique, a commanding presence
and a temper which rarely brooked opposition to his will
—all were qualities which impressed the Oriental mind.
Clarendon made a just estimate when he said[1] that he
greatly admired Stratford's talents but greatly disliked his
character. Stratford had a distinct policy with regard to
Turkey based on a belief in its possible regeneration by
governmental reforms. This belief attached him to his
friend, Reshid Pasha, in his view one of the few Turks
of political ability, and the author of the Charter of
Gulhané (1839), which marked the first stage in Turkey's
westernisation. In 1848, in 1853, and in 1856 he was instrumental in bringing Reshid to power[2]; in 1857 he welcomed, though he did not personally effect, his reappoint-

[1] Maxwell, *op. cit.* II, 159. In 1853 Clarendon wrote: "What a pest
that man is!" *Ibid.* II, 68.

[2] Two letters in *The Layard Papers* show the spirited way in which
Stratford interfered to bring Reshid to power. After his return to
Constantinople in 1848 Stratford wrote to Layard, Nov. 30/50,
private (Add. MS. 38,978): "The first step was to replace Reshid
& Co. in office. That was soon effected..."; and on July 8/53
Alison wrote to Layard (Add. MS. 38,982): "The Sultan suddenly
dismissed the G. Vizier and Reshid P....the Elchee (*i.e.* Stratford)
came down upon His Majesty this morning equally suddenly....The
result of their interview was the rehabilitation of Reshid...". On
Reshid's appointment in 1856, see L. Thouvenel, *op. cit.* pp. 49–52.

ment as Grand Vizier. It has been generally recognised that no small share of the responsibility for the Crimean War rests upon Stratford, who, thoroughly anti-Russian in his political views, rejoiced at a war which might reduce Russia's growing power at the Porte. The very partial success of the Allies in the war; the fact that the few military honours went rather to France than to England; and above all the way in which Napoleon III forced the peace on a warlike England and even proffered friendship to Russia; all these factors, tending to heighten French prestige in the Near East at the expense of Great Britain, contributed to Stratford's acute displeasure which he vented in his private letters. "I was sorry", wrote Layard[1] in June, 1856, during a visit to Turkey, "to find our influence so very low at Constantinople". Stratford's private correspondence explains and illustrates this fact. His influence had suffered from the successful intrigues and newspaper attacks for eighteen months during which an angry country found in him a convenient scapegoat for the failures of the war; *The Times*, in particular, had shown "malice" towards him; consequently "the French have turned the tables on us, and my influence has gone to limbo".[2]

In Thouvenel, who had been sent out in May, 1855, Stratford found an additional cause for complaint. Thouvenel set himself to challenge Stratford's ascendancy and to acquire an ascendancy himself. Thouvenel, complained Stratford,[3] "is remarkably quick in perceiving his opportunity and turning it to account. His countenance

---

[1] *The Layard Papers,* Add. MS. 38,985 (typed copy Add. MS. 38,941 —this contains a few verbal errors). Layard's explanation of our diminished influence at Constantinople was Stratford's system of bullying the Turks.

[2] *The Stratford Papers,* F.O. 352. 44, to Cowley, Feb. 13/56, private.

[3] *Ibid.* F.O. 352. 44, to Clarendon, Apr. 24/56, private.

never betrays him, his language seldom". At the end of July, 1857, Clarendon wrote[1] of a *rixe* between Stratford and Thouvenel as an important cause of the difficulties and dissensions at Constantinople; there are, indeed, sufficient hints in Stratford's private letters to prove the existence of personal no less than official differences between them. On one occasion, for example, when Stratford was expatiating to the Turks on the integrity of the British judicial system, Thouvenel interposed with the remark that "our laws were chargeable with a delay of justice amounting to a denial of it"; "a pleasant colleague", added Stratford; "so coupled here and bespattered at home I have much need of patience".[2] The "moral aggrandizement" and "politico-religious propagandism" of France throughout the Levant formed the theme of a series of Stratford's letters in the years 1856 and 1857 in which he advocated the employment of a newspaper under governmental patronage in order to combat French influence.[3] Later on, in June, 1857, when Thouvenel succeeded[4] in excluding from France and French posts abroad the *Journal de Constantinople* because M. Noguès, its editor, had supported the Turkish view against the union of the Principalities, Stratford was ready to recommend to Clarendon a Mr Edwards from Smyrna who had just acquired an interest in the offending journal. Mr Edwards had a "*smack* of the Levantine in his mode of proceeding",[5] but was eager to direct the paper in

[1] Maxwell, *op. cit.* II, 146.

[2] *The Stratford Papers*, F.O. 352. 44, to Clarendon, Feb. 13/56, private.

[3] *Ibid.* F.O. 352. 44, to Clarendon, Feb. 22/56, private; and F.O. 352. 48, to Clarendon, May 6/57, private, and Oct. 14/57, private.

[4] F.O. 78. 1264, Stratford to Clarendon, June 15/57, no. 530, confidential; and *The Stratford Papers*, F.O. 352. 48, Stratford to Clarendon, Sept. 12/57, private and confidential.

[5] *The Stratford Papers*, F.O. 352. 48, Stratford to Clarendon, Aug. 15/57, private, and Nov. 11/57, private.

British interests, if terms could be arranged. Mr Edwards accordingly came to London, and after a personal interview, Clarendon actually started him off with £2000.[1]

That Stratford was inclined to exaggerate French schemes and French influence in Turkey would seem clear in view of Cowley's penetrating reports of the Emperor's policy and intentions in the Near East. Cowley, writing in May, 1857, did not believe that Napoleon III had any preconceived plan for establishing *exclusive* French influence in Turkey: the Emperor was merely determined that France should be consulted on all European questions and that French dignity abroad should be upheld. Further, Cowley was of opinion that French influence in Turkey might usefully be increased. To the lack of it he attributed the Emperor's denunciation of Turkish rule and his indifference towards the integrity of the Ottoman Empire.[2]

The negotiations which led to the Protocol of Constantinople in February, 1856, revealed clearly to Stratford that his supremacy was challenged. Prokesch and Thouvenel acted together, so that, left in a minority, he "had some rough work with them in the conference".[3] In particular, they stoutly opposed his proposal for a representative system in the Principalities. Thouvenel objected, too, to his claim of a right of military intervention in favour of the Sultan. In justice to Prokesch, Stratford admitted that he had made no hint of any Austrian protectorship.[4] The official views on the future of the Principalities which Stratford received in December, 1855, and in the following January, merely re-echoed his own upon which they were

---

[1] Note 5, p. 102.
[2] See Appendix III (a).
[3] *The Stratford Papers*, F.O. 352. 44, Stratford to Cowley, Feb. 13/56, private.
[4] *Ibid*. F.O. 352. 44, Stratford to Colquhoun, Feb. 16/56, private and confidential.

based and indicated a preference for the *status quo* subject to certain desirable reforms. Stratford was inclined to consider, also, in a very tentative way, an application of the "barrier principle" directed against Russia: by uniting the Principalities, extending the frontier to the Dniester, and creating a "respectable military force".[1] This policy was advocated by Charles Alison, his Oriental Secretary, who was sent in January, 1856, to Bukarest, with Clarendon's consent,[2] to assist Colquhoun in furnishing Stratford with information. Alison upheld Stratford's view that a representative system was desirable, and urged the expediency of a foreign prince "with *arbitrary power* for some time to come".[3] Stratford realised, however, already in February, 1856, that the policy of union would encounter the keen resistance of the Internuncio. Prokesch, who had been appointed in December, 1855, no less than Thouvenel, opposed Stratford's personal ascendancy. He complained[4] that his colleague wished to dominate everything, and in particular, to secure his own nominees as kaïmakams and hospodars in the near future.

He is not an ambassador but a sovereign.... His main desire is to secure for himself a decisive influence in the Principalities.... I have never seen before anyone better in health and more continuously active.

In character the Internuncio was well fitted to enter the lists of diplomacy at Constantinople. Palmerston epitomised his character in 1855—at a time when he was acting as second Austrian plenipotentiary at the Conference of Vienna—in words which, allowing for Palmerstonian passion and exaggeration, assign to him some

[1] *The Stratford Papers*, F.O. 352. 44, Stratford to Clarendon, Mar. 6/56, private.

[2] F.O. 195. 497, Clarendon to Stratford, Jan. 9/56.

[3] *The Stratford Papers*, F.O. 352. 44, Stratford to Clarendon, Feb. 13/56, private.

[4] V.S.A. *Expédition, Varia*, XII, 58, private letter to Buol, Feb. 11/56.

diplomatic qualities: "Prokesch", he wrote,[1] "is on the whole the most roguish diplomatist I ever had to do with. He is a consummate hypocrite, an accomplished actor, destitute of all principle, and utterly regardless of truth". Bulwer, in cautioning Stratford against the current exaggeration of Austrian agents, wrote[2]: "Prokesch himself, tho' a clever and able man, is also a bit of a poet", whilst Stratford commented[3] on his temper thus: "He gets into a heat easily, and like Gunter's mettlesome steed requires to be occasionally 'iced'". In marked contrast to these three dominant personalities and the shuttlecock of their diplomacy stood the well-intentioned Reshid Pasha. The Sultan and Reshid were so weak, reiterated Stratford; Reshid's fear of France was "quite puerile"; "it is only by talking like a bully th. I can keep him at all up to the mark".[4] Nor did Reshid fare better with Thouvenel: "My poor little friend Reshid" (to quote Stratford again[5]) "is frightened out of his wits by 6 ft. 3 of Gallic intimidation". No wonder that Reshid confessed[6] that he "sometimes felt his head as big as a bushel under the expansive influence of business and anxiety".

At the Congress of Paris Great Britain's public attitude was favourable to the Emperor's scheme for the union of the Principalities, but Stratford, doubting the sincerity of Clarendon's support of union at Paris, observed after the peace and pending further instructions a "systematic silence" on the question of union, a silence which did not, however, conceal his personal objection.[7] Thouvenel re-

---

[1] *The Later Correspondence of Lord John Russell*, II, 198.
[2] *The Stratford Papers*, F.O. 352, 48, June 23/57, private and confidential.
[3] *Ibid*. F.O. 352. 48, to Clarendon, July 1/57, private.
[4] *Ibid*. F.O. 352. 48, to Clarendon, May 25/57, private.
[5] *Ibid*. F.O. 352. 46, to Lord Lyons, June 29/57, private.
[6] *Ibid*. F.O. 352. 44, Stratford to Clarendon, Mar. 6/56, private.
[7] Note 3, p. 48

ceived urgent instructions to press union on the Porte and was keenly annoyed at Stratford's official neutrality, especially since despatches from Paris asserted that Great Britain supported union. He protested that nothing could be done without the co-operation of Stratford and insisted that the idea of a foreign prince should be abandoned. He was personally opposed[1] to the policy of union, on the grounds that it afforded France no tangible gain and that it tended more and more to lower French prestige at the Porte. When in August, 1856, Great Britain declared herself against union, Thouvenel's position was rendered more difficult and his chance of success more remote. In September he wrote[2] to Walewski: "Je ne dirai pas que nous ayons perdu du terrain; je reconnais seulement que l'Angleterre et Lord Stratford en ont gagné". For a while Stratford played a passive rôle, whilst Thouvenel urged union on the Sultan and his Ministers, and Prokesch sought to exclude union from the competence of the Divans by an explicit reservation in the electoral firman. An event of some importance modified the situation at Constantinople in November, 1856. To Thouvenel's dismay Reshid Pasha was appointed Grand Vizier, whilst at the same time the Sultan Abdul Medjid, though unwilling,[3] was invested by Stratford with the Order of the Garter. The change of ministry was a serious blow to Thouvenel: Ali Pasha and Fuad Pasha, who fell from power, were in the French interest,[4] but Reshid was essentially Stratford's right-hand man. The failure of Napoleon III to enforce his views in the Bolgrad boundary dispute still further improved Stratford's position at the Porte to the detriment of Thouvenel. The latter had observed[5] with chagrin that

[1] See L. Thouvenel, *op. cit.*, *passim*.   [2] Sturdza, *op. cit.* III, 811.
[3] F.O. 195. 512, Stratford to Clarendon, Oct. 19/56: "I have communicated secretly with the Sultan respecting his investiture. His repugnance to it is decided".   [4] L. Thouvenel, *op. cit.* p. 50.
[5] Sturdza, *op. cit.* IV, 24, to Walewski, Mar. 9/57.

the Bolgrad dispute first united Stratford and Prokesch in an alliance which the union question was to consolidate. In March, 1857, Prokesch noted[1] the "insinuations" of Stratford that some understanding was desirable between the anti-unionist Powers: the Porte and Austria, said Stratford, had positive arguments, the Four (France, Russia, Prussia and Sardinia) had only opinions of doubtful justness. In April he enumerated to Prokesch symptoms of an understanding between the Four Powers, and complained that "only a short time ago Lord Clarendon had expressed himself more than was necessary in favour of a French alliance".[2] That the Internuncio heartily responded to these advances is evidenced by the almost daily private letters which he wrote[3] on the question of the Principalities to his colleague during the summer of 1857. Already in March, Stratford—reacting perhaps to Napoleon's *Moniteur* article on union of February—stated his conviction to Clarendon that Great Britain should not submit to France on the question of union.[4]

You know better than I can pretend to do whether we gained much by playing second fiddle during the war and negotiations. It would be a sad humiliation for England to follow in the wake of a Power which loses no opportunity of influence or ascendancy at our expense.

It is clear that the policy of uniting the Principalities was identified in Stratford's mind with the desire of Napoleon III to force his will on Europe. It was in his opinion imperative that England should "stoutly" join Austria and the Porte in resistance to the French "scheme or fancy",[5] namely union; and he expressed the hope that

[1] V. S. A. *Expédition, Varia*, XII, 60, private letter to Buol, Mar. 25/57.
[2] *Ibid.* XII, 60, private letter from Prokesch to Buol, Apr. 8/57.
[3] These are in *The Stratford Papers*, F.O. 352. 48.
[4] *The Stratford Papers*, F.O. 352. 45, Mar. 25/57, private.
[5] Note 2, p. 109.

his instructions would consider in time the means necessary to this end. Probably he felt some uneasiness on this score since in an interview with the Grand Vizier on March 10, before leaving for Bukarest, Bulwer had spoken[1] about union in a way which varied considerably from the view which he himself understood his Government to hold. Stratford was reassured, however, by Clarendon's reassertion[2] of British opposition to union in April, whilst Turkish anxiety was dispelled by a message in this sense from Palmerston, transmitted by Musurus Pasha,[3] the Armenian Christian who represented Turkey at London. In view of all this it is not difficult to understand why the Grand Vizier, who in February, 1857, was inclining[4] towards French unionist views, on May 1 declared[5] positively that the Porte would never countenance union. When, therefore, the difficulties produced by Vogorides' electioneering became acute, the representatives at Constantinople were already organised into two hostile groups. Thouvenel, supported by the Russian, Prussian and Sardinian Ministers, was ranged sharply in opposition to Prokesch and Stratford, and each group strove, by diplomatic pressure, by ministerial intrigue and by intimidation, to move the Sultan's Government in its own interests.

[1] *The Stratford Papers*, F.O. 352. 48, Stratford to Bulwer, Mar. 13/57.

[2] F.O. 195. 540, Apr. 14/57.

[3] F.O. 78. 1260, telegraphic despatch from Musurus enclosed in Stratford to Clarendon, Apr. 17/57, no. 342, confidential.

[4] *The Stratford Papers*, F.O. 352. 48, Prokesch to Stratford, Feb. 14/57.

[5] *Ibid*. F.O. 352. 48, Prokesch to Stratford, May 1/57.

CHAPTER FIVE

THE DIPLOMATIC RUPTURE AT CONSTANTINOPLE, 1857

"Croyez bien, au reste, que je m'intéresse médiocrement aux Roumains, et, pour être franc, je les ai en guignon."

THOUVENEL to GRAMMONT.[1]

"It is my firm conviction that we ought to join stoutly with Austria and the Porte in resisting the scheme or the fancy—call it what you will—of France in seeking to unite the two Provinces."

STRATFORD to COWLEY.[2]

"Décousu là (Bukarest), et intimidation victorieuse ici (Constantinople), où irons-nous?"

PROKESCH to STRATFORD.[3]

[1] L. Thouvenel, *op. cit.* p. 189.
[2] *The Stratford Papers*, F.O. 352. 46, Apr. 10/57, private.
[3] *Ibid.* F.O. 352. 48, July 13/57.

THE DIPLOMATIC RUPTURE AT
CONSTANTINOPLE, 1857

NO sooner had the Commission reached Bukarest than the struggle began at Constantinople. As early as April Thouvenel demanded of the Porte the dismissal of two Moldavian ministers who had privately declared[1] themselves in favour of union. In May (as has already been noticed) together with his allies he requested that Vogorides should be ordered to suspend his electoral proceedings, with the result that the ambiguous instruction of May 31 was sent to the Commissioners. In June, Thouvenel launched a powerful offensive against the Porte, which began with the demand for the dismissal of Vogorides.[2] In an interview with Photiades, Vogorides' agent at Constantinople, he talked violently of demanding not only the dismissal but the head of Reshid Pasha himself, but, changing his line of attack, he ended by hinting at the bestowal of the Legion of Honour on Photiades and his master as a reward for their support of union.[3] The vigorous and even violent attitude adopted by Thouvenel in June and July, 1857, exceeded in some degree the views held at Paris: "Je vois bien", wrote Benedetti,[4] "que vous ne nous trouvez pas assez fermes!"; and Clarendon believed[5] that probably more moderate counsels prevailed at Paris. Indeed, Walewski informed Cowley confidentially later in the year that Thouvenel had gone to Constantinople with strict instructions to avoid all personal intrigues and controversies and that in using his influence, as he subsequently did in October, 1857, to obtain Reshid

---

[1] F.O. 78. 1260, Stratford to Clarendon, Apr. 6/57, confidential.
[2] F.O. 78. 1264, telegram Stratford to Clarendon, June 5/57.
[3] F.O. 78. 1264, Stratford to Clarendon, June 13/57.
[4] L. Thouvenel, *op. cit.* p. 123, June 20/57.
[5] F.O. 78. 1264, telegram to Stratford, June 13/57.

Pasha's dismissal from office he had acted against those instructions.[1] Two factors in particular explain the vehemence of Thouvenel's actions: first, the acquisition early in June of secret letters incriminating Vogorides, and second, the realisation that only the stoutest efforts could ever prevail against the opposition of Stratford, whom he described as "the sixth Great Power of Europe". Thouvenel's attempt to remove Vogorides failed before the combined resistance of the Porte, Prokesch and Stratford, who acted under express instructions from home.[2] Stratford seems to have been a little impressed by Thouvenel's offensive for he proposed[3] to Clarendon, as an Anglo-French compromise, a scheme based on the principle of uniformity instead of union. The kaïmakam of Moldavia now published his electoral lists, and the elections were accordingly (as prescribed by the firman) to be held some thirty days later. With a positive tactlessness that must have been calculated, Stratford held a "great dinner"[4] at his palace at Pera to celebrate the anniversary of Waterloo.

Undismayed by his first failures, Thouvenel persisted in his endeavours to remedy the irregularities committed in Moldavia. A joint *démarche*[5] by the four unionist representatives on June 25, which urged the Porte to disavow or restrain Vogorides, produced no result, and on July 4, by means of identical notes, they repeated their[6] demand, adding that the Porte should adopt their interpretation of the instruction of May 31. In this emergency the Porte applied to Stratford and Prokesch

---

[1] F.O. 195. 547, Cowley to Clarendon, Oct. 4/57, no. 1382, confidential.
[2] F.O. 78. 1264, telegram received from Clarendon, June 6/57.
[3] F.O. 78, 1264, telegram (confidential), June 11/57, no. 505.
[4] L. Thouvenel, *op. cit.* p. 125.
[5] Identical note printed in S. Wambaugh, *op. cit.* pp. 814–815.
[6] F.O. 78. 1266, Stratford to Clarendon, July 15/57, no. 621.

for advice. For Stratford the situation was difficult owing to "too much zeal on the side of Austria and not a little want of firmness on that of the Porte".[1] Thouvenel was so far successful that the Ottoman Council at a meeting on July 9 actually agreed to accept his version of the instruction of May 31, and to postpone the Moldavian elections for fifteen days in order that the lists might be revised accordingly[2]. Before this decision received the necessary sanction of the Sultan, the Porte proposed confidentially to Stratford that the decision of the Council should be accepted as a reply to the Four. Stratford, however, was suspiciously averse from accepting a decision which, he said, "was not improbably concerted between M. Thouvenel and the party averse to Reshid Pasha in the Cabinet, and to which His Highness had thought it necessary to assent".[1] Together with Prokesch, he refused this proposal and denied the right of the Porte to impose its single decision upon the other parties to the Treaty of Paris—a denial which was unexceptionable, since by treaty the firman was the concern, not of the Porte as suzerain, but of the Porte in concert with the other six signatories. To relieve the tension of the situation, Reshid held a meeting with Stratford and Prokesch in his tent between evening and midnight on July 9.[1] The result was first, a resolution to call a conference of representatives to determine the meaning of the instruction of May 31—a plan which had already occurred to Stratford— and second, the adoption of Reshid's compromise, which he declared indispensable, to adjourn the Moldavian elections for eight days, so that in the interval Vogorides might furnish an explanation of his actions. Thouvenel, together with the other three unionists, promptly refused

---

[1] F.O. 78. 1266, Stratford to Clarendon, July 15/57, no. 621.

[2] L. Thouvenel, *op. cit.* p. 135 and Sturdza, *op. cit.* v, 84, Thouvenel to Walewski, July 9/57.

the conference and clung tenaciously to the decision which he had extracted from the Council. Instructions were sent to Vogorides by telegraph on the 10th to adjourn the elections eight days.[1] Stratford decided to "mark time", leaving on the "Inseparables" the onus of making the next move: "A system of dictation", he wrote,[2] "requires to be met by a firm, though temperate, resistance".

The Porte's vacillation, resulting in two contrary decisions, had embarrassing consequences. It is not certain that Stratford knew immediately the precise nature of Thouvenel's "decision". In his telegrams of the 11th and 15th of July he did not elucidate this point, and it was only on the 17th that he explained[3] that the Council had decided on the 9th to grant a fifteen days' delay. Now arose for Stratford a most awkward dilemma. In his telegram of the 11th,[4] which Clarendon received on the 13th, he had announced the agreement which he and Prokesch had obtained from the Porte, to adjourn the elections eight days. On the 15th, he received a telegram[5] from Clarendon, sent on the 14th, stating that the French Government accepted "the delay" as a complete satisfaction of its demands, on the understanding that, in the interval, irregularities in the electoral lists should be remedied. To Stratford's dismay, however, Thouvenel produced at the Porte a telegraphic instruction from Walewski, "according to which, the delay, described in Your Lordship's message of the 14th, is not the term of eight days, announced in my telegraphic despatch of July the 11th, but one extending to the end of the month".[2] Stratford added that Thouvenel's interpretation rested

---

[1] V. S. A. *Rapports de Constantinople*, XII, 60, enclosure D in Prokesch to Buol, July 18/57.
[2] Note 1, p. 112.
[3] F.O. 78. 1267, to Clarendon, no. 622.
[4] F.O. 78. 1266, to Clarendon.
[5] F.O. 78. 1266.

on his (Thouvenel's) report to Paris of the Council's decision.[1] Under ordinary circumstances this misunderstanding would have been cleared up by telegraphic enquiries at London and Paris in about four or five days, but on the 17th there was insufficient time to adopt this course, unless another postponement of the elections was ordered, since the elections were due to begin on the 19th. Stratford's course seemed clear, especially since advices from Jassy deprecated further delays and since Prokesch's instructions specified the eight days' delay as agreeable to France. He determined, accordingly, to base his actions on his own interpretation of Clarendon's telegram of the 14th, until further instructions arrived.[2]

Meanwhile the Grand Vizier, distracted, and wavering in his allegiance, sought anxiously for some way of escape between the intrigues and threats of Thouvenel on the one hand, and the inexorable will of Stratford on the other. Already in June, Stratford had reported the successful efforts of Thouvenel to form a party in the Council, and, in July, his desire to force a change of ministry at the expense of Reshid Pasha.[3] Nor were these efforts unrewarded.

The Grand Vizier [wrote Stratford on July 17[3]], from some unknown motive, leans to a compromise, and talks of resigning, if too much thwarted in that respect (sc. over the elections).

And Prokesch reported[4] on the 15th of July that the Government seemed unable to resist any longer the pressure of the Four, and that his own and Stratford's support were insufficient to strengthen a ministry which had against it "all the influential people of the country".

[1] Note 2, p. 112.
[2] Note 1, p. 112.
[3] Note 3, p. 113.
[4] V. S. A. *Rapports de Constantinople*, XII, 60, to Buol, no. 44 D.

In particular, Fethi Ahmed Pasha, Master of Artillery and brother-in-law of the Sultan, complained

of the excessive importance attached to the union of the Principalities, a question more Austrian than Turkish, which did not touch any vital interests of Turkey and involved that country in bad relations with both France and Russia.[1]

Indeed, Thouvenel did not neglect any means by which he might win over the Porte to union. He sought access either personally or through his dragoman "to the Sultan at pleasure".[2] He called personally on the Sheik-ul-Islam, "an unprecedented step", alleged Stratford, "on the part of a Foreign Representative".[2] In concert with the other three, and with the assistance of his supporters in the Council, he tried to obtain the dismissal of the Grand Vizier.[3] But Thouvenel's success was very incomplete. Reshid, despite some wavering, remained staunch to the anti-unionists Stratford and Prokesch, for he believed,[4] with some justification, that the French plan of union rested on a belief in the incurability of the "Sick Man".

On the night of the 17th of July, in reply to a note from Stratford protesting against any further postponement of the elections, Reshid suggested, in order to avert a crisis, an adjournment of five days, and declared confidentially that he would resign office unless Stratford consented to this proposal.[5] This threat did not, however, secure Stratford's compliance.

I should deeply lament his mistake, though I could not in conscience surrender an Imperial and European interest to personal feelings.[5]

---

[1] V. S. A. *Rapports de Constantinople*, XII, 60, to Buol, July 22/57, no. 46 B.   [2] F.O. 78. 1268, to Clarendon, Aug. 5/57, no. 688.

[3] F.O. 78. 1267, Stratford to Clarendon, July 20/57, no. 628.

[4] V. S. A. *Rapports de Constantinople*, XII, 60, Prokesch to Buol, July 22/57, no. 46 D.

[5] F.O. 78. 1267, Stratford to Clarendon, July 24/57, no. 643, confidential.

At daybreak on the 18th, Stratford went to Reshid's country house where he found the Internuncio "to all appearance accidentally there", and the Ottoman Council assembled in an adjacent room.[1] Stratford now faced a situation which required immediate decision. The Moldavian elections, delayed eight days, were due to begin on the 19th.

The object of Reshid Pasha and his colleagues in the Government was to throw every particle of responsibility from their own shoulders and to give themselves the advantage of acting in appearance under pressure from England and Austria.[1]

The Grand Vizier and his son, Ali Ghalib Pasha, the Foreign Minister, acted as intermediaries between the Council and the two representatives. Reshid stated that, despite the divergent interpretations of the French and British Ambassadors, he believed an *entente* existed between their Governments. He proposed, therefore, to delay the elections five days, so as to allow time to refer to London and Paris. Stratford suggested that instead of delaying the elections, it might be arranged to lengthen the intervals between the summons of the successive classes of voters. His scheme was adopted and a Memorandum[2] was drawn up consisting of two parts, a Declaration, signed by Reshid and Ali Ghalib Pasha, and the signed Reply of Stratford and Prokesch. The first stated the Porte's proposal of a five days' delay. In the second Stratford and Prokesch expressly assumed responsibility for their action and stated their reasons for not complying with the Porte's proposal: there was no valid argument for further delay, the Four had refused a conference, and the French Government had apparently accepted the eight days' delay as satisfactory. While he was still at

---

[1] F.O. 78. 1267, Stratford to Clarendon, July 22/57, no. 641.
[2] Enclosed in Stratford's no. 641, note 1, *supra*.

Reshid's house Stratford learnt that Thouvenel had received a private audience of the Sultan. Reshid was summoned to the Palace on the following day and defended his policy.

It is interesting by way of comparison to notice Thouvenel's account[1] of the action of Stratford and Prokesch on the 18th. He recounts first how the Porte agreed unanimously to a fifteen days' delay. The result was dramatic.

> Cris, tempête, de lord Stratford et de M. de Prokesch, émoi de Réchid, et, finalement, soumission de ce dernier à ses deux maîtres.

Thouvenel alludes to the Memorandum in which Stratford and Prokesch "déchargent la Sublime Porte de sa responsabilité et la prennent à leur compte"; "la moutarde est montée au nez de l'Empereur", he continued, and the recall of Stratford was essential to the maintenance of the Anglo-French alliance. Not without reason was Stratford "tempted to wish for the quiet times of war".[2]

On July 22 Stratford received a telegraphic despatch from Clarendon[3], who had learnt through Cowley at Paris of the fifteen days' delay promised to Thouvenel.

> We see no objection [he wrote] to the delay of fifteen days to which we understand the Porte has agreed....If the Caimacam proceeds with the Elections notwithstanding... the arrangement made with the Porte, his dismissal will be asked for by the French Government.

In despatches,[4] dated the 22nd and 24th, Stratford justified his actions of the 17th and 18th. On the 25th he pointed out[5] that Clarendon's message above came too

---

[1] L. Thouvenel, *op. cit.* p. 135: letter to the Duc de Gramont, July 30/57.

[2] *The Stratford Papers*, F.O. 352. 48, to Clarendon, July 22/57, private.

[3] F.O. 78. 1267.   [4] Notes 1, p. 116 and 5, p. 115.

[5] F.O. 78. 1267, to Clarendon, no. 648.

late, since the Moldavian elections began on the 19th. Indeed, the elections, resulting in a Rump of separatists, were carried through between the 19th and the 25th of July. The electoral lists included only a minority of those entitled to vote, but even so the majority of these abstained from voting.[1]

Thouvenel, in a letter to the Duc de Gramont, has charged Stratford indirectly with complicity in the elections. He wrote:[2] "M. Alison, secrétaire de lord Stratford, *présidait* les opérations électorales...". Stratford highly estimated Alison's abilities, judgment and linguistic gifts;[3] he had already sent him on a mission to the Principalities in January, 1856, and he hoped to have secured for him the appointment as Commissioner to the Principalities.[4] In July, 1857, acting on his own initiative and without informing Bulwer, he sent Alison to Jassy with instructions[5] to discover what had actually occurred there in the preparation of the electoral lists and to ascertain whether any valid grounds for complaint existed. Alison was (in the wording of his instruction) to provide "satisfactory information for my own guidance", and in particular to answer a number of questions: did the electoral lists conform with the firman? could the Wallachian explanations be applied? does their rejection exclude individuals? should revision of the lists be indispensable, what means would ensure the least delay? have urgent and arbitrary measures been used? Stratford had come to believe that

[1] A good account of the elections is given by S. Wambaugh, *op. cit.* pp. 108–114. See also Prof. T. W. Riker, *op. cit.*

[2] Note 1, p. 117.

[3] Layard, *op. cit.* II, 75–80 and 145–150. Alison was one of the few men who "stood up" to Stratford, who "in his (Alison's) presence became as gentle as a lamb, although a few minutes before he was a roaring lion". Alison became *chargé d'affaires* at Constantinople in Dec./57 and was Minister to Teheran from 1860–72.

[4] Sturdza, *op. cit.* III, 488, Thouvenel to Walewski, May 22/56.

[5] F.O. 78. 1266, instruction to Mr Alison, July 7/57.

there was some foundation to Thouvenel's charges against Vogorides, although he continually asserted that he lacked reliable information. Alison arrived at Jassy on July 13, and it is clear that Vogorides regarded his presence as moral support and as a counterpoise to his opponent Place.[1] On the 14th Alison telegraphed:[2] "the electoral lists cannot be regarded as altogether free from stain and reproach". He discovered that Vogorides was in secret communication with the Porte and that he was aspiring to become hospodar. In a despatch on August 7 he confessed[3] the impossibility of explaining, even by personal enquiries and private observation on the spot, what actually occurred in the framing of the electoral lists and whether the unionists were justified in their loud remonstrances against the kaïmakam. There is no evidence to bear out Thouvenel's assertion that Alison played an active part in the conduct of the elections; nor was he in any sense authorised to do so. He arrived at Jassy too late to be of much use to Stratford, and his mission served to provide yet another ground for difference between Bulwer and Stratford, who admitted later to Clarendon his "oversight" in not informing Bulwer of Alison's mission.[4]

Learning that the Moldavian elections had been held, Thouvenel redoubled his offensive. He had received telegraphic instructions,[5] dated July 27, to demand from the Porte the absolute annulment of the elections, to act together with the Russian, Prussian and Sardinian Ministers, and to threaten a rupture of relations. At midnight of the 28th, Stratford was awakened by the arrival of a

[1] *The Stratford Papers*, F.O. 352. 46, Alison to Stratford, July 13/57.
[2] F.O. 78. 1268, enclosed in Stratford to Clarendon, July 31/57, no. 671.
[3] F.O. 78. 1269, no. 70.
[4] *The Stratford Papers*, F.O. 352. 48, Aug. 10/57, private.
[5] Sturdza, *op. cit.* V, 274.

confidential officer of the Porte, who announced that a few hours earlier, in a formal note, Thouvenel had demanded immediate annulment, adding that his instructions would not allow him to accept either a refusal or delay.[1] In a telegram[2] written at 1 a.m. on the 29th, Stratford outlined the situation and asked for instructions.

The peremptory demand of a single power [he wrote] rests on no title of right and...the Porte would fail in her duty if she did not appeal to all the Powers parties to the Treaty of Peace.[2]

A crisis was, indeed, at hand. Thouvenel was ably backed by the other three Powers. Boutenieff, the Russian Minister, received *via* Vienna special instructions,[3] dated July 27, to co-operate with Thouvenel in breaking off relations. Prussia also co-operated, although with her accustomed caution, since Loftus did not believe (on August 2) that she would break off relations, "a step far too bold and decisive for His Prussian Majesty to adopt".[4] Sardinia was still a self-interested supporter of French policy. Entrenched behind Stratford and Prokesch, the Porte refused[5] Thouvenel's demand, on the 30th, and offered to adjourn the convocation of the Divan if he would agree to refer the electoral difficulties to the Congress of Paris. This Thouvenel declined. Meanwhile, at Bukarest, the Four Commissioners refused (July 29) to recognise the Divan.[6] At the Porte, a ministerial change followed at midnight on the 31st. According to Stratford,[7] Thouvenel wrote to the Sultan, on the previous day, offering the post of Grand Vizier to three of Reshid's rivals in the Council.

---

[1] F.O. 78. 1268, Stratford to Clarendon, July 30/57, no. 644.
[2] F.O. 78. 1267, Stratford to Clarendon, no. 655.
[3] Enclosed in Stratford to Clarendon, July 31/57, no. 668.
[4] F.O. 195. 545, to Clarendon, confidential.
[5] F.O. 78. 1268, Stratford to Clarendon, July 30/57, no. 666.
[6] F.O. 78. 1268, Stratford to Clarendon, July 30/57, no. 665.
[7] F.O. 78. 1268, Stratford to Clarendon, July 30/57, no. 662.

Reshid had shown, in the preceding weeks, a desire to retire from an exacting position in a Government which was becoming unstable by reason of internal dissension and external pressure. Stratford wrote,[1] "It looks as if Reshid had himself obtained the change to escape from further vexation". Thouvenel attributed the change to his own pressure on the Porte.[2] The two explanations, however, are complementary, not mutually exclusive. The change was very incomplete. Reshid retained a place in the Council as President of the Tanzimat, Ali Pasha became Foreign Minister and Mustafa Pasha, ex-Governor of Crete, Grand Vizier. Stratford thought the change "a prelude to a change of political character",[3] but Reshid did not.[3] For the present at least Ottoman policy remained unchanged.

For some time before the storm at Constantinople the French and British Governments had attempted to adjust their differences over the question of union. With this end in view, Cowley paid a visit to London in the middle of June, but, on his return to Paris, he was unable to report to Walewski the likelihood of an understanding. In an interview[4] with the French Foreign Minister, he spoke of the "painful impression" made on his Government by Thouvenel's high-handed conduct, which might lead to "a state of antagonism between the two countries in the East". His Government, said Cowley, could not countenance the demand for the dismissal of the kaïmakam, to which Walewski replied that he could not allow the Porte to stifle public opinion in the Principalities.

Her Majesty's Government [said Cowley[4]] could not help feeling that the two Governments no longer found themselves

---

[1] F.O. 78. 1268, to Clarendon, Aug. 1/57, no. 675.
[2] L. Thouvenel, *op. cit.* p. 146.
[3] F.O. 78. 1268, to Clarendon, July 31/57, no. 674.
[4] F.O. 195. 543, to Clarendon, June 18/57, confidential.

on the same ground of departure, in considering the future state of the two Provinces. Did the French Government still uphold the integrity of the Turkish Dominions as a European necessity, and were they still ready to respect the independence of the Sultan's authority?

He argued that under a native prince union was impracticable, and that, under a foreign prince, it would lead to separation from Turkey, and to similar action in Tunis, Bosnia, Montenegro and Rumelia; "and then what became of the Treaty of 1856 and the solemn engagement to maintain the integrity and independence of the Porte?"[1] Walewski replied[1] that "abstractly speaking" the independence of the Principalities was desirable but that "the moment was not ripe for attempting it".

He could say therefore that the Policy of the French Government was the same as that of H.M.'s Government...and that if union would weaken the authority of the Porte he would abandon it even before the expressed wish of the Divans.[1]

Cowley advocated some common system for the two Principalities, and Walewski suggested separate hospodars over each and a Governor-General over both. But the understanding apparently reached was, as later appeared, superficial. And Walewski's argument was somewhat illogical in professing himself willing to ignore the public opinion which he would not allow the Porte to stifle.

Towards the end of July the British Cabinet found itself involved in a conflict at Constantinople which was neither foreseen nor desired. The immediate reason for this was the alleged misunderstanding arising from Clarendon's telegram to Stratford of the 14th, the responsibility for which rests ultimately on Cowley, who omitted, in his first advice to Clarendon, to specify the period of

[1] Note 4, p. 121.

delay[1] which satisfied the French Government. Stratford's action in preventing further postponement was scarcely, under the circumstances, contrary to his instructions. He had, however, committed his Government to a greater extent than they desired. On the 28th of July Clarendon demanded of Stratford the precise terms of the engagement between Thouvenel and the Porte and further information as to his action in hastening the elections before the French delay of "twenty days" had expired.[2] "The Grand Vizier told the French Ambassador", wrote Clarendon, "that you (Stratford) had been the cause of his breaking his word". The despatch ended with an order firmly to resist the dismissal of the kaïmakam. But when news was received of Thouvenel's request for annulment, ministerial feeling in England definitely supported Stratford. On the back of Stratford's 1 a.m. telegraphic despatch of the 29th of July,[3] there is a note written by Palmerston, dated '30/7/57" and signed "P".

My opinion is that the Porte should be advised by Telegram to decline Compliance with this arrogant (and unjust[4]) Demand which no single Power has a right to make and for which the Five[5] would require strong grounds to be laid before they would make it and even if the Five Powers were to come to the Conclusion that the Elections had been so irregularly and so illegally made as to justify their being annulled they would give that advice in a manner more suitable to the engagement which by the Treaty of Paris they have taken, to respect the Independence of the Sultan.

[1] F.O. 195. 545. Cowley admitted this omission in his despatch to Clarendon, Aug. 4/57, enclosed in Clarendon to Stratford, Aug. 4/57.
[2] F.O. 195. 544. Persigny told Clarendon twenty days. The delay specified should have been fifteen days. Sturdza, *op. cit.* v, 84, Thouvenel to Walewski (telegram), July 9/57.
[3] Note 2, p. 120.   [4] These words were struck out.
[5] There were actually six signatories, excluding Turkey, to the Treaty of Paris. Palmerston probably ignored Prussia, which had not been a member of the Alliance against Russia.

A telegraphic instruction[1] was accordingly sent to Stratford
in this sense. The situation was growing serious. News of
the Mutiny in India had for several weeks reached
England but, as late as June 26, Palmerston had "no
fear of its results".[2] By the end of July facts had shaken
his easy optimism.[2] That was one reason why the conflict
at Constantinople should be ended. Moreover, the union
of the Principalities was for Great Britain a very secondary
question, which would not justify extreme action. Clarendon therefore proposed[3] to Persigny a joint Conference of
the representatives and the Turkish Ministers who drew
up the firman, to interpret that document and to examine
the electoral lists. The French Ambassador thought that
his Government might agree, although Thouvenel had
some weeks previously rejected the same expedient. On
August 3, again, Palmerston and Clarendon held an
interview with Persigny at which they suggested that the
proposed Conference and the Ministerial change at Constantinople might satisfy the French Government.[4] But
their hope proved illusory. In an interview[5] with Cowley,
which "could not but be recriminatory on both sides",
Walewski refused the Conference, unless the elections
were first annulled, and declared the change of ministers
insufficient to satisfy France. Moreover, he said, significantly enough, that "France was not interpreting a
treaty but vindicating her honour". On the same day,
August 4, Clarendon reprimanded Stratford in the following terms:[6]

It seems from your despatch No. 641[7] that the Porte would
very willingly have deferred for five days longer the Mol-

[1] F.O. 78. 1268, Clarendon to Stratford, July 30/57.
[2] *Queen Victoria's Letters*, III, 297.
[3] F.O. 78. 1268, Clarendon to Stratford, July 31/57.
[4] F.O. 195. 545, Clarendon to Cowley, Aug. 3/57.
[5] F.O. 195. 545. Cowley to Clarendon, Aug. 4/57.
[6] F.O. 195. 545.   [7] Note 1, p. 116.

davian Elections, but had yielded to the representations in a
contrary sense addressed to it by Your Excellency and the
Austrian Internuncio; and it is my duty to state to Your
Excellency that Her Majesty's Government much regret that
the Proposal of the Porte in this respect was not accepted.

The great desideratum was that the English and French
Governments should come to an understanding with each
other....If this had been agreed to, all the complications
which have since arisen would have been avoided.

Stratford ably defended himself in a despatch on August
18.[1] He did not doubt that the eight days' delay was
meant in Clarendon's telegram of the 14th of July. Even
Thouvenel's instructions specified "le délai transmis par
La Porte à Jassy" and, it is true, Vogorides was instructed
to delay only eight days, and not any longer period. Again,
the fifteen days' delay was not a binding obligation on the
Porte.

Reshid Pasha has solemnly assured me [Stratford] that he
never gave a promise nor entered into an engagement with the
French Ambassador, as it seems was supposed by the latter,
to whom the conclusion of the Ottoman Council, subsequently
set aside and treated as *non-avenue*, was on no occasion communicated otherwise than confidentially,—never in an official
shape.[1]

These facts, added Stratford, were confirmed by the
Director of Correspondence at the Porte.[1] Moreover,
Stratford had been advised from Jassy not to defer the
elections any longer. His news from Jassy was, however,
entirely conflicting. Vogorides defended himself[2] against
the charge that he had not adopted the Wallachian decisions about the firman, but Gardner, the British consul,[3]
reported that none of the Wallachian decisions was applied.

[1] F.O. 78. 1269, no. 727.
[2] F.O. 78. 1266, Vogorides to his Agent at the Porte, July 13/57.
[3] F.O. 78. 1268, to Stratford, July 9/57.

Alison's reports were often ambiguous and perhaps coloured by the views which he knew Stratford to hold. Stratford's information was such that, if it did not clear Vogorides, it at least discounted the exaggerated charges of Thouvenel. Further—continued Stratford in his defence—the Inseparables had put themselves in the wrong by refusing a conference. And he concluded:

> The responsibility was heavy, but it was forced upon me. ...Had I been guided by instructions immediately applicable to the case, I should not have felt myself at liberty to exercise my own discretion. The information received from Your Lordship by Telegraph, as I understood it, pointed to the position which I maintained.[1]

It is unnecessary to summon counsel in Stratford's defence, but several comments may be offered. Clarendon's contention that, if the delay of five days had been granted, complications would have been avoided, is highly dubious, since, at the end of this delay, the differences about the electoral lists would remain to be settled and Thouvenel had already refused a conference. Again, it does not seem obvious that Stratford should have known that an Anglo-French understanding was "the great desideratum". Stratford was right in perceiving that the real issue in conflict at Constantinople was not the execution of the firman but the union or separation of the Principalities. Finally, it would seem that, although Stratford was perhaps over zealous, Clarendon, with the Mutiny on his hands and the French Government more determined than he had anticipated, was preparing a strategic retreat.

Meanwhile at Constantinople events were quickly reaching a crisis. On the 4th of August, the Porte refused a further demand (August 1) of Thouvenel for annulment, and offered to summon the kaïmakams to Constan-

[1] Note 1, p. 125.

tinople, to hold a personal enquiry, and to annul the elections if illegality was proved.[1] Thouvenel treated this reply as *un refus dérisoire*,[1] and on the 5th, in accordance with instructions and in concert with the Russian, Prussian and Sardinian representatives, broke off relations with the Porte.[2] Prokesch attempted to explain[3] the motives which united the Four: Sardinia and Prussia both hated Austria, Russia wished to break up the Anglo-French alliance, whilst France aspired to supremacy in the Principalities and at the Porte. He rather thought, however, that France had some other motive.

The success of Vogorides in producing an anti-unionist Divan, the determination of the French Government not to countenance irregularities which, if permitted, might defeat its unionist policy, and the efforts of Stratford and Prokesch to outgeneral Thouvenel—all these produced in August, 1857, a serious deadlock. A situation had arisen in which Russia was especially interested. "The Russian Cabinet", so ran a leading article in *The Times*,[4] "is very naturally also endeavouring to regain by astuteness what it has failed to attain by violence". Boutenieff received (as has already been noted) precise instructions to co-operate with Thouvenel. On August 7, Gortchakoff asserted that "Russia could never quietly submit to such a 'soufflet' as the Porte had given her in this affair".[5] Riza Bey, the new Turkish Minister to Russia, who arrived on August 1, was refused an audience of the Czar at which to present his credentials.[6] Moreover, Gortchakoff prevailed upon him to send a non-cypher telegram on the

---

[1] F.O. 78. 1268, Stratford to Clarendon, Aug. 4/57, no. 682.

[2] Sturdza, *op. cit.* v, 388. Copy of identical note presented to the Porte.

[3] V. S. A. *Dépêches à Constantinople*, XII, 61, private letter to Buol, July 31/57.   [4] Aug. 10/57.

[5] F.O. 181. 337, Wodehouse to Clarendon, Aug. 7/57, no. 355.

[6] F.O. 181. 337, Wodehouse to Clarendon, Aug. 7/57, no. 356.

6th, announcing this refusal to the Porte[1]—a step which indicated an open avowal of opposition to Turkey in the Principalities. Once again, as in 1856 during the Bolgrad controversy, Great Britain and France stood sharply opposed, and Russia was concerting with France. A general fear that secret engagements had been made on either side served for a moment to alarm the Powers.

Il doit y avoir [wrote Thouvenel[2]] entre l'Angleterre, l'Autriche et la Turquie, un traité secret, signé sans doute à l'époque de l'affaire de la délimitation de la Bessarabie, et par lequel les trois Puissances, en défiance des résolutions ultérieures du gouvernement de l'Empereur, se sont engagées à empêcher à tout prix l'union des Principautés.

The Porte, too, feared[3] the existence of an offensive alliance of the Four. These suspicions were, however, unfounded. Nor is it true, as Debidour has stated,[4] that, before the rupture at Constantinople, Napoleon III secured Russian co-operation in conference with the Czar at Stuttgart, since the Stuttgart interview took place on September 25, 1857, nearly two months after the crisis at Constantinople. It is true that early in June a meeting between the Czar and the Emperor was much talked of in diplomatic circles at St Petersburg,[5] and when the Czar set out for Kiel later in the month this meeting was thought likely.[6] It did not, however, take place.

One important factor, however, served to relieve the tension of the situation, namely, the disposition of Napoleon III. "The English Alliance, which was never popular in France, would have been shipwrecked then and there

[1] Note 6, p. 127.
[2] To Walewski, Aug. 6/57; Sturdza, *op. cit.* v, 394.
[3] Note 2, p. 115.
[4] *Histoire diplomatique de l'Europe*, II, 172. The error is reproduced in Damé, *op. cit.* p. 122. See Appendix II.
[5] F.O. 181. 337, Wodehouse to Clarendon, June 11/57, no. 273.
[6] F.O. 181. 337, Wodehouse to Clarendon, June 26/57, no. 303.

(August, 1857), had another than Persigny been French Ambassador in London", so wrote Count Vitzthum von Eckstaedt,[1] the Saxon Minister to London. His words attribute too much perhaps to Persigny and too little to the personal inclinations of Napoleon III, for if Guizot's view is right, friendship with England was a "ruling principle" to the Emperor, who attributed the collapse of the Orleanist monarchy to the breakdown of the Anglo-French alliance.[2] Persigny's efforts seem to have played an important part in the reconciliation of the two countries. A firm advocate of the English alliance, Persigny set out for Paris in May, 1857 "to rescue his Emperor out of the hands of the idiots", of whom he conceived Walewski to be the chief.[3] In fact the differences between England and France had been aggravated owing to the unfriendliness existing between Walewski, who wished to strengthen Franco-Russian relations, and Persigny, who was essentially pro-English in policy.[4] On his return to London, Persigny related to Clarendon the substance of his conversations at Paris:[5] the Emperor was convinced that England, France and Russia should settle (*régler*) the affairs of Europe; Persigny warned the Emperor in the presence of Walewski of the dangers he would meet "if he swerved in the least from the path of his true interest which was the English Alliance". The result was that, as early as May, 1857 the Emperor earnestly desired to pay a private visit to the English Court in order to explain his ideas and to resolve mutual differences.[6] Accordingly, on August 6,

---

[1] *Op. cit.* I, 211.   [2] N. Senior, *op. cit.* II, 321.
[3] Vitzthum von Eckstaedt, *op. cit.* I, 213.   [4] *Ibid.* I, 244.
[5] *Queen Victoria's Letters*, III, 294, Clarendon to Prince Albert, May 20/57.
[6] An imprudent *obiter dictum*, made by Palmerston to Persigny and reported to the Emperor, almost led to the abandonment of the Osborne visit. See Col. the Hon. F. A. Wellesley, *The Paris Embassy during the Second Empire*, p. 125.

when a crisis had been reached at Constantinople, Napoleon arrived, closely guarded,[1] at Osborne, where he remained the guest of the Queen until the 10th.

The Emperor desired above all not to shatter his alliance with Great Britain which he regarded as peculiarly his own creation.[2] At meetings with the British ministers on the 7th and 8th of August a compromise was reached.[3] On the 8th he ordered Thouvenel not to leave Constantinople.[4] It became very clear in conversations with the Prince Consort[5] that the two countries failed to see eye to eye over either Turkey or the union of the Principalities. Napoleon maintained that his political view of Ottoman integrity was the same as that of Great Britain although as a private person he despised the Turks.[6] He still upheld his belief in the union of Moldavia and Wallachia under a foreign prince, but realised that without British support union could not be achieved. He was guided at Osborne by the consideration that more important than the future of the Principalities was the continuance of the Anglo-French alliance. Napoleon was becoming greatly embarrassed by the unionist cause to which he had so lightly subscribed in 1856. He was willing enough to modify his original programme: to drop the idea of a foreign prince and even that of one native prince. Buol was not far wrong when

---

[1] Vitzthum von Eckstaedt, *op. cit.* I, 213–214. So vigilant were the French and English detectives in guarding the Emperor from the possible attacks of French or Italian refugees that Persigny himself was arrested as a suspect on his way by fishing boat from Southampton to Cowes on the night of the 5th.

[2] Cp. *ibid.* I, 239: "L'Alliance, je le répète, c'est moi...les deux peuples ne se connaissent pas et ne s'aiment guère".

[3] *Ibid.* I, 225.

[4] V. S. A. *Rapports de Constantinople*, XII, 57, Prokesch to Buol, Aug. 11/57.

[5] The Prince Consort personally (but not officially) disapproved of British opposition to union. See Col. Wellesley, *op. cit.* p. 123.

[6] Martin, *The Life of the Prince Consort*, IV, 101–102.

he said that the crisis at Constantinople marked "the last charge of French Diplomacy to make good its position in the Principalities".[1] In effect this last charge served to cover the Emperor's retreat. The only difficulty that now faced Napoleon III was, how he should yield on the question of union without personal humiliation. The Bolgrad incident had been unpleasant enough, and the French rupture at Constantinople was useful in that he was enabled to withdraw his unionist policy without loss of self-esteem. In securing the annulment of the Moldavian elections at Osborne, he won an immediate success which obliterated his temporary defeat over the union of the Principalities.

No formal engagement was signed at Osborne, but a Memorandum, drawn up by Palmerston on August 9, and subsequently amended by Persigny, states the terms of the compromise reached by the two Powers.[2] Clarendon agreed to advise the Porte to annul the Moldavian elections, so that the electoral firman might be executed anew in accordance with the interpretations of the Commission. In return, Napoleon promised to join with Great Britain in proposing, at the forthcoming Conference, an administrative union of the Principalities which, however, would leave each Principality under its own prince:

It is agreed to be desirable that the two Provinces should have similar organic institutions, and that while retaining their separate Governments, they should have a common system in regard to all matters civil and military to which such a community of system can advantageously be established.[2]

This part of the bargain was to be kept secret for two reasons: first, it was inadmissible that two Powers alone

[1] F.O. 195. 545, Seymour to Clarendon, July 28/57.
[2] See the writer's note, "The Osborne Conference and Memorandum of August, 1857", in *The English Historical Review*, XLIII, 409–412.

should prejudge a question to be decided later at a Conference, and second, "it would never do" (as Napoleon intimated) "for him, and the honour of France, that it should be said, he had come over to Osborne, and then immediately been made to change his mind".[1]

When Napoleon returned to France, news of his success over the Moldavian elections spread throughout Europe. For Clarendon the compromise of Osborne was politically "a godsend",[2] but it was also, immediately at least, a defeat for the English Ministry.[3] It has already been shown that Palmerston vigorously opposed the pretensions of the Four at Constantinople, and since Musurus wrote as late as the 7th of August[4]

I have just seen Palmerston who says Porte is right in refusing the imperious demand...he reiterated assurance of firm support of England,

it is clear that Palmerston's policy was suddenly changed at Osborne. Buol received the news with mixed feelings. He deplored the fact that no guarantee had been extracted from Napoleon, but admitted that he felt "as if a great weight had been removed from his mind".[5] The Porte was thrown into some consternation by the French victory, but Great Britain and Austria hastened to assure it that neither had changed its views on the question of union.[6] Even when the Porte learnt of the secret promise of Napoleon, which Thouvenel officially denied, it was disturbed by the thought that administrative union might easily be

---

[1] Martin, *op. cit.* IV, 106.

[2] *Ibid.* IV, 95.

[3] Greville noted in his *Memoirs*, VIII, 120: "August 20th...As far as outward appearances go, we do not appear to have played a very brilliant part (*sc.* at Osborne) and the Opposition papers think they have got a good case on which to twit Palmerston".

[4] F.O. 78. 1269, Stratford to Clarendon, no. 719, confidential.

[5] F.O. 195. 546, Seymour to Clarendon, Aug. 18/57.

[6] F.O. 195. 545, Clarendon to Stratford, Aug. 13/57, confidential.

translated into something very akin to political union.[1] Walewski commented cryptically on the Osborne agreement,

Il y avait beaucoup de linge sale entre nous, et nous l'avons lavé en famille.[2]

Napoleon's triumph at Osborne has been much exaggerated by contemporaries and by historians. Actually it was no more than a tactical advantage—the annulment of the elections—at the expense of his strategic aim—the political fusion of Moldavia and Wallachia. "France has the formal victory", said Buol,[3] "but one more such victory and the union question is dead". Although he might still hope to stretch the Osborne agreement in the interest of some closer union of the Principalities, Napoleon was morally bound no longer to propose union under a native or foreign prince.

Who, it may be asked, were responsible for the rupture at Constantinople? Contemporary opinion united in blaming Stratford, or Thouvenel, or both. "Half the difficulties which now exist at Constantinople", wrote Clarendon[4] on July 29, 1857, "are owing to the rix(e) between him (Stratford) and Thouvenel, and his doing the right thing always in the wrong way;" and he is reported[5] to have told Persigny in August that "the presence of this old maniac at Constantinople is dangerous". Benedetti assigned[6] all the responsibility to Stratford whose motive in opposing union had always been the desire to bring Reshid back to power and to regain his own supremacy at

---

[1] V. S. A. *Rapports de Constantinople*, XII, 60, Prokesch to Buol, Aug. 14/57 (telegram).

[2] V. S. A. *Rapports de Paris*, IX, 55, Hübner to Buol, Aug. 13/57.

[3] V. S. A. *Expédition, Varia*, XII, 60, private letter from Buol to Prokesch, Aug. 16/57.   [4] Note 1, p. 102.

[5] L. Thouvenel, *op. cit.* p. 165, letter to Thouvenel, Aug. 28/57, from an intimate correspondent at the Foreign Office.

[6] *Ibid.* p. 159, letter to Thouvenel, Aug. 28/57.

the Porte. Count Vitzthum von Eckstaedt[1] was inclined to indict Thouvenel, who "did his utmost to frighten the Divan (*i.e.* the Porte), and remind them of the threats of Prince Menschikoff". *The Times* wrote magisterially on August 10: "The imbroglio which exists at the present moment is to be attributed entirely to the mistaken energy of Constantinopolitan diplomacy." The English Press generally attacked Thouvenel, the French, Stratford; whilst the *Journal de Frankfort* characterised Thouvenel as an *adepte de Mazzini*.[2] Questions were raised in the House of Commons about the differences at Constantinople, in particular by Disraeli; when, however, the question of responsibility for the diplomatic crisis was touched upon in a speech by Lord John Russell on August 14, Palmerston very dexterously turned the attention of a tired House from what he already described as "a mere matter of past history".[3] Modern criticism of the rupture is scanty. The burden of *Trois années de la question d'Orient* is to acquit Thouvenel and to convict Stratford of all responsibility; whilst Sir Herbert Maxwell has written:[4] "Stratford's bearing towards the French ambassador at Constantinople had been the cause of most, if not all, of the trouble with the French government."

In the main, though with certain qualifications, these criticisms must stand. That the Porte itself was the passive tool of the strongest group among the foreign representatives; that Stratford and Thouvenel, as principals, both threw into their struggles at the Porte an excess of zeal and energy beyond the letter of their instructions; and that Prokesch, Stratford's "second", was no less hotheaded than Thouvenel and rather more so than Stratford—all these facts must be admitted. The forcefulness of

---

[1] *Op. cit.* I, 211.   [2] L. Thouvenel, *op. cit.* pp. 166–167.

[3] Hansard, *op. cit.* CXLVII, 1388–1390 and 1687–1690.

[4] *Op. cit.* II, 147.

Thouvenel's conduct sprang from his belief in the moral and legal validity of his argument that Vogorides, in his election proceedings, was violating the express stipulation of the Treaty of Paris that the Divans should freely represent all classes in the country. Thouvenel's case against Vogorides was undoubtedly sound; it is in his methods that he is exposed to adverse criticism. Stratford's case was good where it consisted of objections to Thouvenel's methods—his separate *démarches* apart from other signatories to the Treaty of Paris and his violence and intimidation. His case was otherwise weak against Thouvenel's, inasmuch as it rested on the belief that Vogorides' misdeeds were either non-existent or, at the worst, non-proven. Stratford always complained that he had only conflicting opinions and never reliable evidence of Vogorides' alleged illegalities; he seems, however, never to have lost sight of the ultimate objective of his Government, namely the defeat of the unionist project,[1] and to have believed (as did Clarendon himself[2]) that a separatist Divan in Moldavia, however produced, would be instrumental to that end—an erroneous calculation since the Moldavian Divan, as prepared by Vogorides, could never be accepted as giving the slightest indication of the will of Moldavia. It is only fair in Stratford's defence to note that Thouvenel, inspired by the receipt of documents incriminating Vogorides, was the first to act violently at Constantinople; further, that as early as April, 1857, Stratford predicted[3] in official despatches, that the question of union, if allowed to proceed unchecked, would

[1] He wrote, *e.g.* to Clarendon, July 15/57 (no. 621, secret and confidential): "All parties agree that the Firman is to be carried fairly and fully into effect. They disagree as to the manner of its application in Moldavia, *and I need not repeat that the question of uniting the Principalities under a single Government is the real interest at stake.*" F.O. 78. 1266, italics my own.

[2] See p. 99.   [3] Note 5, p. 105.

produce "a scandalous schism in the face of Europe", and that his Government conspicuously failed to arrive at an early understanding with France. On the other hand, a strong presumption remains that, distrustful of Napoleon III's foreign schemes and becoming keenly anti-French as he had formerly been anti-Russian, Stratford visualised France in the person of Thouvenel as a disturbing influence in European politics which ought to be checked rather than as an ally who ought to be conciliated, and further, as a rival claimant to an ascendancy at the Porte which he had come to regard as his own.[1] In securing the rejection of two distinct proposals to postpone the elections, the one for fifteen, the other for five days, Stratford certainly acted on his own initiative and contrary to the spirit of instructions which, however, he did not formally ignore, since in one instance they were ambiguous in wording and in another instance they were belated. Benedetti's theory of Stratford's actions hardly does justice to the British statesman. First, it does not seem true that Stratford opposed union in order to bring Reshid back to power. Thouvenel himself admitted that it was only just to Stratford to recall that he had *always* opposed union, and the British Government decided definitely against union in August, 1856, three months before Reshid was returned to power. Whilst it is true that the question of union in general and that of the Moldavian elections in particular, involved the issue whether Stratford or Thouvenel should dominate the Porte, it is unreasonable to maintain that Stratford opposed union in order to

[1] Cp. Clarendon's view, stated in January, 1858, in Maxwell, *op. cit.* II, 159: "He (Stratford) has, therefore, consistently and unremittedly hated the French and done his utmost to thwart them; and, having for a number of years occupied the Eastern dunghill without competitors, he could not find an inch of room upon it for the French ambassador, who, being backed by 150,000 men (*i.e.* during the Crimean War), thought he might have *locus standi* there".

improve his own position at Constantinople. On the contrary, the principles which chiefly guided him in his memoranda home recommending future changes in the Principalities, were first, the interests of Turkey, and second, the interests, as he conceived them, of the Principalities themselves. That Stratford wished to maintain Reshid in power—chiefly as a pledge for the execution by the Porte of reforms in accordance with the Treaty of Paris—is true enough. The maintenance of Reshid in office was one issue of importance in his struggles with Thouvenel of June and July. He believed that, had he not acted as he did on July 18, "Reshid would probably have gone overboard with the Moldavian Elections".[1] But it must not be argued further that this consideration conditioned his policy of opposition to Thouvenel;[2] the crucial issue to Stratford was whether or not the political separation of the Principalities could be maintained.

[1] *The Stratford Papers*, F.O. 352. 48, Stratford to Clarendon, July 22/57, private.

[2] *E.g.*, see p. 115, where Stratford expressly states that Reshid's resignation must not be allowed to stand in the way of "an Imperial and European interest".

CHAPTER SIX

THE CONFERENCE OF PARIS, 1858

May 11th, 1858.

Senior. What would you do with the Principalities?

Chrzanowski. If they are united under a foreign prince they are torn from Turkey. If they are united under a native prince he will plunder and oppress them to provide his bribes for the Porte. If they are governed separately they will be under two robbers instead of under one. I really believe that the best course would be to give them over to Austria.[1]

---

[1] N. Senior, *op. cit.* II, 219.

CHAPTER SIX

THE CONFERENCE OF PARIS, 1858

THE crisis precipitated by the Moldavian elections was seemingly ended by the compromise of Osborne. In one respect, however, the reconciliation between the Powers was incomplete: Lord Stratford was not yet convinced that annulment of the elections was either the best, or even the inevitable, expedient. He received a telegraphic despatch[1] from Clarendon on August 11 which stated that the Sultan, having vindicated his independence by resisting the demand of the Four Powers, could therefore without derogation to his dignity consent to annul the elections at the request of the remaining Treaty Powers:

Her Majesty's Government advise the Sultan to annul the elections and permit revisions of electoral lists upon the basis agreed on May 30th (*i.e.* on the view of that agreement held by the Four).

The despatch added further that Austria's co-operation had been demanded, and revealed confidentially (since "it forestalls the decision of the Congress") the Anglo-French agreement to propose for the Principalities a common system under two hospodars. Acutely conscious that his Government had abandoned him at Osborne, Stratford wrote an immediate and vigorous reply,[2] which was seen by Palmerston and the Queen.[3]

Not being ordered to act at once....I presume that you wait for an answer from Austria. I beg leave to submit meanwhile, with all deference, that although the Porte will probably comply, the effect of annulling the elections without enquiry, and revising the lists according to the supposed agreement of

[1] F.O. 78. 1269.
[2] F.O. 78. 1269, to Clarendon, Aug. 11/57.
[3] Pencil note on back of despatch.

May 30th, will, however intended, be in public opinion a complete surrender, that it will probably bring on the resignation of Prince Vogorides, that it will operate very unjustly on all who have been legitimately elected in Moldavia, that it will give to the Porte's instruction of May 30th a meaning not intended by the Internuncio and myself, that it will go far to fix in this Empire the ascendancy of a Power which for the present is justly mistrusted and resisted, and that among its consequences will in all probability be the total exclusion of Reshid Pasha from office.

But Stratford's ominous protestation had no effect upon his Government. On the 13th Clarendon wrote[1] that, although aware of the inconveniences attendant on the policy of annulment,

the good much exceeds the evil, for the good will be permanent while the evil will be temporary.

.   .   .   .

[It is] very important that the Turkish Government should do what we recommend...we rely on your zeal and ability for persuading it to do so.

The effect of this despatch on Stratford is described vividly by Prokesch.

I do not know what Lord Redcliffe will do....Lord Redcliffe thinks that Lord Clarendon would desire even to lay the person of the English Ambassador, as a sacrifice, at the feet of the French Emperor.[2]

On the other hand, Stratford was instructed in another and confidential despatch[3] of the same date, to assure the Porte that the British Government had not changed its opinion as to the impolicy of union. On the 16th, he learnt[4] that

---

[1] F.O. 78. 1269, to Stratford, no. 723.
[2] V. S. A. *Rapports de Constantinople*, XII, 57, to Buol, Aug. 14/57, no. 53.
[3] F.O. 78. 1269, to Stratford.
[4] F.O. 78. 1269, Clarendon to Stratford, Aug. 14/57.

Austria's co-operation was secured, whilst an instruction was sent to Prokesch on the 15th.[1]

By the 16th of August—at the very latest—Stratford had no justification whatever in delaying further the execution of his instruction of the 11th, repeated on the 13th. But he had not yet resigned himself to the performance of an uncongenial task. A despatch,[2] written on the 18th, which can only indicate Stratford's official recalcitrance, ran:

Agreeably to the terms of Your Lordship's telegraphic message dated the 13th Inst, I wait for further instructions....

And this despatch bore in a marginal note an obvious mark of Clarendon's dissatisfaction: "Repeated (*sc.* instructions to annul) in his No. 723 (Clarendon's despatch of the 13th).—Not a word in it to authorize delay. Compare with No. 723". Stratford did not stop at this. On the 19th he wrote[3] that the situation was unchanged, that the Four had not yet resumed official relations with the Porte, and concluded:

I do not feel myself at liberty to take any steps beyond the communication of the Osborne Agreement until I am honored with further instructions.

This was annoying and even perplexing to Clarendon: "What does he mean—Surely the telegram in No. 723 taken with the previous one was clear enough".[4] On August 19 Clarendon reiterated[5] particulars of the secret

---

[1] V. S. A. *Dépêches à Constantinople*, XII, 61, Buol to Prokesch, Aug. 15/57, no. 1.
[2] F.O. 78. 1269, Stratford to Clarendon, no. 728.
[3] F.O. 78. 1269, Stratford to Clarendon, no. 738.
[4] Marginal note written on Stratford's, no. 738.
[5] F.O. 78. 1269, no. 740.

part of the Osborne agreement, and finally on the 21st Stratford declared[1] himself ready to act.

> Now that I have clear instructions, I hasten to act on them in concert with the Aus:rian Minister.

"What does he mean by *now*" (enquired Clarendon in a note on the back of this despatch). "The Inst[ns]. first sent to him are the only ones he has rec[d], and upon wh he condescends now to act. C." He had already expressed his displeasure in a peremptory reply[2] to Stratford's despatch of the 19th.

> We know Instructions were sent to Prokesch on the 15th and we are much surprized at not hearing...that you acted up to them conjointly with him. Do so at once without waiting for further instructions. It is absolutely indispensable that our advice should be taken by the Porte.

On the 22nd—five days at least since the arrival of Prokesch's instructions and eleven since his own arrived —Stratford addressed a Note[3] to the Porte identical with that of Prokesch. The Porte accordingly sent[4] an order to Jassy to annul the elections on August 24. Nor was this too soon. On August 22 Thouvenel was instructed[5] to leave in three days unless annulment was granted. The reprimand[6] which Stratford received from Clarendon— the second within a month—was well merited.

> I have to inform Your Excellency that the reasons alleged by you in your despatch No. 738 of the 19th of August, for not acting upon the instruction which was addressed to you on the 10th ult., are considered to be insufficient by H.M.'s

---

[1] F.O. 78. 1269.
[2] F.O. 78. 1269, Aug. 21/57, no. 742; see also the private letter from Clarendon, certainly stringent in tone, in Maxwell, *op. cit.* II, 147.
[3] F.O. 78. 1269, Stratford to Clarendon, Aug. 22/57, no. 746.
[4] F.O. 78. 1269, Stratford to Clarendon, Aug. 25/57, no. 750.
[5] F.O. 78. 1269, Stratford to Clarendon, Aug. 23/57, no. 748.
[6] F.O. 195. 546, Sept. 9/57.

Government, who regret the delay which took place in advising the Porte to annul the Moldavian Elections.

The fact that his Government had abandoned him at Osborne and that his duty was personally distasteful, is no extenuation of Stratford's official delinquency. His course should have been clear: he might have offered to resign, as Prokesch did,[1] or alternatively, he should have accepted his discomfiture with better grace and expedition.

During September new elections were held in the Principalities. More than ever the desires of the inhabitants turned towards union. Napoleon's name-day, August 25, was celebrated at Bukarest by a unionist procession which included government servants, "chanting Wallachian airs and crying *Vive l'Union*".[2]

The truth [wrote Bulwer] we must acknowledge to ourselves is, that almost every man in this Principality is, or says he is, for uniting the Principalities under a foreign Prince.[3]

Vogorides, with easy adaptability, now worked keenly for union[4] whilst Ghika in Wallachia supported the demand for union, out of necessity, if not from inclination.[3] The French agents—since France after Osborne had less interest in encouraging union—grew more conciliatory and moderate.[3] By an act of tardy justice, and as a result of Stratford's persistent efforts, the Porte had allowed[5] in July, 1857 the return to the Principalities of Wallachian leaders who had been exiled at Russia's command since

---

[1] V. S. A. *Dépêches à Constantinople*, XII, 61, Prokesch to Buol, private letter Aug. 26/57. Prokesch's action in delaying was equally contrary to instructions. On Aug. 22 Seymour telegraphed: "Instructions and of a stringent nature have been sent to the Internuncio to-day for the third time respecting communication to be made to the Porte" (F.O. 195. 546).

[2] F.O. 195. 546, Bulwer to Clarendon, Aug. 25/57.

[3] F.O. 195. 546, to Clarendon, Sept. 4/57.

[4] F.O. 195. 547, Bulwer to Clarendon, Sept. 14/57.

[5] F.O. 195. 543, Stratford to Clarendon, July 6/57.

1848—an action which Bulwer criticised as inexpedient at such a time.[1] Certainly Stratford was wrong[2] in declaring that "the Porte would enlist their gratitude on the side of the Turkish Government", for the exiles became the popular leaders in the new Divans. But the behaviour of those Assemblies in countries unused to representative institutions was generally prudent and moderate,[3] despite Stratford's exaggerated accounts of pro-unionist agitation and intrigue by the French Commissioner and the kaï-makams.[4] Bulwer drew a vivid picture of the elections: there was no minority party because everyone could see that union, supported by the Four Powers, would be the victorious cause;[5] the leading politicians supported union to win popular esteem;[6] none of the peasants elected to the Moldavian Divan could read or write.[7] Even so, Bulwer admitted[5] that "in point of activity, intelligence and even property" the unionist party was the more powerful, "and one which, under ordinary circumstances, it would be wise to conciliate". Irregularities marked the second elections no less than the first: "complete fairness or regularity", wrote Bulwer, "is out of the question".[8] Indeed, the attempt to determine the opinion of the Principalities by representative assemblies was idealistic rather than statesmanlike. As early as January, 1857, Kisseleff ridiculed "the idea of ever arriving at a true knowledge of the wishes of the inhabitants, by the

[1] F.O. 195. 548, quoted in Seymour to Clarendon, Nov. 10/57.
[2] F.O. 78. 1266, Stratford to Clarendon, July 14/57.
[3] F.O. 195. 548, Bulwer to Clarendon, Oct. 23/57, private and confidential, no. 274.
[4] F.O. 195. 546, to Clarendon, Sept. 4/57.
[5] F.O. 195. 548, Bulwer to Clarendon, Oct. 15/57.
[6] F.O. 195. 548, Bulwer to Clarendon, Oct. 7/57.
[7] F.O. 195. 548, Bulwer to Clarendon, Oct. 22/57. Even in 1912 60·7 per cent. of the population over seven years of age were illiterate: see *A Handbook of Roumania*, p. 77.
[8] F.O. 195. 547, Bulwer to Clarendon, Oct. 6/57.

Divans or by any other means", pointing out that, "with few exceptions, views will be given without the giver having the slightest notion on what grounds his opinion is formed".[1] The Divans proved to be almost unanimously unionist. They soon intimated to the Commission their wishes in the form of Four Points:[2] Union, a Foreign Prince not of any neighbouring royal line, a Representative Assembly, and a Collective Guarantee by the Powers.

Providing that Napoleon III honoured the secret part of the Osborne agreement, the continued separation of the Principalities was certain, despite the extreme unionist wishes of the Divans. Although Walewski refused Cowley's request to declare at Bukarest that the French Government would not support a foreign prince, Cowley believed that they would honourably observe the Osborne agreement if left to do so in their own way.[3] For a while, in August, Stratford's behaviour in delaying the annulment of the elections decided on at Osborne, had rendered the position of the British Government with regard to France, in Clarendon's words, "most painful and humiliating".[4] But once the elections were annulled Walewski set himself seriously to execute, in as satisfactory a way as possible, the scheme of administrative union. In an interview with the Czar and Gortchakoff at Stuttgart on September 25, 1857, which Cowley described as "perhaps the greatest external triumph which the Emperor had yet attained", Napoleon III learnt that Russia, although opposed to a foreign prince in the Principalities, was anxious to adopt any French project. Although no precise agreement was made at Stuttgart, Russian co-operation at the future conference was assured.[5] In another direction, too, Walewski pur-

[1] F.O. 195. 537, Cowley to Clarendon, Jan. 4/57, confidential.
[2] F.O. 195. 548, Bulwer to Clarendon, Oct. 23/57, no. 273.
[3] F.O. 195. 548, Cowley to Clarendon, Oct. 31/57.
[4] See Maxwell, *op. cit.* II, 147.
[5] See Appendix II (*a*).

sued a policy of compromise. He replied in moderate terms to the Porte's Circular[1] of September 23, which stated the willingness of the Porte to accept administrative union; further, as will be seen, he entered into negotiations with Count Koscielsky, a secret agent of Reshid Pasha, with a view to a Franco-Turkish understanding. Walewski's aim was, with British, Russian, Turkish and Sardinian support, to propose at the conference a scheme as unionist as possible which Austria, unwilling but isolated, would be compelled to accept.

A change in the Ottoman Council made possible a Franco-Turkish liaison. On October 10 Thouvenel gave a dinner to the French party in the Council, whilst the Sultan unexpectedly dined "with his discarded ministers",[2] of whom Reshid Pasha was the chief. On October 22 Stratford wrote,[3] "Reshid is reappointed Grand Vizier. ...The Sultan has thus asserted his independence, and vindicated his character", whilst he expressly disclaimed any responsibility for the change. Thouvenel had tried to prevent Reshid's return to power by sending M. Outrey, his Interpreter, to the Palace, whilst he went as far as to declare that he could have no confidence in a government of which Reshid was a member, for which he was privately reprimanded by Walewski.[4] Thouvenel was loth to believe the Sultan's assurance[5] that Reshid's appointment had no political significance. He hoped to receive instructions from Paris to protest. Actually, however, Walewski wrote[6] that he was quite willing not only to accept Reshid as Grand Vizier but to concert with him: "Do your best to allow the Grand Vizier to make conces-

---

[1] Sturdza, op. cit. v, 621.
[2] F.O. 78. 1272, Stratford to Clarendon, Oct. 14/57, confidential.
[3] F.O. 78. 1272, to Clarendon.
[4] Note 1, p. 111.   [5] L. Thouvenel, op. cit. p. 194.
[6] Sturdza, op. cit. v, 807, telegraphic despatch Nov. 11/57, referred to in Walewski to Thouvenel, Nov. 27/57.

sions and engagements with us ". At Paris, Count Koscielsky, a naturalised Frenchman better known at Constantinople as Sefer Pasha, in the course of conversations with
Walewski and the Emperor, intimated Reshid's willingness to support the French plan for the Principalities so
long as a foreign prince was not proposed.[1] Thouvenel
protested in despatches[2] to Walewski that these advances
made on behalf of Reshid were not sincere, but Walewski
persisted in his negotiations. He informed Thouvenel in
January, 1858 that he would endeavour to attain at the
conference "union pure et simple, sans prince étranger et
sans hérédité", and added that, if the Turkish plenipotentiary were instructed to support the French plan, he
would try to secure for the Sultan the choice of "prince(s) ",
but that if Turkey supported Austria, he would work for
the election of the princes by the inhabitants themselves.[3]

At Constantinople two events consoled the unhappy
Thouvenel, disapproving as he did not merely of the
Koscielsky negotiations but of the whole tendency of
French policy since the Treaty of Paris.[4] The first was
the departure of Lord Stratford de Redcliffe from
Constantinople on December 12, 1857, the second, the
sudden death of Reshid Pasha in January, 1858. It is not
true that Stratford was recalled by his Government at the
insistence of Napoleon III[5] or that he resigned on leaving
Constantinople.[6] He returned to England on leave, Alison
remaining at Constantinople as *chargé d'affaires*. On
November 3, Stratford had telegraphed to Clarendon
asking for permission to use the leave of absence which

---

[1] L. Thouvenel, *op. cit.* pp. 199–201, Walewski to Thouvenel.
[2] *Ibid.* pp. 203–205, *e.g.* on Dec. 1/57.
[3] *Ibid.* p. 219.
[4] *Ibid. passim.*
[5] E. Bourgeois, *op. cit.* III, 430.
[6] Maxwell, *op. cit.* II, 158.

had been granted to him eighteen months previously; in support of his request he urged the quiet state of public business, "strong private motives", and the condition of his health.[1] Thouvenel suggested in October that Stratford wished to reach London at the same time as Bulwer whose work in the Principalities was ending.[2] Certainly there had been continual differences between the two men, and Clarendon held that Stratford had treated Bulwer "very ill".[3] Moreover Stratford had recently incurred the displeasure of his Government, and Clarendon had broken off personal correspondence with him.[4] In health Stratford had been suffering from "rheumatic vexation", which had made him "half a cripple" in the winter of 1857,[5] but although seventy-one years of age he could scarcely have advanced failing health and declining energy as a motive for resigning his post. Whatever his reasons for desiring leave, he received a private audience of the Sultan and delivered a vigorous lecture, to which Abdul Medjid listened "with gracious though melancholy attention",[6] on the need for greater energy in reform; and on December 10 he bade farewell to the Sultan who wore for the occasion "the Queen's ribband and star of the Garter."[7] Count Buol believed[8] that Stratford's return marked a concession to France, whilst Walewski, who was well aware of the strained relations which existed between Stratford and the Foreign Office, predicted that Stratford's departure would lead to his resignation, which the British ministers

[1] F.O. 78. 1273.
[2] L. Thouvenel, *op. cit.* pp. 181–182.
[3] Maxwell, *op. cit.* II, 146.
[4] *Ibid.* II, 159.
[5] *The Stratford Papers*, F.O. 352. 48, Stratford to Bulwer, Nov. 25/57, private.
[6] F.O. 78. 1274, Stratford to Clarendon, Dec. 2/57, confidential.
[7] F.O. 78. 1275, Stratford to Clarendon, Dec. 12/57.
[8] Hübner, *op. cit.* II, 77.

desired.[1] But the ultimate decision rested with Stratford. According to *L'Étoile du Danube*[2], he made it clear at Constantinople that he would return in three months. Only on the unexpected fall of Palmerston's Government in February, 1858 did Stratford, "as a mark of his sympathy",[3] tender his resignation. This—to his regret a little later—was accepted.[3] News of his retirement, however, was received with satisfaction by the French Government, with joy by Thouvenel, and, if the latter is right, with relief by Abdul Medjid. Stratford abandoned diplomacy, and Sir Henry Bulwer, whom he heartily disliked, replaced him as Ambassador to the Porte.

The Franco-Turkish negotiations conducted through Koscielsky were secretly contrived. Buol suspected some intrigue since he enquired of the Internuncio at the end of November, 1857, whether the Grand Vizier had approved a Franco-Russian plan for the Principalities. Reshid Pasha denied any knowledge of the matter, whilst Clarendon noted: "H. M. G. have no knowledge of any such plan."[4] Walewski's hopes of Turkish support were, however, belied. Thouvenel's scepticism was justified. Fuad Pasha, who was appointed plenipotentiary to the Conference of Paris, promised Thouvenel confidentially that he would support the French project for the Principalities.[5] Fuad was badly received by Napoleon III, partly because of Franco-Turkish disagreements over Montenegro[6], and Benedetti, who was made secretary to the Conference, felt certain that he was bound by engagements made *en*

---

[1] L. Thouvenel, *op. cit.* Walewski to Thouvenel, Dec. 4/57, p. 209.
[2] Sturdza, *op. cit.* VII, 15.
[3] S. Lane-Poole, *op. cit.* II, 446–447.
[4] F.O. 78. 1274, Stratford to Clarendon, Nov. 27/57.
[5] L. Thouvenel, *op. cit.* Benedetti to Thouvenel, May 26/58.
[6] *Ibid.* p. 263.

route at Vienna.[1] Indeed, Fuad had been warmly welcomed at Vienna where he became "the lion of the day"[2].
He received an interview with Count Buol and Baron
Hübner on May 6, dined at Court on the 7th, and was
granted an audience of the Emperor Francis Joseph, who
declared that the Porte should take the initiative at Paris
and that the Austrian plenipotentiary would be instructed
to give his support.[3]

In May, 1858, plenipotentiaries of the seven Powers
signatory to the Treaty of Paris met there to receive the
report of the Commission and to specify in a convention
the definitive organisation of the Principalities. The international differences over the union of Moldavia and Wallachia, which had already been exposed at Constantinople
and within the Commission itself, were no less conspicuous
at Paris. Although morally bound by the Osborne agreement, Napoleon III joined with the Russian plenipotentiary in recording in Protocol I of the Conference the
desirability of union under a foreign prince.[4] It is clear,
however, that since he could not force this plan on Europe,
the Emperor hoped to transform the administrative union
to which he was pledged into something closely approaching
political union.[5] His meeting with the Czar at Stuttgart,
where the future of the Principalities was discussed, did
not result in any precise Franco-Russian scheme,[6] despite
the alarm of the Porte, until reassured by Austria, lest
some scheme was being devised against the Turkish
Empire.[7] Russia, though baulked of any triumph over the

---

[1] L. Thouvenel, *op. cit.* p. 269, Benedetti to Thouvenel, June?/58.
[2] *The Times*, May 12/58.
[3] F.O. 195. 569, Loftus to Malmesbury, May 11/58, confidential.
[4] Hertslet, *British and Foreign State Papers*, vol. XLVIII.
[5] L. Thouvenel, *op. cit.* p. 215. Walewski described administrative
union as "a prelude to a complete and absolute union realisable later".
[6] See Appendix II.
[7] F.O. 195. 541, Seymour to Clarendon, May 12/57, confidential.

rupture at Constantinople, was not dissatisfied with the situation which had arisen out of the question of the Principalities. Since Austria and Turkey had become unpopular in those countries owing to their efforts to manage the Moldavian elections of July, 1857, and since France would lose her popularity if she failed to carry her unionist policy, everything went to support Russia's thesis that her own exclusive patronage was superior to the Collective Guarantee of Europe.[1] Her attitude at Paris, no less than that of Sardinia, was pro-French. Prussia, hesitant and timid, adopted no decided line.[2] Austria, led still by Count Buol, was the uncompromising opponent to union in any form. As early as May, 1857, he had asserted that should union be proposed at Paris and should it receive the assent of every other Power, Austria would withhold her signature to the scheme;[3] and Hübner's instructions[4] ordered him to oppose the introduction of any innovations in the Principalities, such as a common senate at Focşani, which might form the germ of fusion at a later date. Fuad Pasha was conciliatory: as long as the Sultan's suzerainty and the political separation of the Principalities were preserved, he was willing to yield on details.[5] Finally, Cowley, representing Great Britain, sought to uphold the Osborne agreement, and, by mediating between France and Austria, to terminate a question which he felt was becoming "vexatious."

Buol desired that the Conference should proceed to revise the laws of the Principalities in accordance with the Protocol of Constantinople of February, 1856, but Cowley maintained more correctly that the 23rd Article of the

[1] F.O. 195. 548, Wodehouse to Clarendon, Oct. 23/57, no. 470.
[2] Cp. Vitzthum von Eckstaedt, *op. cit.* I, 279.
[3] F.O. 195. 541, Seymour to Clarendon, May 12/57, confidential.
[4] V. S. A. *Dépêches à Paris* (1858), Buol to Hübner, May 12/58, no. 1.
[5] Protocols of the Conference of Paris, 1858, *British and Foreign State Papers*, vol. XLVIII, Protocol 3.

Treaty of Paris should form the point of departure. This article stated that, having received the proposals of the Commission,[1] the Powers should revise the laws and statutes already existing in the Principalities. Walewski, however, produced a project,[2] drawn up in conjunction with the Russian Plenipotentiary, Count Kisseleff, as an *unofficial* plan for general discussion. The project contained an outline of an administrative union of a very comprehensive kind: the Principalities were to retain their separate princes under the suzerainty of the Sultan, but a central commission or "organic body" with large powers, a common title, and a common army and flag, were to be established in addition to common customs, posts, money, telegraph and a supreme court. Although this was not officially proposed by the French Government and indeed lacked any recognised paternity, Walewski declared on May 30 that it contained the *ne plus ultra* of French concession.[3] Fuad was willing to accept the scheme with modifications as a useful beginning.[4] Hübner was instructed[5] on June 1 to oppose the central commission, the title and the flag; whilst Buol condemned Walewski's scheme in vigorous terms as a republican union which "had not even the recommendation of being a monarchical union".[6] Indeed, the language held at Vienna was uncompromising in the extreme, and Bourqueney, the French Ambassador, stated confidentially that he "would not

[1] The Commission's Report, addressed to the Conference on Apr. 7/58, is printed in Sturdza, *op. cit.* VI, 2, pp. 559–672. On the major question of union with or without a foreign prince, the Commission confined itself to recording the views expressed by the Divans.

[2] F.O. 195. 569, enclosed in Cowley to Malmesbury, May 23/58, no. 521, confidential.

[3] F.O. 195. 569, Cowley to Malmesbury, May 30/58, no. 565, secret and confidential.

[4] Note 5, p. 152.

[5] V. S. A. *Dépêches à Paris* (1858), Buol to Hübner, no. 12.

[6] Loftus, *op. cit.* I, 358.

guarantee the maintenance of the peace of Europe for three months ", if Austria refused to discuss Walewski's scheme;[1] whilst on June 5, *The Times* reported from Vienna a violent panic during which private stock was being sold with feverish haste at ruinously low prices. At Paris Cowley was faced by a difficult problem: should he join Austria in resisting any concession to union and show himself less well disposed towards the Principalities than the Turkish Plenipotentiary who was willing to admit the title and perhaps the central commission?[2]

> I am constrained to ask Your Lordship [he wrote to Lord Malmesbury, Clarendon's successor at the Foreign Office] whether it would be prudent to take our stand by the side of Austria and refuse every—even the smallest—concession towards a legislative union of the Principalities. That the Suzerain Power is not prepared to go so far, I have from Fuad Pasha's own lips....Can we show ourselves less favourably disposed towards the Principalities than Turkey?[2]

The possible withdrawal of Austria from the Conference was alarming, and Cowley urged Hübner to join Fuad and himself in a more conciliatory spirit and not to allow France and Russia to break up the Conference.[3] Meanwhile, on June 2, after consultation with the Emperor Francis Joseph, Buol declared that if Fuad accepted the discussion of Walewski's project, Hübner should be instructed to join in the discussion but to withhold his vote in favour of any of its objectionable clauses[4]. Further, Buol in-

---

[1] F.O. 195. 570, Loftus to Malmesbury, June 1/58, no. 119, confidential; cp. Vitzthum, *op. cit.* I, 277.

[2] F.O. 146. 794, to Malmesbury, June 4/58, no. 593, secret and confidential.

[3] F.O. 195. 570, Cowley to Malmesbury, June 3/58, secret and confidential.

[4] F.O. 195. 570, Loftus to Malmesbury, June 2/58, no. 121, confidential.

sisted, with some justification, that the procedure of the Conference should follow the line indicated by Article 23 of the Treaty of Paris. Indeed, it was unfortunate, as Cowley held, that Austria should have objected so suddenly and vehemently to a plan which the French Government had not officially proposed.

At the third session of the Conference (June 5) deadlock occurred when Russia and Sardinia joined Walewski in proposing the discussion of his project, whilst Turkey, Austria and Prussia maintained with Cowley that the Conference should proceed according to the Treaty of Paris to revise the existing laws of Moldavia and Wallachia. Cowley secured the adjournment of the Conference and Walewski became more conciliatory, since he explained to Hübner that his central commission would be merely the guardian of organic law "without governmental, administrative or even legislative powers".[1] Cowley, meanwhile, was instructed to support the Turkish Plenipotentiary, should he accept any modified system of union.[2] On June 8 he wrote:[3]

I learn from good authority that the Emperor has resolved on breaking up the Conferences, if Count Walewski's project is not discussed at the next sitting without reference to the existing laws.... Her Majesty's Government, however much in the right would, I presume, not wish to push matters to extremities on a question of form, and I propose therefore stating to the Conference on Thursday that although Her Majesty's Government consider revision of the laws the most practical mode of proceeding, they will not positively insist on that course, if the majority of the conference prefer an immediate discussion of Count Walewski's project.

[1] F.O. 195. 570, Cowley to Malmesbury, June 5/58, no. 600, secret and confidential.
[2] F.O. 195. 570, Malmesbury to Clarendon, June 7/58, no. 481.
[3] F.O. 195. 570, telegram from Cowley to Malmesbury, June 8/58.

Accordingly, on June 10 Cowley joined with the majority of the Conference in the discussion of Walewski's scheme.

The conflict between France and Austria now centred around the three unionist propositions in Walewski's programme: the title ' United-Principalities ', the central commission, and the common flag. Napoleon tried to persuade Cowley in an interview at Fontainebleau that his programme contained "the mere shadow of union", and that, although he might make concessions on the central commission, he would withdraw his Plenipotentiary from the Conference if the common flag was not allowed.[1] Cowley replied that the British Government's interpretation of the Osborne agreement differed from that of the French Government, that a common flag had not been considered at Osborne, and that the question of the flag was vital to the Emperor of Austria, since his Rumanian-speaking subjects might be tempted to withdraw from his allegiance.[1] Cowley's interview with Napoleon III was unavailing: he made no impression on the Emperor who had, he feared, "a foregone intention to break with Austria"—an intention, however, which Napoleon denied.[1] Cowley drew up a memorandum outlining a central committee which was merely a guardian of organic laws, and his contribution was received with satisfaction by Fuad and with relief by Hübner.[2] But the common flag was the decisive issue. Cowley thought that Austria's objections were "legitimate", and Fuad intimated that he would rather leave Paris than consent to a common flag.[2] On June 21 Hübner was instructed to assent to the amended title *Principautés-Unies de Moldavie et Valachie* and to

[1] F.O. 146. 795, Cowley to Malmesbury, June 15/58, no. 669, secret and confidential.
[2] F.O. 195. 570, Cowley to Malmesbury, June 16/58, no. 675, secret and confidential.

Cowley's central commission, provided that the common flag was not proposed at the Conference:

The flag is inadmissible, even if the Porte yields. If France makes it a *conditio sine qua non* throw the responsibility of the rupture as much as possible on her. If she yields on this point, grant the title and the central divan with as limited powers as possible.[1]

Fuad had already signified his willingness to accept the first two points. The difficulty was that the question of the flag had become one of *amour-propre* with Napoleon III. The central commission which had been abandoned was "of Imperial and not of Walewskian origin".[2] Would he, by breaking up the Conference and at the risk of a European war, seek again (as in August, 1857) to vindicate his honour?

Complaints were made at the Porte about the conduct of Fuad Pasha, by both the Internuncio and the French Ambassador, who within the same hour demanded his recall for precisely opposite reasons: the one, because Fuad had consented to the central commission, the other, because he was too much opposed to French views.[3] On June 21, Lord Malmesbury described[4] to Cowley an interview at which the Duc de Malakoff, the French Ambassador, declared the intention of France to end the Conferences rather than give way on either the title, the commission or the flag.

The Count declared that he did not take the same view as we did on the spirit of "the Agreement of Osborne", for that no pledge had therein been given of a political separation of the Provinces. He added that if we continued to oppose his project France would return to her original view of having a Foreign Prince.[4]

[1] V. S. A. *Dépêches à Paris* (1858), XII, 64, telegram from Buol.
[2] Malmesbury, *Memoirs of an Ex-Minister*, New edition, p. 439.
[3] F.O. 195. 570, Paget to Malmesbury, June 23/58, no. 15.
[4] F.O. 195. 570, no. 548.

Buol regarded this threat as "a moral impossibility".[1]
Malmesbury replied to Malakoff that it was unfair for the
French Government to declare "Those who are not for
us are against us", and that "a difference of opinion as to
the nature of a Roumanian Principality inferred an unfriendly feeling on the part of Great Britain against
France." He concluded:

I stated to the Duc de Malakoff what were Lords Palmerston's and Clarendon's[2] positive recollections of what took
place at Osborne, that they had put them down in writing,
and that any reserve then made for an administrative union
inferred of itself a political separation. I impressed upon him
the circumstances which caused the Osborne Agreement,
after which we immediately fulfilled our part by annulling the
late elections. We had done this and now asked France to
keep her pledge.[3]

Cowley learnt that a Council of War was to be held at St
Cloud on the morning of the 24th. He, therefore, in
accordance with his instructions,[3] handed to Walewski
on the evening of the 23rd a copy of the above men-
tioned despatch from Malmesbury. Walewski observed
that "it contained matter on which he could engage
a polemical discussion if necessary".[4] He adopted, however, an attitude of reserve, and Cowley, learning that
the Emperor was displeased with Walewski because of
the modifications of his project, feared that a determination had been taken to break up the Conference, if
the common flag was not conceded.[4] Cowley's position

---

[1] V. S. A. *Dépêches à Paris* (1858), XII, 64, telegram Buol to
Hübner, June 27/58.

[2] On June 13/58 Clarendon wrote to Malmesbury: "If Walewski
tries to wriggle out of the agreement come to at Osborne last year,
pray do not hesitate to call me as a witness." Note 2, p. 157.

[3] Note 4, p. 157.

[4] F.O. 195. 570, Cowley to Malmesbury, June 25/58, no. 742,
secret and confidential.

was extremely embarrassing: in the event of a crisis becoming inevitable, should Great Britain, he asked, support either France or Austria?[1] Although he believed with some justification that the Emperor was exceeding the terms of the Osborne agreement in demanding a common flag, he advised that in the event of a crisis Great Britain should acquiesce in the French plan. The attitude of Fuad would depend on his action; the abstention of Austria from the Conference would not, he argued, wreck the Conference; but the withdrawal of France, followed by a declaration in favour of union under a foreign prince, would shatter the Conference and cause "all sorts of complications in the East".[1]

Already attempts had been made to find a compromise which both France and Austria might accept. Count Hatzfeldt's scheme[2] that, when acting in common, the two armies should carry their separate flags side by side, though recommended to Napoleon by Walewski, was opposed by Austria; Malmesbury's suggestion that the common flag should contain the Ottoman Crescent met with the approval of the Porte but not of either Austria or France.[3] It was Cowley whose imagination, tact and prudence produced a solution. His idea that the separate flags of each Principality should carry a permanent pennant received Napoleon's assent, and he terminated the dangerous controversy by suggesting to Buol that in accepting the pennant the Emperor Francis Joseph should state that the abandonment of the common flag by Napoleon III was personally agreeable to him.[4] In this way the difficult question of *amour-propre* was over-

[1] Note 4, p. 158.
[2] F.O. 195. 570, Cowley to Malmesbury, June 28/58, no. 760, secret and confidential.
[3] F.O. 195. 570, Cowley to Malmesbury, June 22/58, no. 722, secret and confidential.
[4] Loftus, *op. cit.* I, 363.

come and a dispute settled which might easily have resulted in war. Cowley was complimented by his chief on
the convention which marked the end of the discussions:

I send you back the *projet de convention* for the Principalities [wrote Malmesbury[1] on July 30], and wish you joy
of having ended this work;

and on September 7 he wrote,[1] "All the good in it (*sc.*
the Convention) is yours." Buol was "radiant with satisfaction"[2] at this successful conclusion of the struggle,
whilst Hübner declared, with dramatic irony, that union
would never develop out of the Convention of Paris.[3]

The polemics of the Conference chamber ended in
a controversy of pamphlets. On August 4, Buol instructed[4] Hübner to secure a printed refutation of a
brochure called *L'Autriche et les Principautés Danubiennes*[5]
which had just appeared at Paris. In June another brochure
entitled *L'empereur Napoléon III et les Principautés
Roumaines*,[6] attributed by Hübner[7] to an official pen, had
declared that war with Austria was imminent and had
caused a moment's panic on the *Bourse*.[7] Hübner executed
his instructions, for on November 5, Buol received[8] forty
copies of a brochure printed at Paris at the cost of 240
francs, 95 centimes.

The work of the Conference of Paris was embodied in a
Convention signed by the seven Powers on August 19,
1858.[9] All the existing privileges of the Principalities were

[1] Malmesbury, *op. cit.* p. 442.
[2] Loftus, *op. cit.* I, 365.
[3] V. S. A. *Rapports de Paris* (1858), IX, 57, to Buol, Aug. 26/58, no. 85.
[4] V. S. A. *Dépêches à Paris* (1858), XII, 64, no. 6.
[5] Published in Sturdza, *op. cit.* VII, 363.
[6] *Ibid.* VII, 232.
[7] Hübner, *op. cit.* II, 192.
[8] V. S. A. *Dépêches à Paris* (1858), XII, 64, Buol to Hübner, Nov.
5/58, no. 4.
[9] Hertslet, *op. cit.* II, 1329.

placed under a Collective Guarantee, whilst Turkish suzerainty was reaffirmed. That suzerainty was defined to
mean the right of the Sultan to invest (though not to
reject) the life hospodars chosen by the Assembly of each
Principality; to receive an increased annual tribute (but
no extraordinary tribute payable on the appointment of
hospodars); to apply to the Principalities all the Porte's
treaties which did not infringe their local immunities, and,
finally, to concert with the hospodars measures of defence.
Moldavia and Wallachia secured autonomy, representation
at the Porte by *capou kiayas* (*chargés d'affaires*) through
whom appeals against the violation of their privileges
might be made to the Porte and the other guaranteeing
Powers. The existing militias of the Principalities were to
receive an identical organisation so as to form for defensive
purposes two corps of one army, and a permanent "blue
pennon" was to be attached to their existing standards.
A supreme court was to be established at Focşani, on
the frontier between Moldavia and Wallachia, where also
a central commission should meet. This body, composed
of sixteen members chosen by the hospodars and assemblies of both Principalities, was to watch the execution of
the stipulations of the Convention, codify common laws
and *prepare* legislation common to both Principalities for
the consideration of the separate governments. In these
particulars only had unionist innovations been made.

The union question was apparently solved after two
years of international controversy. The Convention arranged (in Article 49) in accordance with the *Règlement
Organique* for the appointment in each Principality of a
kaïmakamie or interim commission composed of three
ministers who held office under the hospodars of 1856:
the President of the Divan, the Grand Logothète and the
Minister of the Interior. It remained for the kaïmakamie
to draw up the electoral lists and to hold the elections

for the assemblies at which life hospodars would be elected.

The provisions of the Convention were not applied without difficulties and disputes. Count Buol objected to the use by each Principality of the title " United-Principalities " to describe its own separate acts and refused to grant visas to passports bearing that superscription;[1] the British law officers of the Crown declared that each Principality was at liberty to use the heading "United-Principalities" above that of its own name,[1] a view which the French Government endorsed.[2] Bulwer, as Ambassador at Constantinople, wrote that all the consuls in the Principalities, with the exception of the French who were working for a democratic election,[3] agreed that illegalities were being committed by the kaïmakams in both Principalities;[4] the irregularities in Moldavia increased since the kaïmakamie had split into two groups, the larger of which wanted union and usurped the authority of the third kaïmakam;[5] unless some action was taken, advised Bulwer, the Porte's authority in the Principalities would be lost and Turkey and Austria would refuse to recognise the assemblies.[3] Walewski at Paris urged that the Powers should "wink at" the alleged illegalities, on the ground that once new hospodars were appointed a legal state of things would be restored,[2] whilst Malmesbury, anxious to prevent the Porte from annulling the elections, proposed with Walewski's half-hearted concurrence the reopening of the Conference of Paris.[6] By the 31st of December the Moldavian elections were finished and the Metropolitan declared the proceedings to have been so illegally conducted

[1] F.O. 195. 575, Loftus to Malmesbury, Nov. 17/58.
[2] F.O. 195. 575, Cowley to Malmesbury, Dec. 7/58.
[3] F.O. 195. 575, Bulwer to Malmesbury (telegram), Dec. 20/58, secret and confidential.
[4] F.O. 195. 575, Bulwer to Malmesbury (telegram), Dec. 15/58.
[5] F.O. 195. 575, Bulwer to Malmesbury (telegram), Dec. 3/58.
[6] F.O. 195. 575, Malmesbury to Bulwer, Dec. 28/58.

that he would not preside over the assembly.[1] In a tele-graphic despatch marked "most secret and confidential"[2], Bulwer urged Malmesbury not to be misled by the French suggestion of letting the Moldavian elections stand; he predicted that union would follow and possibly separation from the Porte: "the example of Servia with Milosh at its head",[3] he wrote, "generates suicide. Bulgaria will follow Servia". Malmesbury advised that the Porte should accept the elections as valid, that once the hospodars were elected the likelihood of union would end, and that the Conference should meet again to deal with the situation.[4] Count Buol wished to prevent a reopening of the Con-ference. Intent, owing to the condition of Italian affairs, on preserving good relations with France, he desired to avoid open discussions with her; moreover he declared that the Porte had the right to refuse to invest hospodars if the Con-vention of Paris was in any way violated by the elections.[5]

The threatening difficulties over the affairs of the Prin-cipalities were cast into the shadow by more serious inter-national complications, for on January 12, 1859, Malmes-bury wrote: "a war is imminent between Austria and France".[6] The Porte meanwhile decided not to annul the elections, but reserved her right to withhold investiture.[7] The "ultra-democratic" or national party dominated in the Moldavian assembly, and on January 17, Colonel Alexander John Cuza was unanimously and unexpectedly elected hospodar. Bulwer wrote that Cuza "was chiefly

[1] F.O. 195. 614, Bulwer to Malmesbury (telegram), Jan. 8/59.
[2] F.O. 195. 614, Jan. 8/59.
[3] In Serbia on Jan. 3, 1859, the Prince, Alexander Karageorgevitch, had been forced to abdicate and Milosh Obrenovitch was welcomed back as Prince after an absence of twenty years: see H. W. V. Tem-perley, *History of Serbia*, pp. 238–239.
[4] F.O. 195. 614, Malmesbury to Bulwer, Jan. 13/59.
[5] F.O. 195. 614, Loftus to Malmesbury, Dec. 28 and Dec. 29/58, both confidential.   [6] F.O. 195. 614, to Bloomfield.
[7] F.O. 195. 615, Bulwer to Malmesbury (telegram), Jan. 14/59.

known as a card player and as having headed the insur-
rection in 1848 ";[1] and Baron Eder, the Austrian consul at
Bukarest, hardly an impartial critic, believed that he
"preferred Jamaica rum to public affairs".[2] These views
do less than justice to the man who became the first
prince of the United-Principalities. He had been raised to
the rank of colonel by Vogorides, but resigned his office
as Prefect of Galatz in protest against the corrupt mal-
practices of the kaïmakam; he was a unionist member of
the Divan *ad hoc*; and later, in 1864, he issued an agrarian
law which, with all its defects, did at least emancipate the
Rumanian peasant.[3] The Porte was disposed to regard
the election of Cuza as illegal, while Austria raised
technical questions: had Cuza, asked Buol, the private
fortune required by the terms of the Convention?[4] An
entirely new situation was created, however, when on
February 5 Cuza was unanimously elected hospodar of
Wallachia.

The idea of a double election has been attributed to
French and Russian agents in the Principalities,[5] but it is
difficult to accept this view in the light of the precise report
of Eder.[6]

I can say positively that the day before the election no one
knew that the elections would be held that day and also that
Cuza would be elected. No organ of a foreign Power was
engaged in producing this result. It was spoken about but
not believed in.

Cuza accepted the joint hospodariate, although he read an
address at Jassy praying to be allowed to abdicate in
favour of a foreign prince. The Porte protested against

[1] F.O. 195. 615, to Malmesbury, Jan. 18/59 (telegram).
[2] V. S. A. *Rapports de Bukarest* (1859), to Buol, Apr. 16/59, no. 34 B.
[3] For a review and criticism of this law see Ifor L. Evans, *op. cit.*
ch. II.   [4] F.O. 195. 615, Cowley to Malmesbury, Jan. 19/59.
[5] Debidour, *op. cit.* II, 182.
[6] V. S. A. *Rapports de Bukarest* (1859), to Buol, Feb. 15/59, no. 15.

the double election, and now favoured the reunion of the
Conference, which it had previously opposed,[1] whilst
Austria broke off consular relations with the Principalities.[2]
Asked again their opinion on a matter relating to the
Convention of Paris, the British law officers were of
opinion "that it is not according to the terms of the
Convention to elect the same person in both Provinces",
and they added that since Cuza had accepted the hospo-
dariate of Moldavia he should refuse that of Wallachia.[3]
The Porte's proposal for a conference was accepted by
the Powers. The French Government made no secret of
its views and strove keenly and with success to win over
the British Government to its policy. In an interview with
Cowley,[4] Walewski declared that they were faced with
faits accomplis; if a fresh election were ordered by the
Conference, either Cuza would be re-elected or the
Wallachian assembly would refuse to obey the instruction
of the Conference, and how, he asked, was the Conference
to enforce its authority? The Emperor, he continued,
would never concur in the forcible execution of the
decision of the Conference against the will of Wallachia.
"Could not the Convention be modified?", he asked,
to which Cowley answered that conventions "were not
lightly to be set aside" and that "the game in the
Principalities was the game of independence". The
Prussian Government favoured the double election.[5] At
St Petersburg Gortchakoff thought that the Convention
could not be strained to admit the double nomination; the
Convention was *un œuvre informe*, and he accepted the
reopening of the Conference.[6] Further, he warned the

[1] F.O. 195. 615, Bulwer to Malmesbury (telegram), Feb. 8/59.
[2] V. S. A. *Rapports de Bukarest*, Eder to Buol, Feb. 12/59, no. 19.
[3] F.O. 195. 615, Malmesbury to Bulwer (telegram), Feb. 9/59, no. 108.
[4] F.O. 195. 615, Cowley to Malmesbury, Feb. 11/59, confidential.
[5] F.O. 195. 615, Bloomfield to Malmesbury, Feb. 19/59, confidential.
[6] F.O. 195. 616, Crampton to Malmesbury, Jan. 26/59.

Powers that, in the event of either Austria or the Porte intervening by force of arms in the Principalities without the previous consent of the other guaranteeing Powers, Russia would not content herself with "a mere verbal protest".[1]

The attitude of the British Government averted the revival in a serious form of the old cleavage between the Powers. On February 21 Malmesbury instructed Bulwer to persuade the Porte to recommend to the Powers the acceptance of Cuza as sole hospodar as an exceptional case, providing that positive assurances were given that no foreign prince would be allowed, that the two assemblies should continue, and finally, that the Sultan's suzerain rights should remain untouched.[2] This, he declared, was the inevitable solution, and the Porte should initiate the proposal to preserve its own dignity. In a later despatch[3] he added that England "will not stand a Hospodar being forced down the throats of the Roumans, but on the other hand we cannot force the Porte to submit to a breach of a Treaty we have so lately made". The Porte, abandoned by Great Britain and by Austria, whose Italian difficulties were proving acute, made some show of further resistance. For the third time in three consecutive years the question of the Principalities produced an international crisis out of which war might have developed. Cuza, with an eye to the possible seizure of Bukovina while Austria was occupied elsewhere, concluded two "conventions"[4] with the Hungarian revolutionary, General Klapka, in May, 1859; whilst at his request Napoleon III sent 10,000 rifles to the Principalities.[5] The question was whether Russia would

---

[1] F.O. 195. 616, Crampton to Malmesbury, Feb. 16/59.
[2] F.O. 195. 615, telegram.
[3] F.O. 195. 616, to Bulwer, Mar. 6/59 (telegram), private.
[4] For a copy of these "conventions" see Damé, *op. cit.* pp. 422–424.
[5] See note 4 above and D'Hauterive, *The Second Empire and its Downfall*, letter from Napoleon III to his cousin, Prince Napoleon, Mar. 18/59.

seize a favourable moment to intervene to revise the Treaty of Paris. Gortchakoff had avowed indirectly to Sir John Crampton, the British representative at St Petersburg, that the treaty needed revision.[1] He gave France a secret assurance, the nature of which was not generally known, that he would not support Austria in Italy as he had done in 1848 by withdrawing his Minister from Turin.[2] On April 30 Malmesbury wrote in some alarm to Bulwer:[3]

You are quite aware whence and how the peril will come upon the Porte if it is so mad as to refuse [*sc.* to accept Cuza]. Austria cannot help them....Urge them to give way. The Austrians entered Piedmont yesterday.

Fortunately the Russian Government, whose influence at Constantinople was visibly increasing without the need for military display, was not bent upon war. According to Walewski, Russia had declared that she was "not ready" and that complications in Eastern affairs would at that time be very disagreeable to her.[4] France, further, wished to localise the war in Italy and instructed her agents in the Near East to avoid provoking demonstrations.[5] It was in vain that the Porte complained that the conduct of the guaranteeing Powers towards itself was worse than that of Russia alone in former times,[6] for without strong foreign support it had no alternative to submission. On May 31, 1859 it accepted Cuza's double election, issued *two* firmans of investiture, and summoned Cuza to Constantinople, to which he came, for the ceremony of investiture. At the Conference of Paris, which had met in April, the seven

---

[1] F.O. 195.616, Crampton to Malmesbury, Mar. 16/59, confidential.
[2] F.O. 195. 618, Lord John Russell to Crampton, June 24/59, reporting a conversation with Brunnow, Russian Minister at London.
[3] F.O. 195. 617.
[4] F.O. 195. 617, Cowley to Malmesbury, May 12/59.
[5] F.O. 195. 617, Bulwer to Malmesbury, May 13/59.
[6] F.O. 195. 617, Bulwer to Malmesbury, May 1/59.

Powers stated that the Convention of Paris had been violated, but recognised the double election of Cuza as an exceptional case.[1]

The political union of Moldavia and Wallachia, which Napoleon's direct diplomacy had failed to accomplish, was thus realised, thanks to the astuteness of the Principalities themselves, and to the preoccupation of Austria, the principal opponent of Rumanian aspirations. The pretensions of the Principalities were by no means yet satisfied. Cuza sought to accredit an official agent in Great Britain with a view to encouraging commerce, but the British Government refused to infringe in this way the Porte's right of controlling foreign affairs.[2] The central commission at Focşani proposed the union and independence of the Principalities and the disregard of the Convention.[3] No further concessions were immediately forthcoming from the Powers. In December, 1861, however, the Sultan granted a firman[4] which allowed the temporary suspension of the central commission and the union of the two separate assemblies into one Chamber at Bukarest. The cause of Rumanian independence was all but won: in 1866 the United-Principalities received a foreign prince, whilst in 1878, with the abandonment of the Sultan's suzerainty, the independence of the Principality of Rumania was fully achieved.[5]

[1] Protocols of the Conference are printed in Hertslet, *The Map of Europe by Treaty*, II, 1376.

[2] F.O. 195. 619, Churchill to Russell, Sept. 29/59, confidential, and Russell to Churchill, Oct. 18/59.

[3] F.O. 195. 619, Bulwer to Russell, Sept. 2 and Nov. 27/59.

[4] Hertslet, *op. cit.* II, 1498.

[5] It is not believed that the independence was limited by the conditional form of recognition granted to Rumania with a view to safeguarding the rights of religious minorities. According to the predominant opinion of international lawyers, the possible non-fulfilment of these obligations would not give the Powers the right to withdraw the recognition once accorded. See Oppenheim, *International Law*, 4th edition (1928), vol. I, p. 147.

APPENDIX ONE

THE BEGINNING OF
BRITISH CONSULAR
RELATIONS WITH
THE PRINCIPALITIES:
FRANCIS SUMMERERS
AND WILLIAM WIL-
KINSON

APPENDIX ONE

THE BEGINNING OF BRITISH CONSULAR RELATIONS WITH THE PRINCIPALITIES: FRANCIS SUMMERERS AND WILLIAM WILKINSON

THE origin and early history of British consular relations with Moldavia and Wallachia have hitherto remained somewhat obscure. Great Britain was the last of the Great Powers to begin official relations. In 1781 Russia succeeded in appointing a consul-general at Bukarest, not without the keen resistance of the Porte, which realised that Russia's ostensibly commercial agents would interfere in political matters; in the following year Austria appointed a "secrétaire aulique pour les affaires du commerce"; the Empire was represented by an agent in 1784, and Prussia by a consul three years later; finally, the French Government sent a *consul résident* in 1798.[1] All these agents received *Bérats* (*exequaturs*) from the Sultan. The only published authority for the beginning of British consular relations is *An account of the principalities of Wallachia and Moldavia: with political observations relating to them*, first published in 1820, by William Wilkinson, who described himself as formerly British consul-general at Bukarest. On page 183 he wrote:

A British consul-general was for the first time appointed in 1802 to reside at Bukorest, chiefly for the purpose of facilitating the overland communications between England and Turkey. After the peace of Tilsit he was recalled, and the consulate was renewed in 1813, with the additional motive of promoting commercial intercourse with the principalities.

Further, in an appendix to his work, Wilkinson published a copy of the *Bérat*, dated May 24, 1814, which he himself received from the Porte on his appointment as consul-general, in succession, so the document states, to Francis Summerers, who had resigned the office bestowed on him by a *Bérat* of

[1] G. Bengesco, *op. cit.* p. xii. Only the first part of Prof. Iorga's study of Anglo-Rumanian relations has so far appeared, namely, *Les premières relations entre l'Angleterre et les pays Roumains du Danube* (1427 à 1611), printed in C. Bémont, *Mélanges d'Histoire*.

January 6, 1802. The examination of the Diplomatic Correspondence from Constantinople and Vienna to the Foreign Office from 1799 until 1815 and of the correspondence of Francis Summerers which has been preserved at the Public Record Office, makes it possible to describe more fully than Wilkinson has done the somewhat anomalous beginnings of British consular relations with the Principalities.

Francis Summerers was a Greek, "born a gentleman", but engaged in mercantile pursuits when Lord Elgin, who arrived at Constantinople in 1799 as Ambassador Extraordinary and Plenipotentiary to the Porte, took him into the service of his Embassy as a dragoman.[1] According to Summerers' own accounts, Elgin sent him to Bukarest in February, 1800, as a "Gentleman of his Embassy", with a view to facilitating the passage of couriers to and from Constantinople *via* Bukarest and to serving the interests of the Government, and of the Levant and East India Companies.[2] Summerers explained that he had not been invested with consular powers because of the war and further because it was desirable not to give Russia any cause for jealousy or complaint.[3] He states that in 1801 Lord Elgin nominated him his *Agent diplomatique*, and promised to apply to the Foreign Office on his behalf for a consular appointment.[2] Subsequently Elgin applied to the Porte for the recognition of Summerers as consul-general in the Principalities; the Porte willingly complied, issuing the usual *Bérat* in his favour, and Summerers, formally recognised by the hospodar of Wallachia as British consul, placed the British arms over his door.[3] In September, 1805, Summerers drew up a memorial, a précis of which (for he was inclined to verbosity) was sent to the Foreign Secretary by Charles Arbuthnot, Elgin's successor at the Porte. In this document,

---

[1] F.O. 78. 71, Summerers to Wellesley, May 28/10.
[2] F.O. 78. 46, précis of Memorial from Summerers enclosed in Arbuthnot to Lord Mulgrave, Sept. 18/05, no. 18.
[3] F.O. 78. 71, Summerers to Wellesley, Feb. 26/10. One of Summerers' brothers, the "Chevalier de Kirico", was Russian consul at Bukarest at the time Summerers was sent there.

after outlining his official relations with Lord Elgin, Summerers requested a suitable appointment such as he had been led to expect. He pointed out that his "pension" (salary) as a Gentleman of the Embassy was 3000 piastres (about £200)[1] a year during 1800, 1801 and 1802, and 4000 in 1803; from 1803 until 1805 he had received no salary at all, and since it cost him 12,000 piastres to maintain his official position, he had incurred debts to the extent of 25,000 piastres (about £1700). In a covering despatch to this memorial Arbuthnot wrote: "Summerers acts as H.M.'s Consul at Boucarest,...I do not believe that as yet it (*i.e.* his appointment) has ever received the sanction of His Majesty's Ministers"; it would be, he added, "a great detriment" to the service of the Government and the East India Company if there was not some public agent at Bukarest, but there was no need to pay Summerers so large a salary as he asked.[2]

That Summerers' mission to the Principalities arose chiefly out of the need for an efficient postal system between Constantinople and London *via* Vienna which might be used also by the Government in India and the East India Company, is perfectly clear. The establishment of some such system formed part of Lord Elgin's instructions in 1799,[3] and he set himself immediately to consider schemes of improvement. There was no regular postal service from the East to Constantinople except from Smyrna; westwards from Constantinople there was only the "German post" under the control of Austria which was guaranteed security by treaty with the Porte. The Austrian couriers, however, travelled unguarded and assumed no responsibility for loss by robbery.[4] "Nothing of the sort", wrote Elgin, "can be so arbitrary and so irregular as the

[1] Lord Elgin, who was himself unable to maintain his position on the salary of £4400 allowed him, commented in 1801 on the high prices and the adverse rate of exchange, the rate being then 15 piastres to the pound, whereas before the war it was 12: to Grenville, Mar. 25/01, separate, in F.O. 78. 31.

[2] Note 2, p. 171.

[3] F.O. 78. 24.

[4] F.O. 78. 38, Elgin to Hawkesbury, Jan. 15/03, separate.

Austrian post ".[1] Again, in July, 1800, he complained[2] that
letters were opened and withheld, and "even newspapers
(were) purposely kept back", notwithstanding that Austria
was at that time an allied Power. Elgin's real difficulty was
that the Porte depended very largely on the foreign representatives for news, and as both Austria and Russia had systems
of their own, they were first to receive the news and thus had
"an incalculable advantage in acquiring influence at the
Porte".[2] The route, times and cost of Austrian couriers, as
given by Elgin,[1] may be shown thus:

Constantinople to Bukarest (6–7 days) 267 piastres for an express
Bukarest to Hermanstadt   (7–8 days) 40 or 50   ,,   ,,
Hermanstadt to Vienna   (7–8 days) 60   ,,   ,,

In addition, an *ad valorem* consulage of 1 per cent. was charged
on articles carried. Alternatively to the Austrian post Elgin
could employ his own messengers as the East India Company
usually did: these were faster but more expensive:

Constantinople to Bukarest (5–6 days)
Bukarest to Hermanstadt   (2–3 days)
Hermanstadt to Vienna   (6–7 days) Total cost 500 piastres.

Elgin considered the possibility of a Turkish post which would
have the advantage that "the Turks (in contrast to Tatar
messengers) do consider letters as well as any other deposit
sacred while entrusted to them".[1] This scheme was impracticable, and Elgin therefore proposed some British controlled
system: an "agent or consul" might be appointed at Semlin
or Hermanstadt,[3] and messengers might convey despatches to
and from either place.[1] The Marquis of Wellesley, as Governor-
General of India, was also pressing for a British postal system

[1] F.O. 78. 24, Elgin to Grenville, Dec. 28/99, no. 20.
[2] F.O. 78. 29, Elgin to Grenville, July 23/00.
[3] Both Semlin and Hermanstadt lay within Austrian territory, the
first on the south side of the Danube a little to the west of Belgrade,
the second a few miles north of the Red Tower Pass through the
Transylvanian Alps; Semlin stood on the Nish-Belgrade route,
Hermanstadt on that *via* Burgas and Bukarest. The post was beset

from Constantinople to London.[1] Finally, in July, 1800, Elgin established a King's Messenger, "one Duff" by name, at the Turkish frontier (probably at Hermanstadt); on the first of each month he was to proceed to Vienna, from which he would return on the 15th.[1] On his own showing Summerers had already reached Bukarest in February, 1800, although curiously enough Elgin makes no reference to his mission in his correspondence of 1800 and complaints about the post continued until the end of that year, for Lord Grenville, the Foreign Secretary, complained in a despatch of December 9, 1800, that he had received no despatches from Elgin of a date later than October 9, notwithstanding that many had been sent.[2] Of Summerers' activities at Bukarest in 1801 there can be no doubt whatever, for there are two statements of account relating to him[3] which were paid by the Embassy:

(1) "Expences attending the Establishment of the Agent for forwarding Packets at Buccorest from february to December 1801 inclusive". (This was an itemised account amounting to a total, including Summerers' salary, of 3357 piastres.)

(2) "Expences attending the expeditions [sc. of correspondence] from Buccorest from Febry. to the end of December 1801". (This was again an itemised account and amounted in all to 3536 piastres, 30 paras.)

Wellesley noted with satisfaction the success of the monthly messenger service, and on March 31, 1802, Elgin commented on "the exactness and unexampled celerity" with which his despatches had reached England since the appointment of Summerers as "agent at Buccarest"; he urged the "indispensable necessity of continuing the Establishment"; he did

by difficulties other than those given above: armed bandits, for example, blocked the line of communication for three weeks at Burgas and Rodosto in 1800, whilst in 1805, owing to the intoxication of a King's Messenger, despatches were stolen near Hermanstadt and apparently read by the Austrian Government before their return some days later.

[1] F.O. 78. 29, Elgin to Grenville, July 23/00.

[2] F.O. 78. 31, Elgin to Grenville, Feb. 5/01.

[3] F.O. 78. 36, Elgin to Lord Hawkesbury, Mar. 31/02, no. 41; the statements of account are enclosed.

APPENDIX I   175

not consider that the duties necessarily required an English-
man: Summerers was "sufficiently respectable", he was
assiduous, zealous and in every way deserving of the Government's "favour and confirmation".[1]

There is no doubt that Lord Elgin did his best to secure for
Summerers an adequate and regular consular appointment at
Bukarest, for on the eve of his departure from Constantinople
on January 15, 1803, he wrote[2] to Lord Hawkesbury, the
Foreign Secretary:

I have the satisfaction of informing Your Lordship, that from
the Sanction given by Government, & the East India Company
to the establishment of an agent at Buccarest, and the increasing
importance of that Place since the navigation of the Black Sea
is opened,[3] I have applied & obtained from the Porte, a consular
Barat [sic] for that Situation which will be delivered in a few
days. Meanwhile as no instructions have been received on the
enquiries contained in my despatch No. [4] relative to the
appointments of that establishment, I have been induced to
address a letter of which the annexed is a copy to Mr Sumerer
on my departure from hence.

The despatch referred to in the above is very probably that
of March 31, 1802, which has been quoted; at least there is no
other despatch in the Turkey correspondence answering to
the reference. Further, it is clear from Elgin's account that
the Sultan's *Bérat* could not have been issued to Summerers
in January, 1802, the year given by Wilkinson (and generally
accepted) as marking the beginning of British consular relations; indeed, an unpublished[5] copy of Summerers' *Bérat*

[1] F.O. 78. 36, Elgin to Lord Hawkesbury, Mar. 31/02, no. 41; the
statements of account are enclosed.

[2] F.O. 78. 38, no. 75. A copy of the letter from Elgin to Summerers,
written in French and dated Jan. 8/03, is enclosed.

[3] By an Act of the Sultan, Oct. 30, 1799, British merchant ships
were allowed to enter the Black Sea: Hertslet, *Treaties, etc., between
Turkey and Foreign Powers*, p. 269.   [4] Left blank.

[5] F.O. 78. 71. The copy, which is an English translation, is enclosed
in Summerers to Hamilton, Apr. 17/10; there is also here enclosed
a copy of the firman ordering the hospodar of Wallachia to receive
Summerers as consul.

bears the date January 17, 1803, which accords with Elgin's account above, whilst the difference between Wilkinson's monthly date—January 6—and the January 17 of the unpublished copy may be due to the conversion of an original Turkish date into the Russian and western (Gregorian) calendars. Elgin's letter to Summerers alluded to above was dated January 8, 1803: Elgin informed him that he had instructed Mr Tooke, the East India Company's agent at Constantinople, to pay him a salary of 4000 piastres as from January 1, 1802, as well as expenses for Janissaries, Couriers, Estafettes and the expedition of packets generally; until the Government had decided on his position he was to receive 4000 piastres a year and his expenses, *which were to be limited to the expedition of correspondence*.[1]

Recognised by the Porte and the local authorities in the Principalities as consul-general, Summerers, apparently on his own initiative, extended the sphere of his activities, which involved him, according to his own statements, in considerable expenditure. He not only carried out his duties in connection with the post, but entertained British merchants and travellers, and spent relatively large sums on secret service work which consisted chiefly in collecting evidence of French and Russian intrigues. He conducted a regular correspondence with Arbuthnot, and with Adair and Jackson, British representatives respectively at Vienna and Berlin, whilst in 1805 he addressed despatches directly to the Foreign Secretary. His financial condition grew more and more stringent, whilst the Government at home remained oblivious of, or at least disinterested in, his well-being. This was not due to silence on his part, for from 1805 until 1810 he strove by continual appeals to attract official attention to his financial position. Although both Elgin and Arbuthnot had officially favoured his claims to some regular consular appointment, no instruction or reference to his position was forthcoming, the reasons being chiefly the quick succession of Foreign Secretaries,[2] and the more serious

[1] Note 2, p. 175 (my italics).
[2] Between the years 1799 and 1810 there were nine different Foreign Secretaries.

matters connected with the French war. From Summerers' own statements it would seem that he received no official payments between 1803 and 1805: it is clear, however, that three sums were paid by the Embassy at Constantinople in 1804–5; these amounted to 4337 piastres for messenger and Janissary expenses.[1] He was paid no salary during this period, and for salary in 1802 he received 3000 instead of 4000 piastres. In consequence, Summerers fell increasingly into debt, being forced to contract loans at the rate of 12 per cent. compound interest. In a *mémoire* addressed to the Foreign Secretary, Charles Fox, in 1806, he stated that his debts incurred through official business amounted to £2000 and that his creditors pursued him *à outrance*; his *mémoire* further contained a quotation from Elgin's letter of January 8, 1803 (somewhat distorted in his own favour), and requested payment in respect of salary and extraordinary expenses.[2] Later in the year (in August) he declared that his debts amounted to "over £3500".[3] Arbuthnot did his utmost in despatches home to ameliorate Summerers' financial condition. In August, 1806, he declared that Summerers was zealous and active and deserved better treatment than he had received;[4] in the following January he stressed the importance of keeping Summerers at Bukarest, and reported that he had paid him 6000 piastres and that he would be compelled, owing to the urgency of the case and out of common justice, to act without instructions in paying him all his arrears of salary.[5] Summerers accordingly received another 6000 piastres, so that his salary at the meagre rate of 4000 piastres, as arranged by Lord Elgin in 1803, was now paid up to the end of 1806. Summerers later regarded the 12,000 piastres which he had received from Arbuthnot as equivalent to one year's salary.[6]

[1] F.O. 78. 48, enclosed in Straton to Lord Harrowby, Jan. 25/05, no. 5.
[2] F.O. 78. 53. The *mémoire* was dated Apr. 2/06.
[3] F.O. 78. 53.
[4] F.O. 78. 51, Arbuthnot to Fox, Aug. 25/06, no. 54.
[5] F.O. 78. 55, Arbuthnot to Howick, Jan. 15/07, no. 6.
[6] F.O. 78. 71, Summerers to Wellesley, Feb. 26/10.

During the years 1806–7, owing to the turn of Napoleonic policy, the Principalities became suddenly involved in international politics. Summerers devoted himself to the task of discovering the aims and reporting the activities of French and Russian agents: thus he gave Arbuthnot early information of the intention of the French Ambassador to demand the recall of the hospodars,[1] and sent Adair at Vienna an able account of the flight of the hospodar Ypsilanti.[2] With the Russian occupation of the Principalities Summerers demanded of Adair letters of credence from the Government, since the Sultan's firman, he declared, no longer served to accredit him.[3] Somewhat embarrassed by this request, since any recognition of existing affairs in the Principalities would offend Austria, whilst at the same time he desired reports from Bukarest, Adair sought permission from General Michelson, who was in charge of the occupation, for Summerers to remain at Bukarest as Resident. Summerers' information proved incorrect, however, for General Michelson informed Adair that the Principalities were still acknowledged part of the Turkish Empire.[4] When the Turks advanced into Wallachia against the Russians, Summerers hurriedly left Bukarest, leaving his horses, house and effects to be plundered by Cossack troopers.[5] From July until September, 1807, he was at Vienna, where Adair provided him with a passport, dated September 24, which styled him "His Majesty's Resident" at Bukarest, and sent him with despatches to Malta and with verbal communications to Sir Arthur Paget at the Dardanelles.[6] Learning that Sir Arthur Paget was in London, he gladly set out from Malta, reaching London in June, 1808. Here he

---

[1] F.O. 78. 51, Arbuthnot to Fox, Aug. 25/06, no. 54.

[2] F.O. 7. 80, Adair to Fox, Sept. 13/06, separate, no. 2.

[3] F.O. 7. 83, Adair to Howick, Feb. 11/07, and Mar. 5/07.

[4] F.O. 7. 83, Adair to Howick, Mar. 28/07, separate.

[5] Summerers interpolated an account of his hurried departure from Bukarest in 1807 and the loss of his effects in statements under heading I of his accounts: see note 1, page 179.

[6] F.O. 78. 66, Summerers to Hammond, Feb. 13/09: the passport is enclosed.

devoted strenuous and persistent efforts to secure satisfaction of his financial claims. His correspondence between 1808 and 1810, which has been preserved, is wearisome in its continual reiteration week after week, in letters to successive Foreign Secretaries and Under-Secretaries, of claims to the payment of salary since 1803, to his extraordinary expenses, and even to the interest charges which he had incurred in the public service. At length, in February, 1809, the Foreign Office instructed him to forward particulars of the monies he claimed, and he did so in a voluminous document which tabulated his expenditure from 1803 until 1808 under thirteen heads.[1]

The following is the "Résumé of Mr Summerers' Expenses" which was drawn up by the Under-Secretary, Hamilton, and sent to the Foreign Secretary, Lord Bathurst:[2]

Ordered to be pd. by Ld. Elgin		150. 11. 0.
Presents etc. in Wallachia and Moldavia		932. 18. 10.
Do. to Turkish Pashas		578. 10. 4.
Journies for public serv.		759. 0. 0.
Expedns. into provinces		524. 0. 10.
Secretary etc.		665. 6. 8.
Secret service G.		662. 8. 10.
H.	(473. 19. 4.[3])	473. 9. 11.
I.		2122. 5. 5.
K.	(823. 3. 7.[3])	872. 15. 7.
Expenses in public service		1305. 12. 11.
Correspondence Vienna		552. 3. 5.
		£9550. 1. 2.

Summerers stated under heading I that one of his principal instructions was to learn in detail the conduct of Russia in the Principalities and neighbouring countries. Heading G described his secret activities in detecting and counteracting French intrigues: these included, for example, efforts to intercept or retard French couriers *en route* between Constantinople

[1] This document is contained in F.O. 78. 66.
[2] Enclosed in an undated letter from Hamilton to Bathurst.
[3] These are the correct figures which Hamilton inaccurately transcribed.

and Vienna by means of disguised emissaries sent to await their passage on the roads. Hamilton took exception to Summerers' references to "the consul and the consulate", and described him as "Resident at the Court of the Prince of Wallachia".[1] It appears that Summerers never received any satisfaction of his claims: the Foreign Office declared that no precedent existed for the payment of interest charges and that they would consider his claim only if he could show the authority of Lord Elgin or of Arbuthnot by which he incurred these debts.[1] Although, as a result of his persistence, his case was referred to Arbuthnot[2] and the Foreign Office demanded a statement of his accounts again in May, 1810,[3] apparently no decision in his favour was made; the collection of Summerers' correspondence at the Public Record Office ends abruptly with a letter of July 24, 1810, in which he demanded permission of the Foreign Secretary to go to Constantinople with a view to joining the Grand Vizier's army, if no settlement of his claims was forthcoming.[4] Canning's recommendation[5] in 1809 that Summerers should have a pension was not carried out. In fact the Foreign Office appears neither to have recognised him to be in the Government service nor even to have issued him the usual discharge.

To what extent were Summerers' claims fair and reasonable? Little weight can be given to his own assertions that he was personally incorruptible and that he had not abused his consular position to enrich himself through private trade as was the custom amongst Greek consuls in the Near East,[6] but in his favour it must be admitted that both Lord Elgin and Arbuthnot wrote highly of his character and abilities, and that Adair, too, approved his activities. The Foreign Office was certainly negligent in dealing with the question of his

[1] Enclosed in an undated letter from Hamilton to Bathurst.
[2] F.O. 78. 66. Note by Wellesley on the back of a letter from Summerers dated Dec. 9/09.
[3] F.O. 78. 71, Summerers to Culling Smith, May 28/10.
[4] F.O. 78. 71, to Wellesley.
[5] F.O. 78. 66. Note on back of letter from Summerers, June 27/09.
[6] Note 1, p. 171.

status and salary; and it is certain that the lesser servants of the Foreign Office, such as attachés at the Constantinople Embassy, received niggardly and inadequate salaries at this time. Even so, Summerers' expenditure, as described by himself, was on a grand scale for one who received no instruction to spend money on secret service, and who, indeed, was ordered in 1803 to restrict his expenditure to the business connected with the postal system.

A word may be added about Summerers' successors at Bukarest. William Wilkinson was appointed consul by the Levant Company in October, 1813,[1] and was accredited by the Porte in the following year. E. L. Blutte, an attaché at the Constantinople Embassy, in accordance with official instructions, was sent to Bukarest by Sir Stratford Canning, Ambassador at the Porte, in 1826.[2] He carried out the duties of British consul, and collections of his despatches are preserved. In succession to Blutte, who died at his post in 1834, Robert Colquhoun was appointed consul. He was the first British consul to the Principalities to be appointed by the King in the normal official manner.[3]

[1] F.O. 78. 81, Wilkinson to Hamilton, Oct. 21/13, enclosing an open letter to the Foreign Secretary, in which he offered to act for the Government at Bukarest.

[2] F.O. 78. 134, J. Planta to Blutte, Oct. 11/25 and F.O. 78. 146, Blutte to George Canning, May 19/26.

[3] F.O. 78. 242, Palmerston to Colquhoun, Nov. 17/34.

APPENDIX TWO

THE STUTTGART
INTERVIEW, 1857

APPENDIX TWO

THE STUTTGART INTERVIEW, 1857

THE two, hitherto unpublished, copies of despatches given below from Lord Cowley, Ambassador at Paris, in 1857, afford evidence upon a rather obscure incident, namely, the Stuttgart interview between Napoleon III and the Czar Alexander II. Count Walewski and Prince Gortchakoff were present. Many topics seem to have been discussed including the future of the Principalities. The meeting took place on September 25, 1857, that is, *after* the Osborne agreement,[1] so that, morally at least, Napoleon III was at that time pledged to administrative union of the Principalities without a single prince.

In two respects the evidence supplied by the two despatches of Cowley given below conflicts with known information about the interview. Debidour, after ante-dating the interview to *before* the rupture at Constantinople of August 5, 1857, states in his *Histoire diplomatique de l'Europe*, II, 172:

> Le czar promettait à l'empereur des Français de ne pas contrarier sa politique en Italie; ce dernier s'engageait à ne pas abandonner la nation roumaine.

It is very unlikely that any such definite, though verbal, agreement was actually made. Moreover, according to Cowley, Russia reserved her judgment on the desirability of union and certainly wished to avoid union under a foreign prince, whilst France herself was indisposed to press for union which had become almost impracticable. Napoleon III declared at Osborne that Russia was "even against the union".[2] Lord Wodehouse, Minister at St Petersburg, noted, on October 23, 1857, the "rigid silence" of the Russian Government on the question of union, "so much so that only the Emperor and Gortchakoff know which way they will vote in Paris",[3] and he added that even the diplomatic staff were not informed. Even if Napoleon III wanted to secure at Stuttgart Russian neutrality in the event of a war against Austria in Italy (and Debidour

[1] See note 2, p. 131.
[2] Martin, *The Life of The Prince Consort*, IV, 102.
[3] F.O. 195. 548, to Clarendon.

gives no evidence for this supposition), it does not seem that his support of union would have been an acceptable *quid pro quo* to the Czar. Certainly at the Conference of Paris in 1858 Kisseleff, on behalf of Russia, joined Walewski in stating (as is recorded in Protocol I[1]) the desirability of union under a foreign prince. But since Napoleon III's hands were tied by the agreement made at Osborne, this must be regarded rather as Russian concurrence in a policy incapable of realisation.

There appears to be no reference to the Interview in the *Cambridge History of British Foreign Policy*, vol. II, whilst Bourgeois, in his *Politique étrangère*, III, 429, refers to it with studied vagueness. A full account is given in Charles-Roux, *Alexandre II, Gortchakoff et Napoléon III*, bk. III, ch. i. According to Charles-Roux, the discussions concerned the affairs of Naples, Poland, Montenegro, and the Principalities "which interested France even more" (*sc.* than Russia). He refers to three unsigned protocols or minutes of the interview in the Russian archives, which outline three general aims: Franco-Russian co-operation in the Near East; co-operation in case of any disruption of Turkey; and common action by ministers and consuls in the Near East, France refraining from religious propaganda. Charles-Roux does not believe that any agreement, bearing upon the later French war against Austria of 1859, was made at Stuttgart, although he records that the Czar admitted significantly that he did not wish "recommencer l'année 1849" (*sc.* when he supported Austria against the revolted Hungarians). Further, he quotes, though without comment, statements of Gortchakoff after the interview in which the latter claimed agreement with France on all outstanding questions—a claim which the Prince Consort believed to be exactly the reverse of the truth and which Cowley's despatch No. 1419, given below, seems to refute.

Indeed, the biographer of the Prince Consort was probably right when he said that the Stuttgart meeting had no definite political results.[2] It provided one of those occasions, so beloved of Napoleon III, at which he was able to discuss, in generalities,

---

[1] See note 4, p. 151. [2] Martin, *op. cit.* IV, 133.

the future political condition of Europe. Stuttgart, taken together with the Osborne meeting, was really significant as an indication of Napoleon III's personal ascendancy. It was strangely reminiscent of the Tilsit interview fifty years previously: Napoleon III was repeating the action of Napoleon I in extending the hand of friendship to the Power which he had just defeated.

The copies given below are transcripts taken from the drafts received by Lord Stratford de Redcliffe at Constantinople, in F.O. 195 (Turkey).

(a) *Lord Cowley* to the *Earl of Clarendon, K.G.*,
October 4/57, no. 1379.[1]

My Lord,

I saw Count Walewski the day before yesterday for the first time since his return from Stutgart.

H E's observations respg what passed at the meeting of the two Emperors were almost entirely confined to his appreciation of the persons whom he met in the Wurtemburgh Capital. If any political questions were discussed at Stutgart, he was silent in regard to them, with two exceptions to which I purpose alluding in other despatches and Y L will, I feel confident, approve my own reserve, in not shewing the least anxiety to know more than C Walewski chose to impart. From H E's tone however I am disposed to think that whatever may be his own sentiments in regard to them, neither the Czar nor those who accompanied H M have made a favourable impression upon the Emperor Napoleon, & this opinion is confirmed by what I have heard from others.

It would appear from C Walewski's statement that the Emperor Napoleon was recd. in the German States through which he passed with a degree of enthusiasm for which H M was not prepared, & which embarrassed him not a little. H M was met and complimented by Princes of the reigning Family in all the German States, through or near which he passed, to commence with the Prince of Prussia, who was the bearer of an autograph letter from the King, his Brother.

I could not help contrasting to C Walewski the conduct of

[1] F.O. 195. 547.

Russia at the present moment, with her conduct when the Emperor Napoleon assumed the Imperial Diadem, & I said that I considered the meeting at Stutgart to be perhaps the greatest external triumph which the Emperor had yet attained, and the position of Russia to be equally humiliating. C Walewski did not disagree from this estimate of the Imperial Meeting.

I have, etc.

(signed) COWLEY.

(b) *Lord Cowley* to the *Earl of Clarendon*, *K.G.*, October 13/57, no. 1419. Confidential.[1]

My Lord,

As a sequel to my preceding despatch I beg to add in a more confidential form that during the conversation with C Walewski therein recorded, I said to H E that I had until now abstained from motives of delicacy from putting any questions to him relative to what had passed between himself & Prince Gortchacoff when they had met at Stuttgardt, but that having heard that the latter had boasted that there was a complete understanding between the French & Russian Govts on several European questions, that of the future organisation of the Pties being among them I could no longer refrain from asking H E whether such was the case, observing that it was due to H M's Govt to be correctly, if confidentially, informed on this very important matter.

There was a momentary embarrassment in Ct Walewski's answer; not I believe arising from any intention to deceive me on main points, but from a feeling that he had courted explanations from Prince Gortchacoff and had perhaps been more ardent in his expressions of regard for Russia than he was content tha I should know. He denied at once there being any understanding between the French & Russian Govts but he said that it was natural that the question of the Pties should have been discussed between himself & Prince Gortchacoff (a proposition in which I at once acquiesced) and that he had thereupon taken an opportunity of asking the Russian Minister's notions in regard to it. Prince Gortchacoff had replied that he had formed no

[1] F.O. 195. 548.

opinion upon the matter and should form none until the Divans according to the stipulations of the Treaty of Paris had had an opportunity of expressing their wishes. It was true, Prince Gortchacoff said, that the Russian Plenipotentiaries had pronounced themselves at Paris to be favourable to the Union, but that declaration was subject to further enquiry, and until that enquiry had been made, Russia reserved her final judgment. The Russian Commissioner had sided with the French Commr in protesting against the legality of the Moldavian Elections, because those Elections were so conducted that the wishes of the inhabitants of Moldavia could not have been fairly ascertained, but it was not intended thereby to express any opinion respecting the future organization of the provinces themselves. If however the French Govt had any proposal to make, the Russian Govt would examine it with all the attention it merited. For himself he looked upon the organic statutes of the Pties as the point of departure.

C Walewski added that Prince Gortchacoff was so prolix of his words while making this statement that it was easy to gather from him that he was opposed to the Union of the Pties under a Foreign Prince, and that he had therefore observed to him at once that he saw that the Russian Govt was not in favour of such an issue from the question. Prince Gortchacoff, H E continued, had not denied the truth of this remark, but had still maintained that the Russian Govt was perfectly free to take any course which on further consideration they might deem desirable. He had, moreover, said that Russia would never give her assent to any Prince governing the Pties who was not of the Greek religion; he had added that the Emperor of Russia would never permit a Russian Prince to take the Govt, and had asked where there was any other Prince to be found. "I may then assume" Count Walewski describes himself to have said to the Russian Minister "that you are not prepared to force the hands of the Porte in order to effect the Union of the Provinces". "Exactly so" replied Prince Gortchacoff. "That will suit us perfectly" rejoined C Walewski; "we think the Union desirable, but if it can only be obtained by force, we are not ready to make war upon the Porte for the purpose".

Prince Gortchacoff again asked C Walewski whether he had any project, assuring him that Russia *would adopt it*; but the latter replied that it would be at all events premature to form one before the decision of the Divans was known.

I cannot conclude this despatch without observing that C Walewski's satisfaction while recounting to me his conversation with Prince Gortchacoff was very apparent, and is a fresh proof to me of his intention to abandon the Union. He went so far as to say that he had attained the conviction that, even if France had persisted in her views respg the Union, she would have been deserted by Russia at the last moment.

I have, etc.

(signed) COWLEY.

APPENDIX THREE

NAPOLEON III AND
TURKEY, 1857

APPENDIX THREE

NAPOLEON III AND TURKEY, 1857

THE two, hitherto unpublished, despatches from Lord Cowley given below are such able and closely reasoned studies of Napoleon III's feelings and attitude towards the Ottoman Empire in general and the Principalities in particular that, although despatch (*b*) has already been cited by F. A. Simpson in his *Louis Napoleon and the Recovery of France*, pp. 364–5, and quotations from each have been made in the present essay, it is thought worth while to reproduce them verbatim.

Despatch (*a*) deals with French policy in the Near East and reveals the Emperor's attitude towards the integrity of the Ottoman Empire; despatch (*b*) describes interviews which Cowley held with Walewski and the Emperor, at both of which French views with regard to the union of the Principalities and the Emperor's interest in the cause of nationality are exposed.

The copies given below are taken from the drafts received by the Foreign Office, in F.O. 27 (France).

(a) *Lord Cowley* to the *Earl of Clarendon*, K.G., May 11/57, no. 753. Most Confidential.[1]

My Lord,

Although I should have had no difficulty, as far as my own personal convictions went, in replying at once to Your Lordship's Despatch No. 590[2] of the 13th Ultimo, marked "Most Confidential", in which Your Lordship adverting to the anxiety felt by the Porte at the supposed designs of the French and Austrian Governments to extend their influence in Turkey, instructs me to report to Your Lordship any observations I may have to offer upon this subject, I have deemed it more respectful to Her Majesty's Government, and more becoming the importance of the matter on which Your Lordship has done me the honor to ask my opinion, to make such further enquiries before stating it, as would enable me to confirm or correct my previous

[1] F.O. 27. 1196.
[2] This is in error for no. 540: a copy of this despatch is in F.O. 27. 1176.

impressions. My observations will of course relate to France alone.

I do not believe that the Emperor has any preconceived plan of establishing exclusive French influence in any part of the Turkish Dominions; if for no other reason, because His Majesty knows it to be impossible. On the other hand it would be idle to deny, that the Emperor is determined that France shall be consulted, and that her voice shall be heard on all questions of European interest. He is convinced that the Governments, which preceded him, fell because they neglected to uphold the dignity of France and he is resolved to recover for her that position in the Councils of Europe, which had been lost through the feebleness of others. No doubt, if he could exercise ascendancy either in Turkey or elsewhere he would do so. What Government exists that would not do the same thing?

I cannot help calling to mind, the warnings addressed on all sides to Your Lordship, as the late War progressed, and as French troops were poured into Turkey, respecting the intentions of the French Government, and their designs upon the East. I have now present to my memory one remarkable letter, in which the position of the different Corps of the French Army, was likened to the claw of the Bird, whose emblem they bore, ready to seize its devoted prey. Your Lordship was told, that Turkey was only about to change masters,—that France was substituted for Russia,—yet when the time came France was of all the Allies the most eager to quit the Turkish Territory, and to leave matters to settle themselves with Russia as best they might. Does this look like a desire for political ascendancy in Turkey?

But supposing the desire to exist of what avail is it? Did it succeed in obliging the British Fleet to quit the inner waters of Turkey, and the Austrian Troops the Principalities, and in giving Bolgrad to the Russians? Has it prevented the return of Reshid Pacha to power? Has it placed the monetary affairs of Turkey, and the construction of Railroads in the hands of French Capitalists? Has it obtained the consent of the Porte to the construction of the Suez Canal?

The determination however to uphold the dignity of France, to which I have referred above, leads the Emperor without doubt to anticipate the discussion of questions, which might otherwise never present themselves for solution, and to ask for premature decisions, which it is highly inconvenient to give. But this conduct is dictated far more by the apprehension of these questions being decided to the exclusion of France, than by a desire of deciding them to the exclusion of others.

Your Lordship is aware how openly and confidentially, the Emperor has expressed himself towards Her Majesty's Government with respect to his ideas,—I can hardly call them plans for the future—how many and varied have been the conversations both in regard to passing events, and to those yet in the womb of time, with which His Majesty has honored me, and I would ask Your Lordship confidently whether such conduct does not at least lead to this conclusion—that whatever may be the desire of His Majesty, he has the full conviction that he cannot establish French ascendancy, either in Turkey or elsewhere, to the extinction of that of Great Britain.

Indeed, My Lord, I could almost wish, that the influence of France in Turkey, tempered as it would always be by the firm and unabated vigilance of Her Majesty's Representative at Constantinople, were greater than it is; for it is to the want of it, and to the jealousy and irritation engendered by that want, that I attribute in great measure the ill-will which, it is useless to conceal it, the Emperor entertains towards the Porte. Had the Turkish Ministers shown themselves more ready to listen to the—call it as you will—the behests or advice of France, I doubt whether the Emperor would condemn as sweepingly as he does, the whole system of Government in Turkey, and teach himself, as is rapidly coming to pass, to look with complacency on the dismemberment of an Empire, for the preservation of which hardly a year has passed since he was in arms.

With a character such as that of the Emperor, there is as much danger in curbing too tightly the influence of France, as there would be folly in giving the reins to her complete ascendancy. It is no easy matter to steer between the two systems. It requires temper, caution, and perhaps some amount of forbearance on the part of those who have to deal with French Agents, but I believe it to be the safest course to pursue, and such as the Emperor merits at our hands. With regard to Turkey particularly, your Lordship must not think, that while Turkey is expressing anxiety of the ascendancy of French interests on the one side, France is silent respecting the extension of British influence on the other; and, to speak frankly, although I rejoice at it, there cannot I think be much doubt as to which side of the two statements the balance of truth would incline.

With respect to the question more immediately raised by the correspondence of the Porte, inclosed in your Lordship's Despatch No. 540[1], of the desire of the Emperor to unite Servia Montenegro the Herzegovine and a part of Bosnia into one Sclavonic Principality, I can only state my total ignorance of it, if it exists, but the agglomeration of people of the same race under one rule is a theme so consonant to the Emperor's ears, that His Majesty would be likely to listen with complacency to any scheme the basis of which is the restoration of nationality. On the other hand His Majesty's conviction that the Turkish Empire cannot last, that Mahommedanism and civilization cannot coexist and that it would be a blessing for the world in general were the Crescent everywhere replaced by the Cross, leads him too easily to dispose, by anticipation, of the component parts of an Empire, the dissolution of which he pre-conceives.

To sum up I have more fear of French intrigues than of French influence. No nation can be influential whose Government does not pursue a steady, straightforward, honest policy. This has never been, and without a miracle, never will be the course of France, and I am cognizant of no country where her influence has been permanently and steadily maintained. If there had been one nation more likely than another to undergo this influence, it would have been Turkey, where France was the first recognised protectress of the Christian religion. But the advantages which this acknowledged right gave her, she has managed to forfeit, and I do not fear her recovery now, of that which under far more favorable circumstances, she did not know how to keep.

I have, etc.

(signed) COWLEY.

[1] Note 2, p. 192.

(b) *Lord Cowley* to the *Earl of Clarendon*, *K.G.*, May 12/57, no. 759. Confidential.[1]

My Lord,

I stated to Your Lordship at the end of my Despatch No. 681 of the 29th Ultimo that I proposed giving you the substance of a conversation which I had with Count Walewski respecting the future administration of the Principalities. Since then the subject has been more than once resumed between us, and it is my purpose in the present Despatch to lay before Your Lordship a general summary of what passed on the first and on subsequent occasions.

The apprehensions which I have long entertained, that if the attitude of the two Governments on this question, as well at Constantinople as in the Principalities, was not already antagonistic, it was too likely to become so, led me to take a favorable opportunity of expressing those apprehensions to Count Walewski. The French Government, I observed to His Excellency, had given unequivocal proof of their desire to see the two Provinces united under one Chief, and one Administration; while Her Majesty's Government entertained the conviction that the realisation of such a project would be the first step towards the dismemberment of the Turkish Empire, the integrity of which it had been the object of the late war to preserve. Now would it not be prudent, I asked, that the two Governments, while there was yet time for calm deliberation, should examine the question in all its bearings. I was most anxious that it should not remain in its present state, until the Congress should be called to pronounce its judgement, and I considered that some attempt should at once be made by the two Governments to reconcile their conflicting opinions. If the two Governments were unfortunately to remain separated on this question, let each at least have the consolation of feeling, that every effort had been made to prevent it. What I ventured to suggest was, that the two Governments, without touching in the first instance the political part of the question, should confine themselves to examining its practical possibilities, that is should enquire into the means of organising a united Government, that would satisfy the two Principalities and the Porte.

[1] F.O. 27. 1196.

If upon examination it was found, that such a scheme offered but little chance of success, it was to be hoped that the French Government would desist from recommending it. If on the other hand the difficulties were found to be none, or easily to be overcome, the political bearings of the question, as connected with the future destinies of the Turkish Empire, might be taken into the calm and impartial consideration of the two Governments. Since neither had any direct interest at stake, since the object of both was the general good, it might be hoped that their deliberations would lead to a decision satisfactory to the Principalities themselves, and compatible with the sovereign dignity of the Porte.

Count Walewski received my observations in very good part, and he said that he responded cordially to the sentiments which had dictated them. On the first occasion, while not exactly objecting to an early examination of the question, His Excellency expressed doubts, whether it would not be advisable to wait until the Divans had pronounced themselves, but upon reflection, and after conversing with the Emperor, he appears disposed to listen at once to any suggestions that Her Majesty's Government may have to make. He seems fully alive to the grave consequences which may follow a decided antagonism of the two Powers, in regard to the question of the Union. I wish I could add that I saw any real intention on his part, of allowing it to be judged by its merits. I should deceive Your Lordship if I did not add that to me it is evident that the hope of the French Minister is, that Her Majesty's Government will adopt the views of France.

The position taken by Count Walewski is this. His Excellency maintains that the French Government were originally indifferent upon the question; and that although it had been put forward by them at the Vienna Conferences, and was reproduced in the memorandum submitted for the approval of Her Majesty's Government before the opening of the Paris Congress, yet that in fact it had been determined not to insist upon it, should it meet with any opposition from Her Majesty's Advisers; but that Your Lordship having signified both to the Emperor and to himself your acquiescence in it on your arrival in Paris, it had been warmly taken up by the French Government, both during the sitting of the Congress and since: that under these circumstances some indulgence was due to the French Government on the part of that of Her Majesty, since the interest of the former in this question originated in the supposition that they were acting in complete unison with the sentiments of Her Majesty's Government.

I replied, that, admitting that Your Lordship had in the first instance been favorably inclined towards the Union, your opinions had been already shaken, before you left Paris, by the observations that had been made to you by Aali Pasha. That you had agreed that the question of the Union could not be excluded from the consideration of the Divans, but that you had said no more upon the subject in Paris, because it had been distinctly understood that the question should not be discussed for the moment. That on your return to England, the future administration of the Provinces had undergone the careful consideration of Her Majesty's Government, and that in the month of August I had been instructed to lay before His Excellency the reasons which induced Her Majesty's Government to think that the Union would not be compatible with the general interests of Europe, and to express the hope that the French Government would concur in the validity of them. Nothing could have been more frank and unreserved than the conduct of Her Majesty's Government in this matter.

Count Walewski said that he did not recollect my having spoken to him; but there can be no question upon this point, because I placed in his hands copies of Your Lordship's despatch No. 862[1] of the 21st of August last, and of the Memorandum annexed to it; and although I did not for reasons explained in my despatch No. 981 of the 24th of the same month, include the last paragraph of your No. 862 in the copy of it which I gave to Count Walewski, I yet took care, both then and since, to let His Excellency know verbally the opinion of Her Majesty's Government, as set forth in that Paragraph.

Having touched upon the impulse given to the agitation of the question by the open declaration of the French Government in favor of the Union, Count Walewski maintained that, agreeing as they did in the project of the Union upon its political merits,

[1] The despatch No. 862 referred to is dated Aug. 22/56 not Aug. 21; one copy of this is in F.O. 27. 1115, another is in F.O. 195. 508, from which a passage is produced on p. 70 of the present essay.

they were driven to make a public manifestation of their opinion, in consequence of the covert steps taken by Turkey and Austria to prevent its realisation, and he asked how it was possible that France, supported as she is in this question by Russia, Prussia, and Sardinia, could recede, as it were at the bidding of Austria, from a position which she firmly believes to be for the advantage of the Principalities. How could she give way, to a Power, which openly declared that the Union can only be accomplished by passing over her body?

Her Majesty's Government, Count Walewski thinks, should make allowance for this situation, more particularly if it becomes strengthened by a declaration of the Divans in favor of the Union.

But while persisting in the course which he has begun, Count Walewski is by no means insensible to the complications which may arise, should the two Governments find it impossible to come to a common understanding upon the eventualities which may occur. If Her Majesty's Government can be persuaded to support the Union in conjunction with the French Government, His Excellency is convinced that it will no longer be opposed by the Porte; whereas even the neutrality of Her Majesty's Government would encourage the Turkish Ministers to resist, and if the Sultan were to place his veto upon the project, the question would arise as to his right to do so, a question which he should be sorry to see discussed by a conference.

I observed in reply, that all that Count Walewski had said only convinced me more and more that I was right, in recommending an early examination of the whole question. I never could believe, that two Governments so amicably disposed towards each other, as were the Governments of France and England, could not come to an understanding upon a matter, which interested neither except in a general point of view. But to arrive at this understanding, there must exist a real desire to examine the question upon its merits and to abjure all foregone conclusions. For instance, had the French Government, I enquired, ever given a thought to the next step to be taken, supposing that the Union was thought desirable and practicable? What was the idea of the French Government? How was the Union to be carried out?

Count Walewski seemed to catch at this remark, as if he saw in it a means of approximation with Her Majesty's Government.

His Excellency said, that the French Government had formed no opinion whatever upon this subject, except that the reins of Government must not be confided to the hands of a Foreign Prince. He had lately written to Monsieur de Talleyrand, to give every discouragement to this idea, which had been unfortunately connected with the Union in the minds of the Unionists, and he had instructed Monsieur de Thouvenel to assure the Porte, that France was quite ready to agree that the question of the nomination of a Foreign Prince should be excluded from the deliberations of the Divans. If then Her Majesty's Government had any proposals to make, which while uniting the two Principalities under one Government, would give that security for the continued Suzeraineté of the Sultan, about which Her Majesty's Government were so anxious, the French Government would willingly listen to them, and he thought they would easily understand each other. Count Walewski added, that his latest advices from Vienna led him to hope that the Austrian Government were not indisposed to some sort of compromise.

Since I commenced writing this Despatch, I have had an opportunity of ascertaining the Emperor's sentiments in connection with the subject matter of it. His Majesty began the conversation himself and I took the liberty of expressing myself to him in the same terms as I had previously used to Count Walewski. His Majesty said that he entirely agreed with me in the propriety of an early exchange of opinions between the two Governments on the questions relating to the Principalities: he admitted the difficulties which surrounded them; but nothing fell from him which would justify me in saying, that if the Divans pronounce in favor of the Union, His Majesty will not give them all the support he can. He dwelt long, and with considerable animation upon the fact that the Great Powers of Europe having invited the people of Moldavia and Wallachia to express their wishes in respect to their future Government, could not with consistency or honor, turn a deaf ear to their aspirations. But what, I said, if those aspirations went far beyond an administration in common of the two Principalities: if under the term "union", the word "independence" was concealed; if the Government of a single chief meant separation from Turkey. The Emperor could not deny that such might be the aim and scope of the Unionists, but His Majesty would not allow that it was a reason for opposing them. He said that the mal-administration of the Turks was such that it was impossible that Christian Powers should not sympathise with those Christian subjects of the Sultan, who asked for a better Government. His Majesty could understand that Turkey, Austria, and Russia, should oppose the Union of the Principalities, because in Union there would be strength, and it must be the desire of those Powers, each for its own specific reasons, to keep those Provinces in a state of weakness; but for his own part he was convinced, that the surest barrier against the future encroachments of Russia, was to be found in strengthening the Principalities, and as this was the principal object which England and France must have in connection with those countries, he conceived that their true policy was to aid in developing those resources which produce strength.

The fact is, that the Emperor, although he does not avow it, would not see with disfavor a separation of the Principalities from Turkey. His whole policy therefore, with regard to those Provinces, is actuated by other motives than those of Her Majesty's Government; or rather I should say that He does not feel the same necessity that exists, for preserving the Ottoman dominions intact. Such being the case it is difficult to argue with His Majesty, for, on this question at least, his philanthropy far exceeds his respect for Treaties.

I have thus endeavoured, I fear at a length which will try Your Lordship's patience, to place before you the opinions and the probable conduct of the Emperor and his Government in respect to the question of the Union. In a word, I am convinced that they will continue to encourage the notion in the Provinces themselves, and that they will leave no stone unturned, if the Divans declare in its favor, to induce the Conference to confirm that decision. It would be a useless waste of time to enquire into the causes which have led to this policy; but much I think is to be attributed to a personal feeling of the Emperor in regard to Turkey, and to his avowed respect for nationalities; something perhaps to a morbid dread of being supposed to cede in every question to Great Britain. But if the word Union is premised as granted, my impression is that at this moment it is still in the power of Her Majesty's Government to make the Union itself as harmless as possible. It will be for Your Lordship, and for Her Majesty's Government to consider whether the attempt shall be made; or whether the passive resistance of the Porte is to be encouraged.

If the latter course is adopted, it seems to me that measures should be taken to prove the difficulties of bringing Wallachia and Moldavia under the rule of a native Boyard of either Country. For this purpose, if the Divans pronounce themselves, as is natural they should do, for the abstract principle of the Union, they should I conceive be asked separately, whether each is ready to submit the country which it represents to the administration of a Prince of the other;—to accept a Government formed of elements taken from the other;—to consent to the Capital of the other being the seat of Government. Questions of this nature, judiciously asked, would, I cannot doubt, soon produce divergence of opinion between the two Divans, and when the Conference meets, would aid the arguments of those members of it, whose Governments are opposed to the project. It may also be argued in conference, that the opinions of those countries which border the Principalities, and particularly of the Porte, are entitled to greater consideration, than the opinions of those, who are but onlookers from a distance. In short, if Great Britain, Austria, and Turkey remain united, there can be little doubt that they can prevent the accomplishment of the Union.

But it would not be wise to neglect the reverse of the picture. Supposing the Divans to pronounce themselves decidedly in favor of the Union, and a majority of the Conference to do the same thing, and that the Union is prevented by the passive resistance of the minority, what will happen? Will not a permanent agitation be established in the Principalities, an agitation that would certainly be fomented by French and Russian Agents? May this not lead to outbreaks against the authority of the Porte, and will Christian Europe under such circumstances, sanction the repression of those outbreaks by Turkish troops? I cannot help asking myself these questions and many others which naturally suggest themselves, because it appears to me that Her Majesty's Government must deliberately look these and other eventualities in the face, before their final determination is taken. It is not for me to speculate on public opinion in England of which Her Majesty's Government must be the best judges; but I should neglect my duty, did I not tell Your Lordship, that the

Emperor and his Government count upon it in the calculations which they make for the future. Let a majority of the Divan, they say, pronounce themselves for the Union, and no Government in England can resist it.

It is not my purpose to examine now, what may or may not be done, if on the whole Her Majesty's Government are of opinion that a compromise with France is desirable. The choice must first be made between concession and resistance.

I have, etc.

(signed) COWLEY.

BIBLIOGRAPHY

The unpublished sources given below are those used in the present essay. A few geographical studies have been included in the list headed "Rumanian History". For a full bibliography, particularly of French works, up to the year 1907, see George Bengesco, *Bibliographie franco-roumaine*, 2nd edition, 1907. The Bibliographical Notes to Professor N. Iorga's *A History of Roumania* provide a list of recent French and Rumanian works on Rumanian history.

I. DOCUMENT SOURCES

A. *Unpublished*

(a) Public Record Office.

F.O. 195. Embassy Correspondence (Turkey). This contains the official instructions from the Foreign Office to the Ambassador at Constantinople and copies of despatches bearing on Near Eastern questions drawn from various representatives abroad. (At the Cambridge Gaol.)

F.O. 78. General Correspondence (Turkey). This contains the despatches from the Ambassador at Constantinople together with many enclosures in the form of memoranda, notes, etc. relating to the business of the Embassy. (At Chancery Lane.)

F.O. 27. (France) 1163–1171, Paris Conference Drafts: despatches from Lord Clarendon to Lord Palmerston, written from Paris during the meeting of the Congress, February–March, 1856. (At Chancery Lane.)

F.O. 181 (Russia). Correspondence in August, 1857, from Lord Wodehouse, Minister at St Petersburg, to the Foreign Office. (At the Cambridge Gaol.)

F.O. 97. 402–404. "Reports from Mr Blutte and others, the proceedings of the Russians in Moldavia and Wallachia 1828–1836". Blutte was British consul at Bukarest. (At Chancery Lane.)

F.O. 196. 29–31. Sir Stratford Canning Letter-Books 1848–49. Stratford arrived at Constantinople as Ambassador on June 26/48; these books contain copies of his despatches home kept at the Embassy. (At the Cambridge Gaol.)

Stratford Canning Papers[1], F.O. 352. 43–48, for the years 1856–57. (At Chancery Lane.)

The Bloomfield Papers, F.O. 356. 12–13. These form the official correspondence for the years 1856–57 from Lord Bloomfield, who was Minister at Berlin. (At Chancery Lane.)

(b) *Vienna State Archives* ⎫ These contain the correspon-
Expédition, Varia, 1856–58 ⎬ dence between the Foreign
Rapports de Constantinople, ⎭ Minister and Internuncio at
1856–58 Constantinople.

Dépêches à Paris ⎫ These contain the correspondence be-
and *Rapports de* ⎬ tween the Foreign Office and Hübner
Paris, 1856–58 ⎭ at Paris.

Rapports de Bukarest, 1859. Consular correspondence.

(c) *The Layard Papers* (at the British Museum). These occasionally throw a sidelight on affairs at Constantinople. Austen Henry Layard (later Sir) served as an attaché, first unpaid and then paid, at the Constantinople Embassy from 1847–52, and was Liberal M.P. for Aylesbury from 1852–57.

B. *Published*

Actes et documents relatifs à l'histoire de la régénération de la Roumanie, edited by G. Petresco, D. A. Sturdza and D. C. Sturdza. 9 vols. 1888–1901. (This collection is an invaluable source for the history of the Principalities up to 1859; it contains copies of the early treaties with the Porte; a great number of pamphlets written by Rumanian leaders and others in favour of union, especially during the years 1856–58; and it contains copies of much official correspondence between Thouvenel and the French Foreign Office.)

British and Foreign State Papers, edited by Sir E. Hertslet:
  Vol. XLV. Protocols of the Conference of Vienna, 1855.
    XLVI. ,, Congress of Paris, 1856.
    XLVIII. ,, Conference of Paris, 1858.
    XXXII. Copy of the *Règlement Organique* for Moldavia.

Documents pour servir à l'histoire de l'application de l'article 24 *du Traité de Paris en Moldavie*. London. 1857. (The contents of this small volume are described by its subtitle: *Doléances du Parti National de l'Union adressées aux*

---

[1] These have been described in the footnotes as *The Stratford Papers*.

Puissances Garantes du Traité de Paris et à la Commission Européenne réunie à Bucarest. (These documents are concerned chiefly with Vogorides' electioneering.)

Hansard, *Parliamentary Debates* (3rd series).

Hertslet, Sir E. *The Map of Europe by Treaty.* 4 vols. 1875–91.

Hertslet, L. *Treaties, etc., between Turkey and Foreign Powers,* 1535–1855. 1855.

Martens, G. F. von, and others. Various collections of treaties. (For a list of the various collections see Sir E. Satow, *International Congresses,* p. 168.)

Parliamentary Papers, LV. 265–270. Instructions to Lord John Russell for the Conference of Vienna, Feb. 22/1855.

Wambaugh, S. *A Monograph on Plebiscites with a Collection of Official Documents.* 1920. (This contains copies of the electoral firman of Jan. 13/56, of the Protocols of the Commission in the Principalities, a part of the Report of the Commission, *etc.*)

II. OTHER AUTHORITIES

A. *Diplomatic History*

Auerbach, B. *Les races et les nationalités en Autriche-Hongrie.* 2nd edition. 1917.

Bernstorff, Count A. von. *The Bernstorff Papers,* by C. Ringhoffer. 1908. English translation. 2 vols. 1908.

Bourgeois, E. *Manuel historique de Politique Étrangère.* Vol. III. 6th edition. 1924.

Bulwer, Sir H. L. *Life of H. J. Temple, Viscount Palmerston.* 3 vols. 1870–74. (This biography ends at the year 1847.)

Cambridge History of British Foreign Policy. Vol. II. 1922–23.

Cecil, Algernon. *British Foreign Secretaries, 1807–1916.* 1927.

Charles-Roux, F. *Alexandre II, Gortchakoff et Napoléon III.* 1913. (This affords a good picture of Franco-Russian relations after the Crimean War.)

Debidour, A. *Histoire diplomatique de l'Europe.* 2 vols. 1891.

Driault, E. *La Question d'Orient depuis ses origines jusqu'à la paix de Sèvres.* 8th edition. 1921.

Eckstaedt, Count Vitzthum von. *St Petersburg and London, 1852–64.* English translation. 2 vols. 1887.

Friedjung, H. *Der Krimkrieg und die österreichische Politik.* 1911.

Greville, C. C. F. *The Greville Memoirs.* Vol. VIII. 1888.

Guedalla, P. *Palmerston.* 1927. (This work has little value to the student of foreign policy, but, impressionistic though it is, it is the only modern biographical account of Palmerston the man.)

Hearnshaw, F. J. C. (editor). *Prime Ministers in the Nineteenth Century.* 1926. (Contains a lecture on Palmerston by P. Guedalla.)

Holland, Sir T. E. *A Lecture on the treaty relations of Russia and Turkey from 1774 to 1853.* 1877. (A brief essay by a jurist.)

Hübner, Comte A. de (editor). *Neuf ans de souvenirs d'un ambassadeur d'Autriche à Paris sous le Second Empire,* 1851–1859. 2 vols. 1904. (Written in diary form by Count J. A. von Hübner, who was Ambassador at Paris from 1851–59, and edited by his son.)

Iorga, N. *Actes et fragments concernant l'histoire des Roumains.* 3 vols. 1895.

—— *Correspondance diplomatique roumaine sous le roi Charles Ier* (1866–1880). 1923.

—— *Histoire des relations Russo-Roumaines.* 1917.

—— *Histoire des relations entre la France et les Roumains.* 1918.

—— *Histoire des relations entre l'Angleterre et les Roumains.* (Only the first part is published, in C. Bémont, *Mélanges d'Histoire.* 1913.)

La Gorce, P. de. *Histoire du second Empire.* 7 vols. 1894–1905.

Lane-Poole, S. *The Life of Lord Stratford de Redcliffe.* 2 vols. 1888. (This work, written only eight years after Stratford's death and mainly biographical in aim, has little to say on the diplomacy of Stratford's last two years, and does not mention, for example, the rupture at Constantinople in 1857.)

Layard, Sir A. H. *Autobiography and Letters.* 2 vols. 1903. (Throw interesting sidelights on the personalities at the British Embassy at Constantinople.)

Letters of Queen Victoria. Vol. III. Edited by A. C. Benson and Viscount Esher. 1907.

Loftus, Lord A. *The Diplomatic Reminiscences of Lord Augustus Loftus, P.C., G.C.B.* 1837–1862. (First Series.) 2 vols. 1892.

Malmesbury, Earl of. *Memoirs of an Ex-Minister.* 2 vols. New edition. 1920.

Martin, Kingsley B. *The Triumph of Lord Palmerston.* 1924. (A study of public opinion in England before the Crimean War.)

Martin, Theodore. *The Life of His Royal Highness the Prince Consort.* 5 vols. 1875–80.

Maxwell, Sir Herbert. *The Life and Letters of George William Frederick fourth Earl of Clarendon.* 2 vols. 1913. (This contains useful letters showing the relations between Stratford and Clarendon.)

Morny, Duc de. *Extraits des Mémoires: une Ambassade en Russie.* 1892.

Nesselrode, Count. *Lettres et Papiers du Chancelier Comte de Nesselrode.* Vol. IX. 1904.

Russell, Lord John. *The Later Correspondence of Lord John Russell,* 1840–1878. 2 vols. 1925. Edited by Dr G. P. Gooch.

Satow, Sir E. *International Congresses.* 1920. (Foreign Office Handbook, No. 151.)

—— *An Austrian Diplomatist in the Fifties.* 1908. (A brief essay on Hübner.)

Senior, N. W. *Conversations with M. Thiers, M. Guizot, and other distinguished persons, during the Second Empire [from 1852 to 1860].* Edited by M. C. M. Simpson. 2 vols. 1878.

Simpson, F. A. *The Rise of Louis Napoleon.* New edition. 1925.

—— *Louis Napoleon and the Recovery of France,* 1848–1856. 1923.

Sproxton, C. *Palmerston and the Hungarian Revolution.* 1919.

The Cambridge Historical Journal, vol. II, no. 2, "Treaties of Guarantee", by J. W. Headlam-Morley; vol. I, no. 3, "Instructions of Rechberg to Count Thun (4 Dec. 1859)", by E. F. Malcolm-Smith.

The English Historical Review, vol. XLII, 227–44, "The Concert of Europe and Moldavia in 1857", by T. W. Riker; vol. XLIII, 409–12, "The Osborne Conference and Memorandum of August, 1857", by W. G. East.

Thouvenel, L. *Trois années de la question d'Orient* 1856–1859. 1897.

—— *Pages de l'histoire du Second Empire, etc.* 1903.

Weld, Stuart F. *The Eastern Question and a Suppressed Chapter of History: Napoleon III and the Kingdom of Roumania.* 1897.

(The author charges Kinglake with having suppressed reference to the question of uniting the Principalities in his *The Invasion of the Crimea* (8 vols.), and gives a brief and enthusiastic account of Napoleon III's policy with regard to this question.)

Wellesley, Col. the Hon. F. A. (editor). *The Paris Embassy during the Second Empire.* 1928. (Selections from the papers of Earl Cowley, who was Ambassador at Paris from 1852 until 1867.)

B. *Rumanian History*

Academy of Bukarest. *Bulletin de la Section Historique.* 1913, *etc.*

André, L. *Les états chrétiens des Balkans depuis 1815.* 1918.

Bellesort, A. *La Roumanie contemporaine.* 1905.

Benger, G. *Rumania in 1900.* 1900.

Bibesco, Prince de. *Règne de Bibesco.* 2 vols. 1893. (An account of the hospodariate of Prince George Bibesco in Wallachia from 1843–48; it is partisan in spirit but contains documents in the form of letters and Russo-Turkish treaties.)

Carra, J. L. *Histoire de la Moldavie, et de la Valachie: avec une dissertation sur l'état actuel de ces deux Provinces.* 1777.

Damé, F. *Histoire de la Roumanie Contemporaine.* 1900. (A good general introduction to Rumanian history.)

D'Hauterive, E. *The Second Empire and its Downfall.* English translation, 1927. (Contains newly published correspondence between Napoleon III and his cousin Prince Napoleon.)

Eliade, P. *De l'Influence française sur l'esprit publique en Roumanie.* 1898.

Evans, Ifor L. *The Agrarian Revolution in Roumania.* 1924. (A study of post-war agrarian changes.)

Iorga, N. *A History of Roumania. Land, people, civilisation.* English translation, 1925. (A learned national history by the greatest living Rumanian historian.)

Martonne, E. de. *La Valachie.* 1902. (A geographical study.)

Miller, W. *The Ottoman Empire and its Successors, 1801–1927.* 1927.

—— *The Balkans.* (3rd edition.) 1923.

Newbigin, M. I. *Geographical Aspects of Balkan Problems.* 1915.

Nitz, E. *Militärgeographische Beschreibung von Rumänien.* 2 vols. 1919. (With useful maps.)

Pârvan, Vasile. *Dacia.* 1928. (A study of pre-historic and Roman civilisation in the Carpatho-Danubian countries.)

Pittard, E. *La Roumanie.* 1917. (An anthropological and ethnological study.)

Rumania. *A Handbook of Roumania.* 1920. ("Prepared by the Geographical Section of the Naval Intelligence Division, Naval Staff, Admiralty"; contains a useful geographical summary, statistics, and a Note on Maps, p. 199.)

Rumania: An Economic Handbook. (Special Agents' Series, No. 222.) 1924. Washington. (This contains a number of small scale maps showing, for example, the distribution of population, forests and wheat acreage.)

Seton-Watson, R. W. *The Rise of Nationality in the Balkans.* 1917.

—— *Roumania and the Great War.* 1915.

—— "Roumanian Origins," *History*, vol. VII, no. 28.

Sturdza, A. A. C. *De l'histoire diplomatique des Roumains*, 1821–1859. 1907. (The subtitle of this work, which contains some excellent portraits of Moldavian princes, is *Règne de Michel Sturdza.* Sturdza ruled as hospodar of Moldavia continuously from 1834 until 1849.)

Wilkinson, W. *An account of the principalities of Wallachia and Moldavia: with political observations relating to them.* 1820. (A rather unscientific study, interesting as an early English account and written by the British consul in the Principalities. It gives a sketch of economic activities.)

Xénopol, A. D. *Histoire des Roumains de la Dacie Trajane.* 2 vols. 1896. (This is still the best general history of the Principalities.)

Zallones, M. P. *Essay on the Fanariotes.* Translated from the French. 1826.

I N D E X

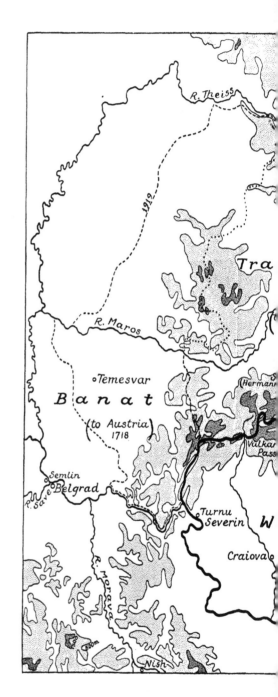

MAP
TO ILLUSTRATE
THE UNION OF
MOLDAVIA AND
WALLACHIA IN
1859

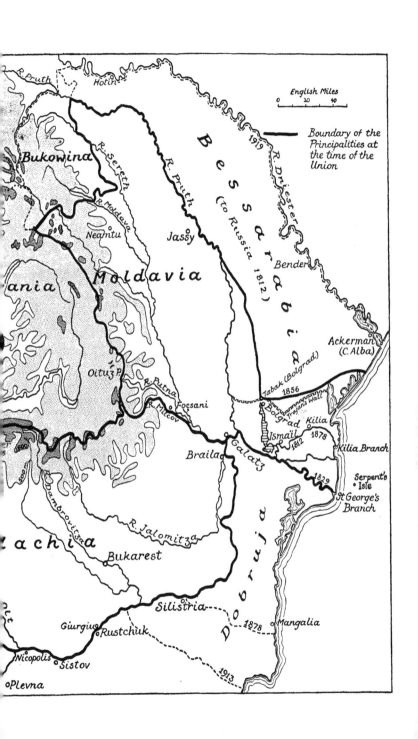

English Miles
0   20   40

Boundary of the
Principalities at
the time of the
Union

R. Pruth

Hotin

Bukowina

R. Sereth

R. Moldava

Neamtu

R. Pruth

Jassy

B e s s a r a b i a
(to Russia 1812)

1919

R. Dniester

Bender

Moldavia

Ackerman
(C. Alba)

Oituz P.

R. Putna

R. Mitcov

Focsani

Tabak (Bolgrad)

1856

Trajan's Wall

Bolgrad

Kilia

Ismaïl

1878

1812

Kilia Branch

Braila

Galatz

1829

Serpent's
Isle

St George's
Branch

ania

R. Jalomitza

achia

Bukarest

D o b r u j a

Silistria

1878

Mangalia

Giurgiu

Rustchuk

Nicopolis

Sistov

1913

Plevna

www.ingramcontent.com/pod-product-compliance
Ingram Content Group UK Ltd.
Pitfield, Milton Keynes, MK11 3LW, UK
UKHW042142280225
455719UK00001B/47